FAL
CTHULHU
APOCALYPSE

ROSS RICHIE
chief executive officer

MARK WAID
editor-in-chief

ADAM FORTIER
vice president,
publishing

CHIP MOSHER
marketing director

MATT GAGNON
managing editor

JENNY CHRISTOPHER
sales director

Office of publication: 6310 San Vicente Blvd, Ste 404, Los Angeles, CA
90048-5457.

A catalog record for this book is available from the Library of Congress and
on our website at www.boom-studios.com on the Librarian Resource Page.

First Edition: June 2009

10 9 8 7 6 5 4 3 2 1
PRINTED IN KOREA

Story by **MICHAEL ALAN NELSON**
Art by **MATEUS SANTOLOUCO**

Colors by **EDUARDO MEDEIROS** (Chapter 1)
Colors by **MATEUS SANTOLOUCO** (Chapter 2-4)

Cover by **JEFFREY SPOKES**

MARSHALL DILLON
Letterer

MATT GAGNON
Editor

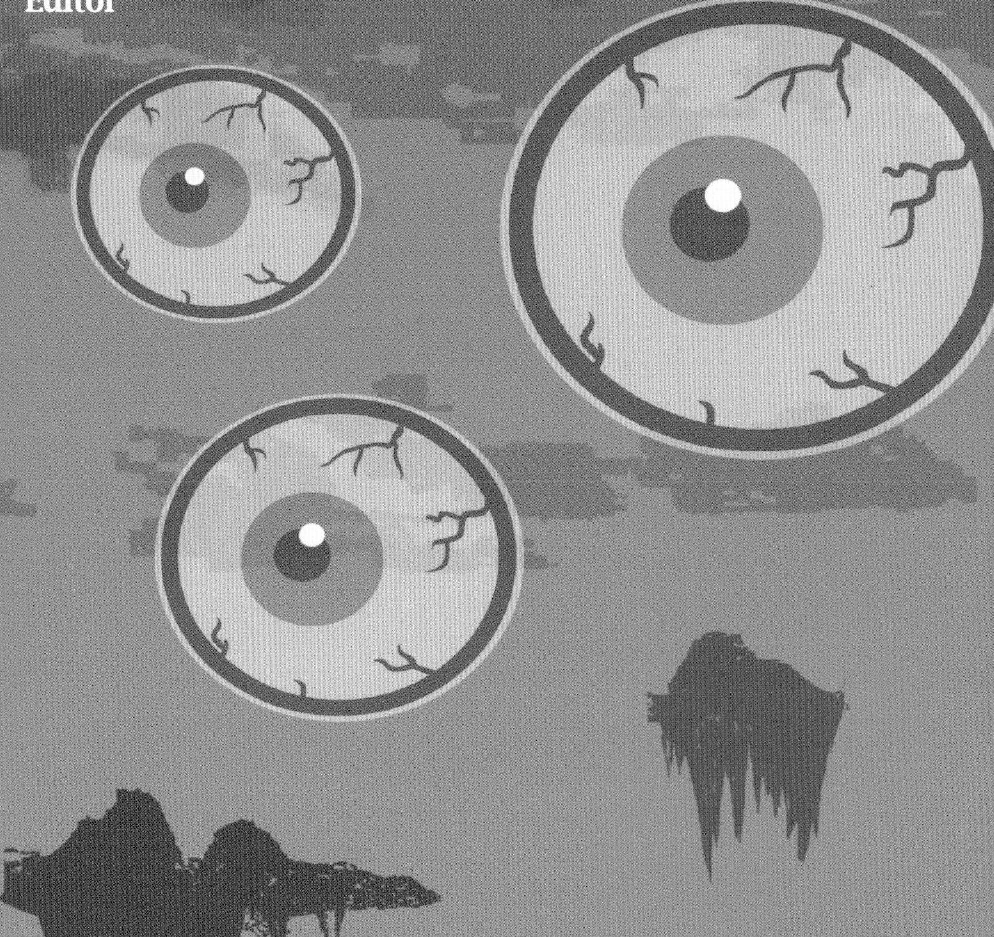

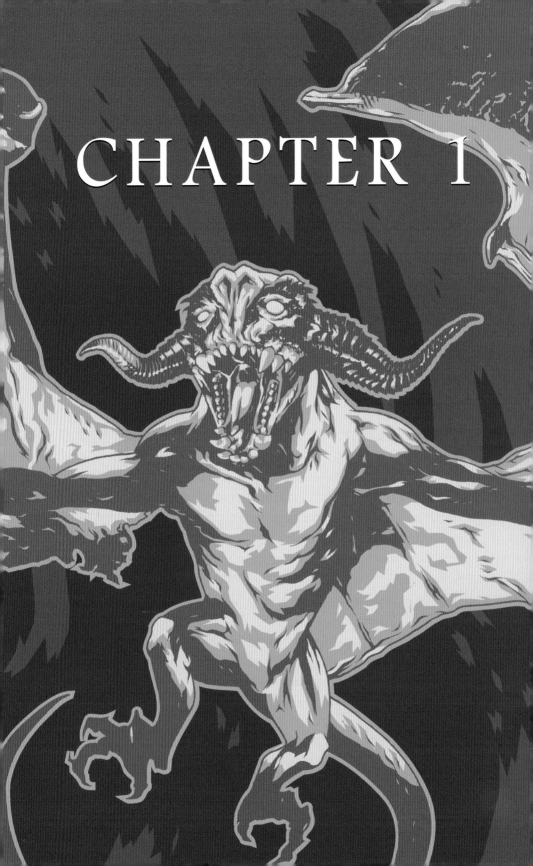

CHAPTER 1

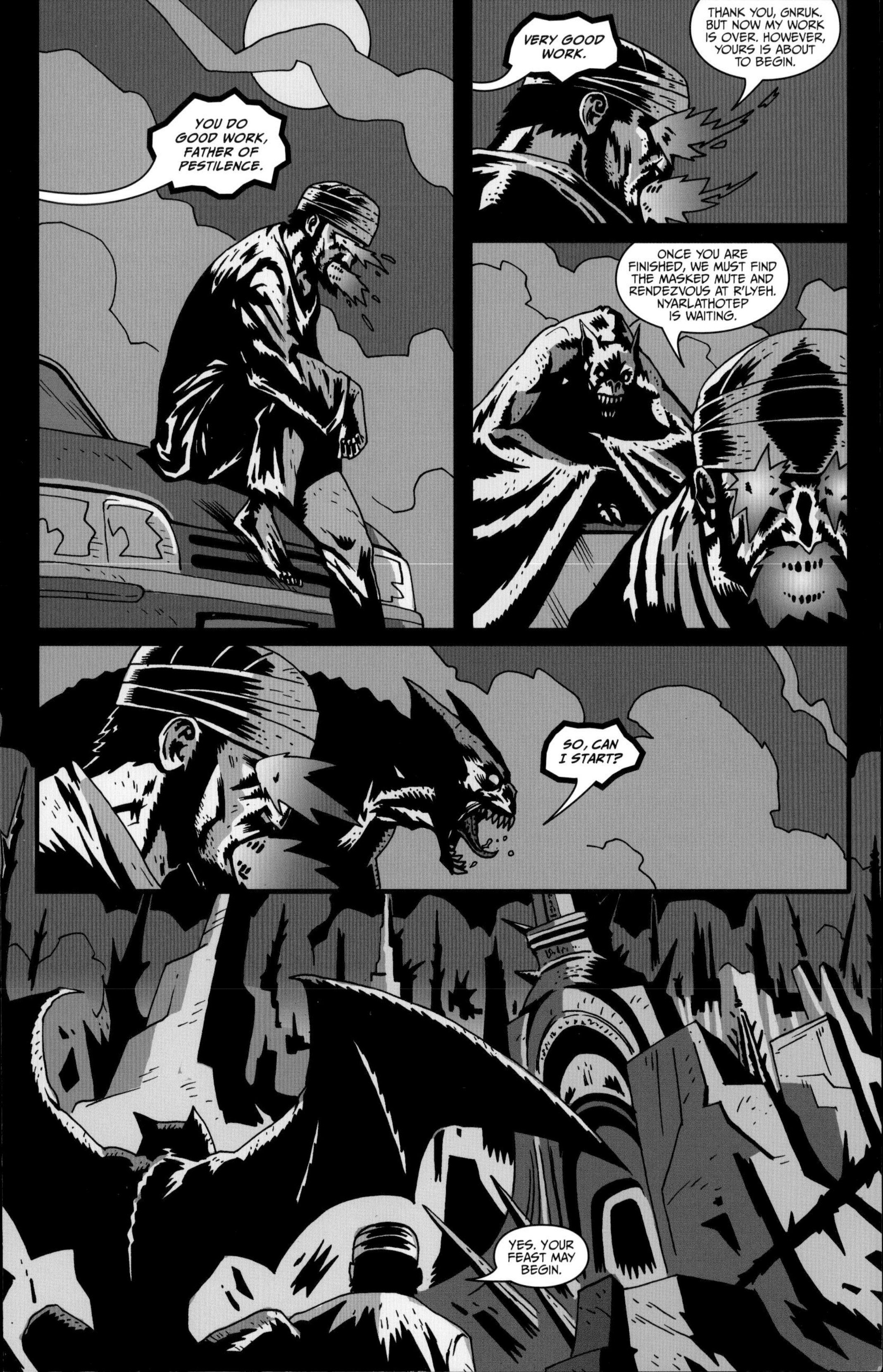
YOU DO GOOD WORK, FATHER OF PESTILENCE.
VERY GOOD WORK.
THANK YOU, GNRUK. BUT NOW MY WORK IS OVER. HOWEVER, YOURS IS ABOUT TO BEGIN.
ONCE YOU ARE FINISHED, WE MUST FIND THE MASKED MUTE AND RENDEZVOUS AT R'LYEH. NYARLATHOTEP IS WAITING.
SO, CAN I START?
YES. YOUR FEAST MAY BEGIN.

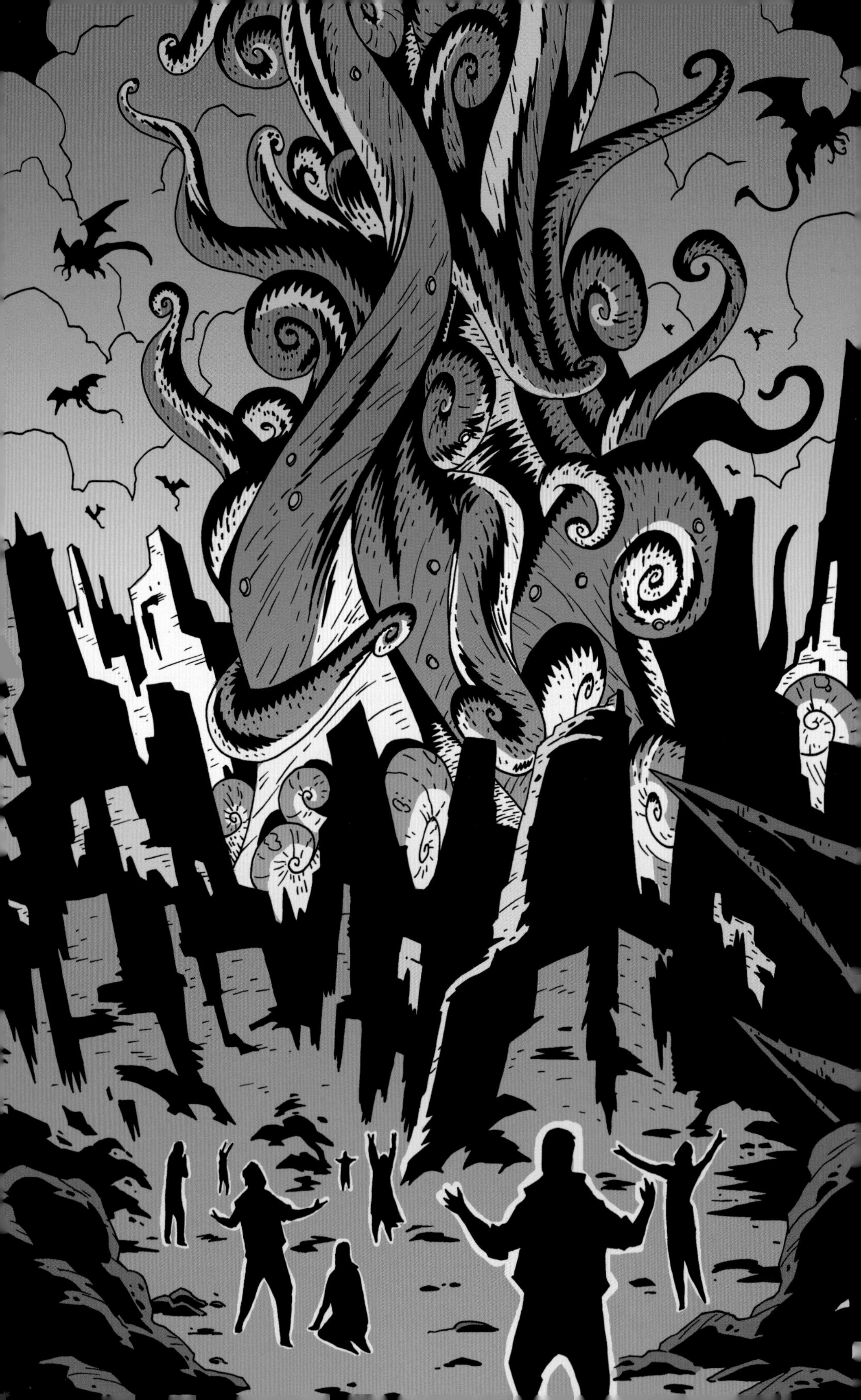

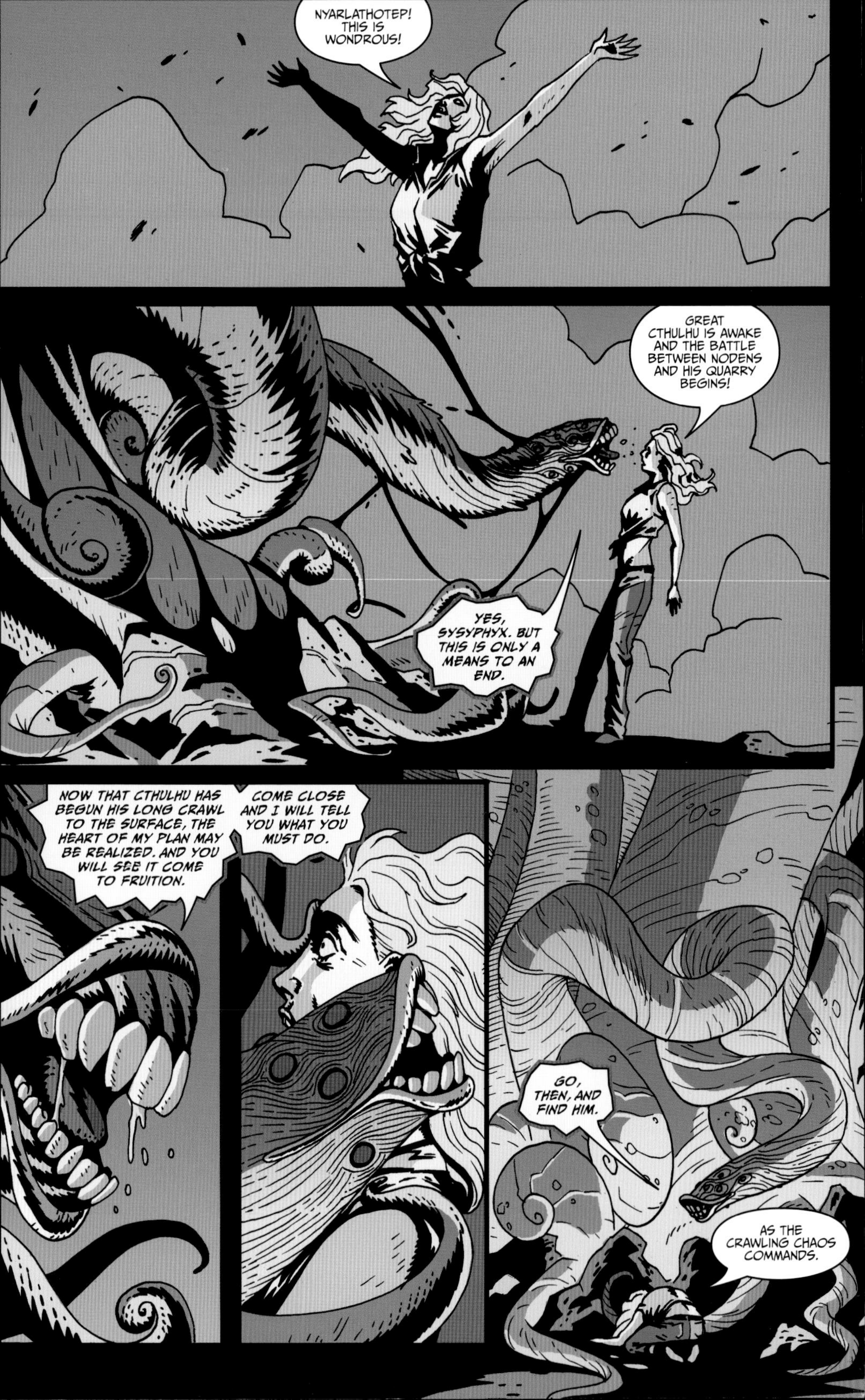
NYARLATHOTEP! THIS IS WONDROUS!
GREAT CTHULHU IS AWAKE AND THE BATTLE BETWEEN NODENS AND HIS QUARRY BEGINS!
YES, SYSYPHYX. BUT THIS IS ONLY A MEANS TO AN END.
NOW THAT CTHULHU HAS BEGUN HIS LONG CRAWL TO THE SURFACE, THE HEART OF MY PLAN MAY BE REALIZED. AND YOU WILL SEE IT COME TO FRUITION.
COME CLOSE AND I WILL TELL YOU WHAT YOU MUST DO.
GO, THEN, AND FIND HIM.
AS THE CRAWLING CHAOS COMMANDS.

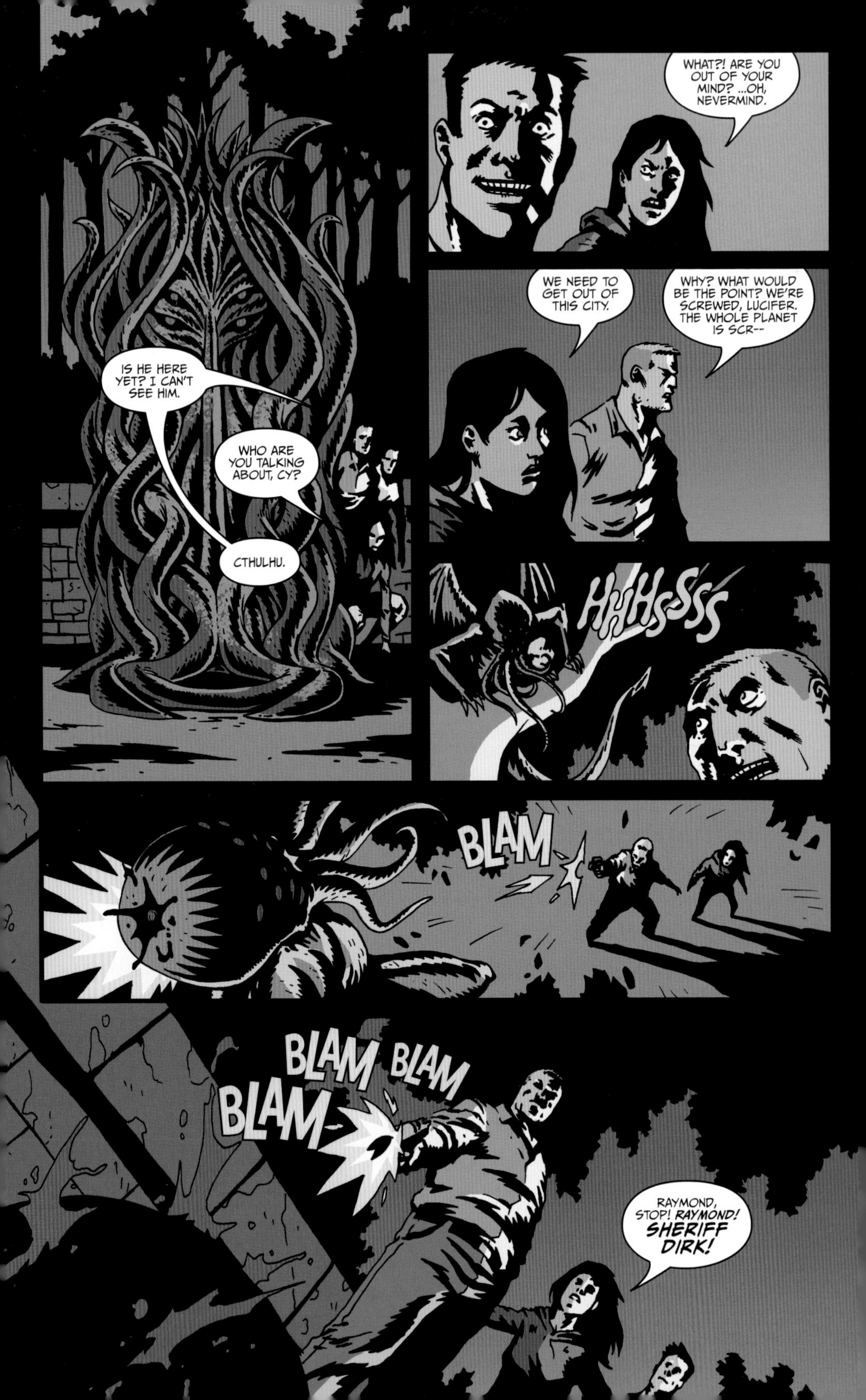
IS HE HERE YET? I CAN'T SEE HIM.
WHO ARE YOU TALKING ABOUT, CY?
CTHULHU.
WHAT?! ARE YOU OUT OF YOUR MIND? ...OH, NEVERMIND.
WE NEED TO GET OUT OF THIS CITY.
WHY? WHAT WOULD BE THE POINT? WE'RE SCREWED, LUCIFER. THE WHOLE PLANET IS SCR--
HHHSSSS
BLAM
BLAM BLAM BLAM
RAYMOND, STOP! RAYMOND! SHERIFF DIRK!

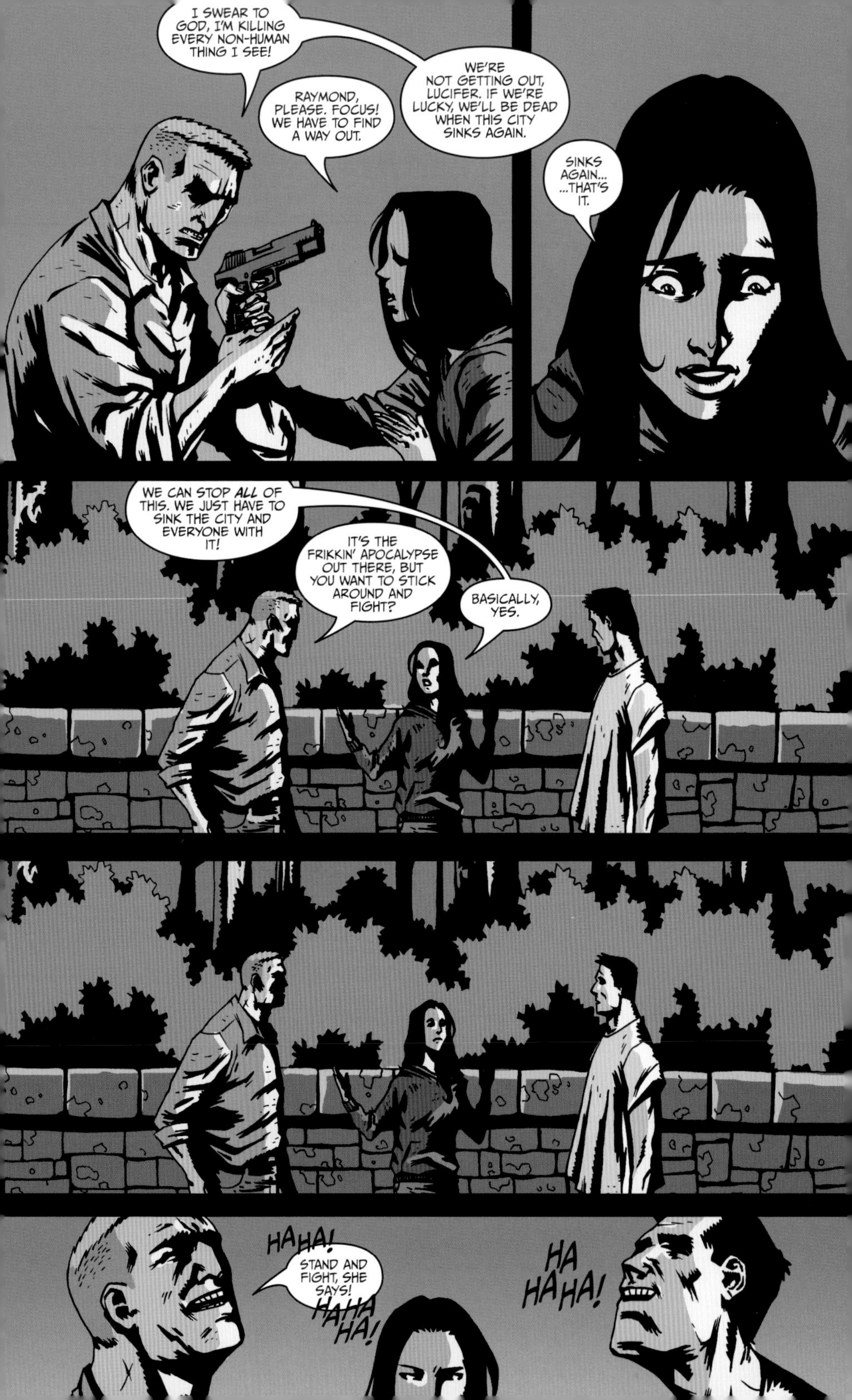
I SWEAR TO GOD, I'M KILLING EVERY NON-HUMAN THING I SEE!
RAYMOND, PLEASE. FOCUS! WE HAVE TO FIND A WAY OUT.
WE'RE NOT GETTING OUT, LUCIFER. IF WE'RE LUCKY, WE'LL BE DEAD WHEN THIS CITY SINKS AGAIN.
SINKS AGAIN... ...THAT'S IT.
WE CAN STOP ALL OF THIS. WE JUST HAVE TO SINK THE CITY AND EVERYONE WITH IT!
IT'S THE FRIKKIN' APOCALYPSE OUT THERE, BUT YOU WANT TO STICK AROUND AND FIGHT?
BASICALLY, YES.
HAHA!
STAND AND FIGHT, SHE SAYS!
HAHA HA!
HA HAHA!

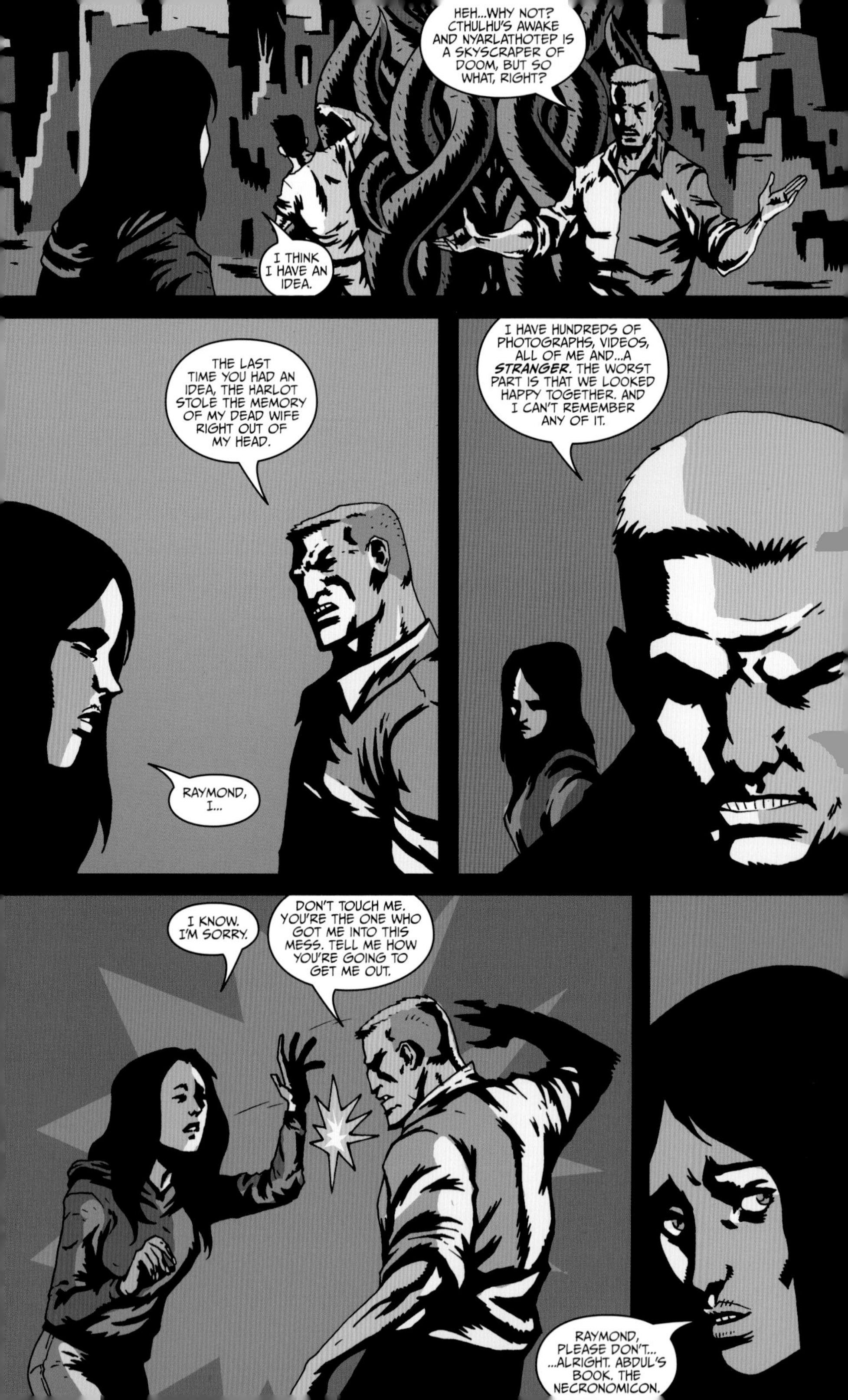
HEH...WHY NOT? CTHULHU'S AWAKE AND NYARLATHOTEP IS A SKYSCRAPER OF DOOM, BUT SO WHAT, RIGHT?
I THINK I HAVE AN IDEA.
THE LAST TIME YOU HAD AN IDEA, THE HARLOT STOLE THE MEMORY OF MY DEAD WIFE RIGHT OUT OF MY HEAD.
RAYMOND, I...
I HAVE HUNDREDS OF PHOTOGRAPHS, VIDEOS, ALL OF ME AND...A STRANGER. THE WORST PART IS THAT WE LOOKED HAPPY TOGETHER. AND I CAN'T REMEMBER ANY OF IT.
I KNOW. I'M SORRY.
DON'T TOUCH ME. YOU'RE THE ONE WHO GOT ME INTO THIS MESS. TELL ME HOW YOU'RE GOING TO GET ME OUT.
RAYMOND, PLEASE DON'T... ...ALRIGHT. ABDUL'S BOOK. THE NECRONOMICON.

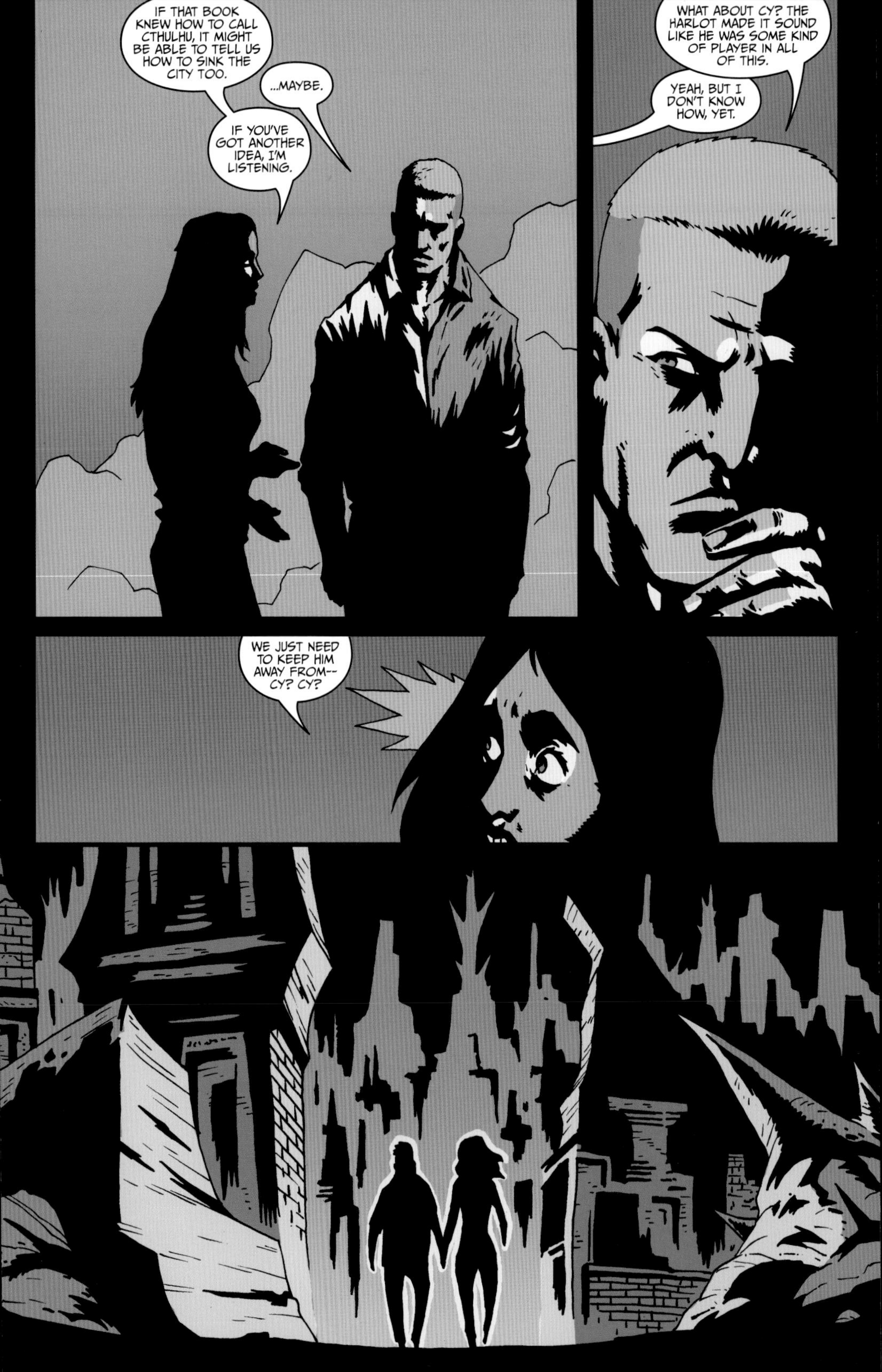
IF THAT BOOK KNEW HOW TO CALL CTHULHU, IT MIGHT BE ABLE TO TELL US HOW TO SINK THE CITY TOO.
...MAYBE.
IF YOU'VE GOT ANOTHER IDEA, I'M LISTENING.
WHAT ABOUT CY? THE HARLOT MADE IT SOUND LIKE HE WAS SOME KIND OF PLAYER IN ALL OF THIS.
YEAH, BUT I DON'T KNOW HOW, YET.
WE JUST NEED TO KEEP HIM AWAY FROM-- CY? CY?

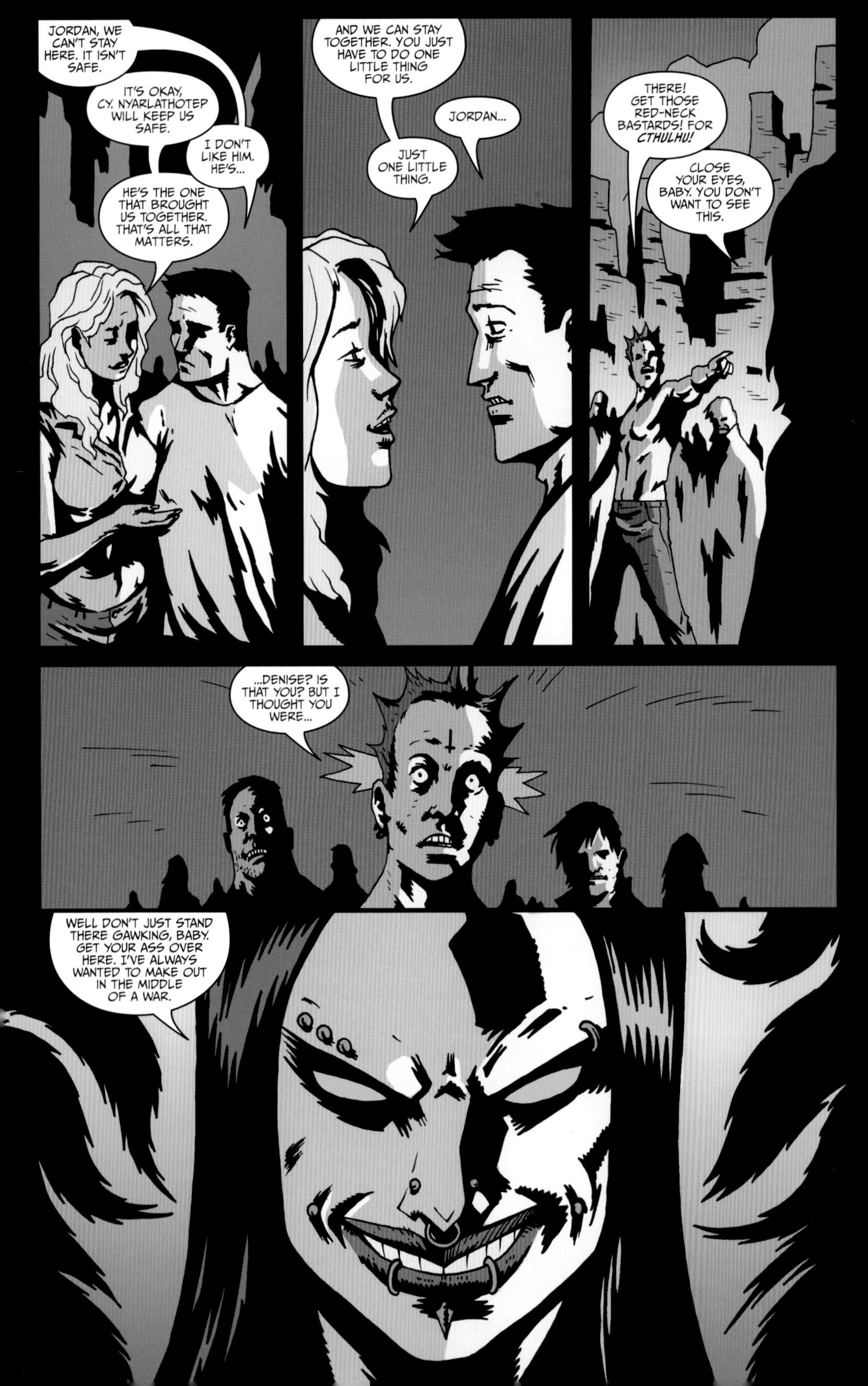
JORDAN, WE CAN'T STAY HERE. IT ISN'T SAFE.
IT'S OKAY, CY. NYARLATHOTEP WILL KEEP US SAFE.
I DON'T LIKE HIM. HE'S...
HE'S THE ONE THAT BROUGHT US TOGETHER. THAT'S ALL THAT MATTERS.
AND WE CAN STAY TOGETHER. YOU JUST HAVE TO DO ONE LITTLE THING FOR US.
JORDAN...
JUST ONE LITTLE THING.
THERE! GET THOSE RED-NECK BASTARDS! FOR CTHULHU!
CLOSE YOUR EYES, BABY. YOU DON'T WANT TO SEE THIS.
...DENISE? IS THAT YOU? BUT I THOUGHT YOU WERE...
WELL DON'T JUST STAND THERE GAWKING, BABY. GET YOUR ASS OVER HERE. I'VE ALWAYS WANTED TO MAKE OUT IN THE MIDDLE OF A WAR.

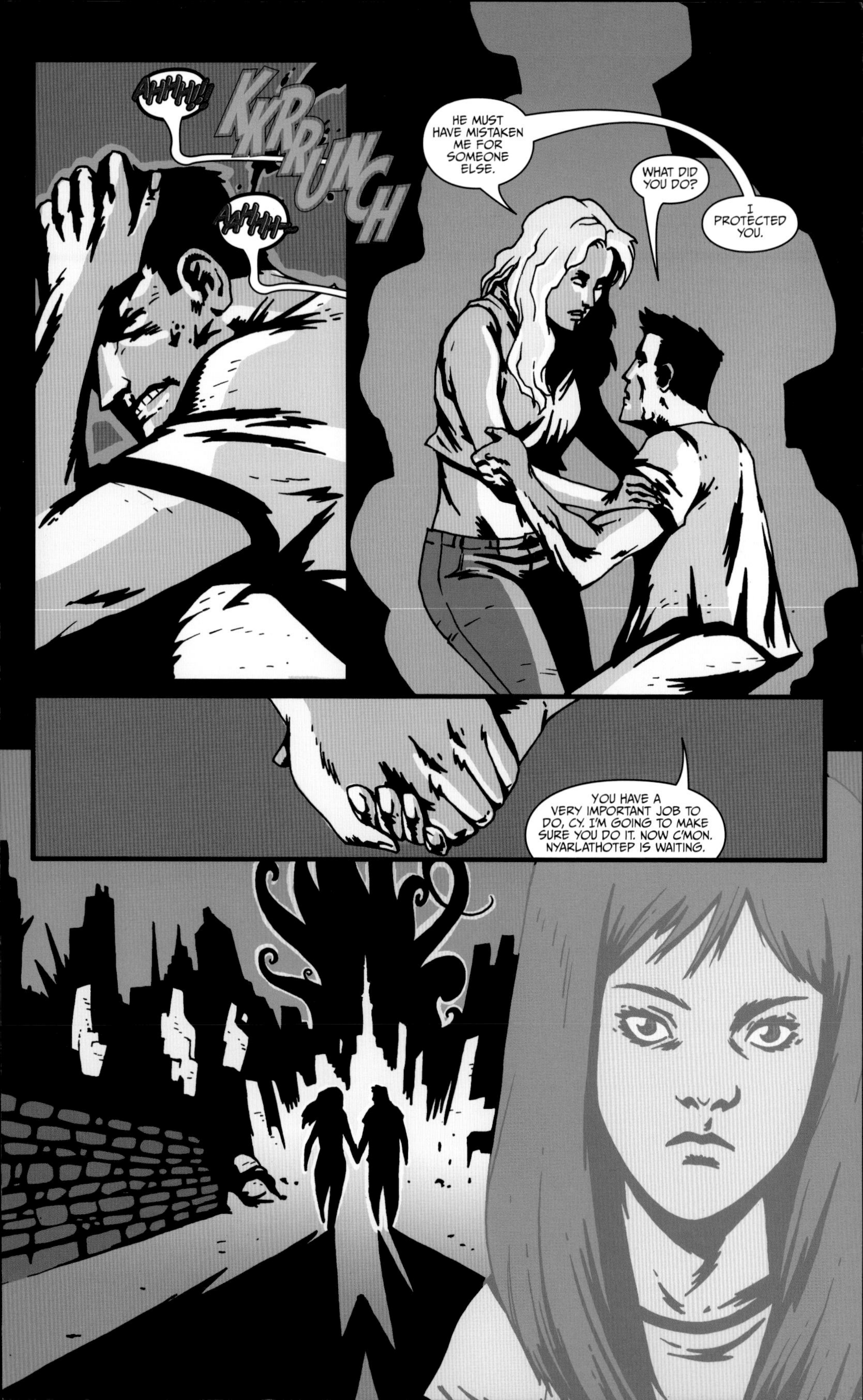
AHHH!!
KKRRUNCH
AAHHH—
HE MUST HAVE MISTAKEN ME FOR SOMEONE ELSE.
WHAT DID YOU DO?
I PROTECTED YOU.
YOU HAVE A VERY IMPORTANT JOB TO DO, CY. I'M GOING TO MAKE SURE YOU DO IT. NOW C'MON. NYARLATHOTEP IS WAITING.

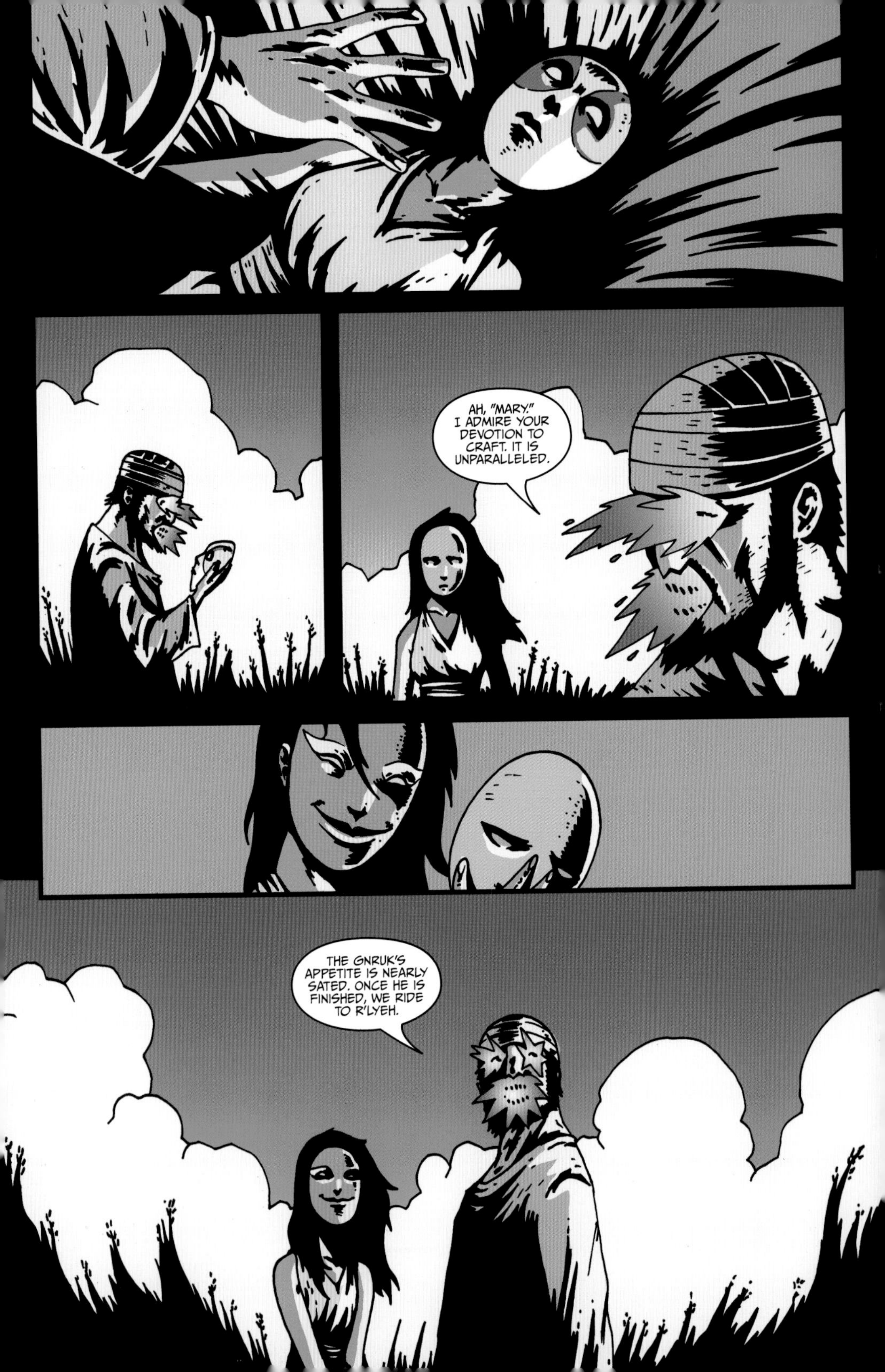
AH, "MARY." I ADMIRE YOUR DEVOTION TO CRAFT. IT IS UNPARALLELED.
THE GNRUK'S APPETITE IS NEARLY SATED. ONCE HE IS FINISHED, WE RIDE TO R'LYEH.

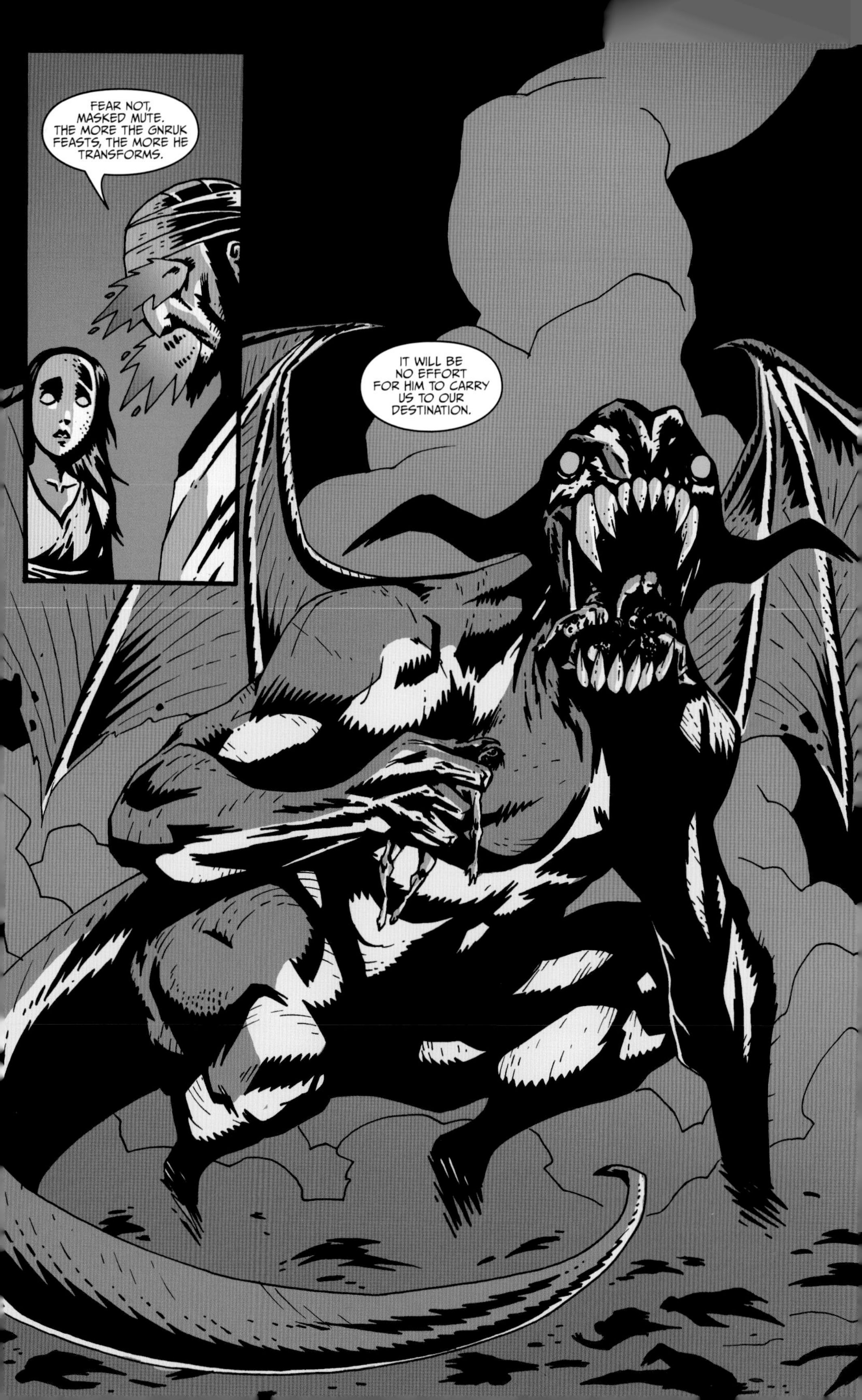
FEAR NOT, MASKED MUTE. THE MORE THE GNRUK FEASTS, THE MORE HE TRANSFORMS.
IT WILL BE NO EFFORT FOR HIM TO CARRY US TO OUR DESTINATION.

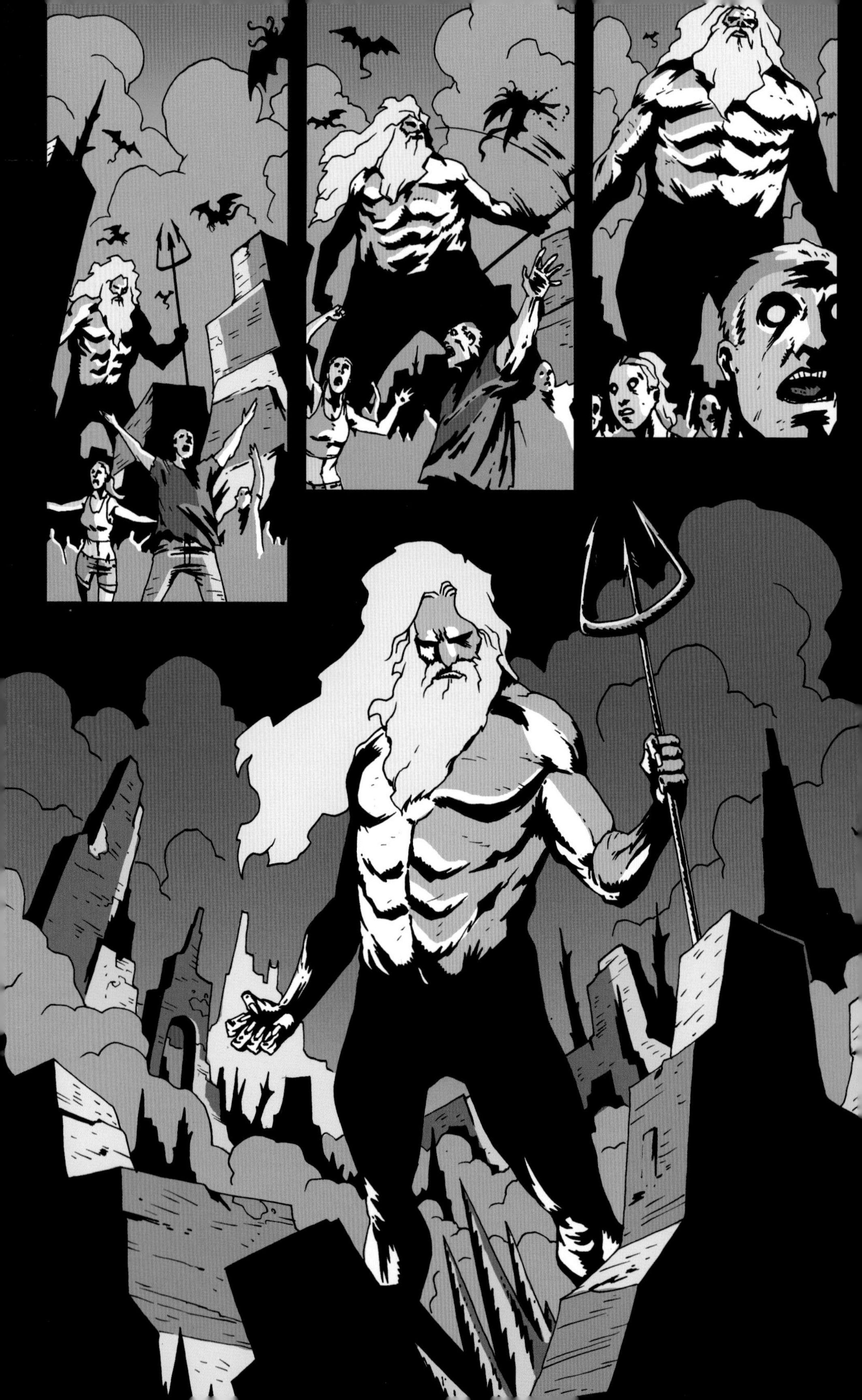

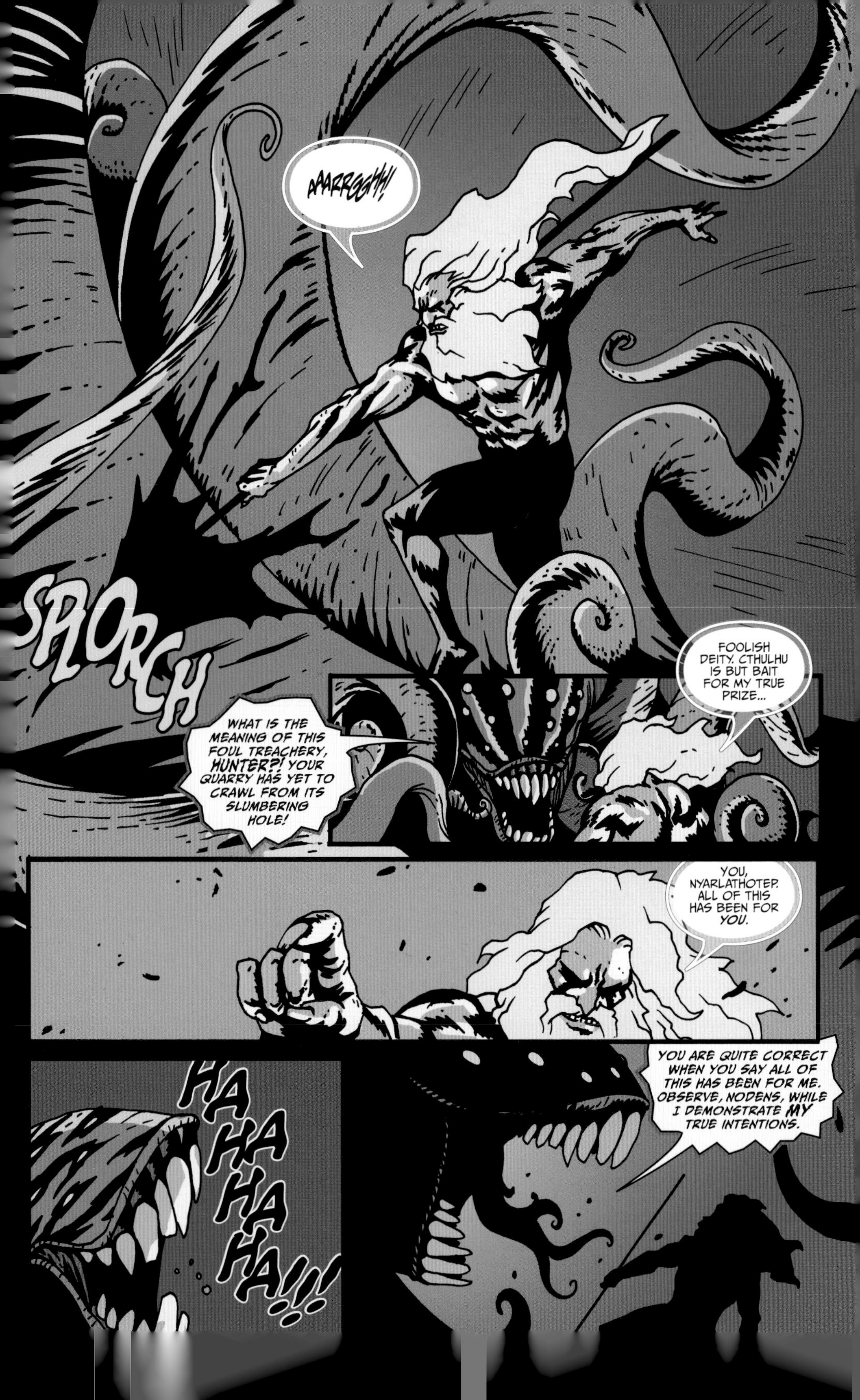
AAARRGGHH!
SPLORCH
FOOLISH DEITY. CTHULHU IS BUT BAIT FOR MY TRUE PRIZE...
WHAT IS THE MEANING OF THIS FOUL TREACHERY, HUNTER?! YOUR QUARRY HAS YET TO CRAWL FROM ITS SLUMBERING HOLE!
YOU, NYARLATHOTEP. ALL OF THIS HAS BEEN FOR YOU.
HA HA HA HA HA!!!
YOU ARE QUITE CORRECT WHEN YOU SAY ALL OF THIS HAS BEEN FOR ME. OBSERVE, NODENS, WHILE I DEMONSTRATE MY TRUE INTENTIONS.

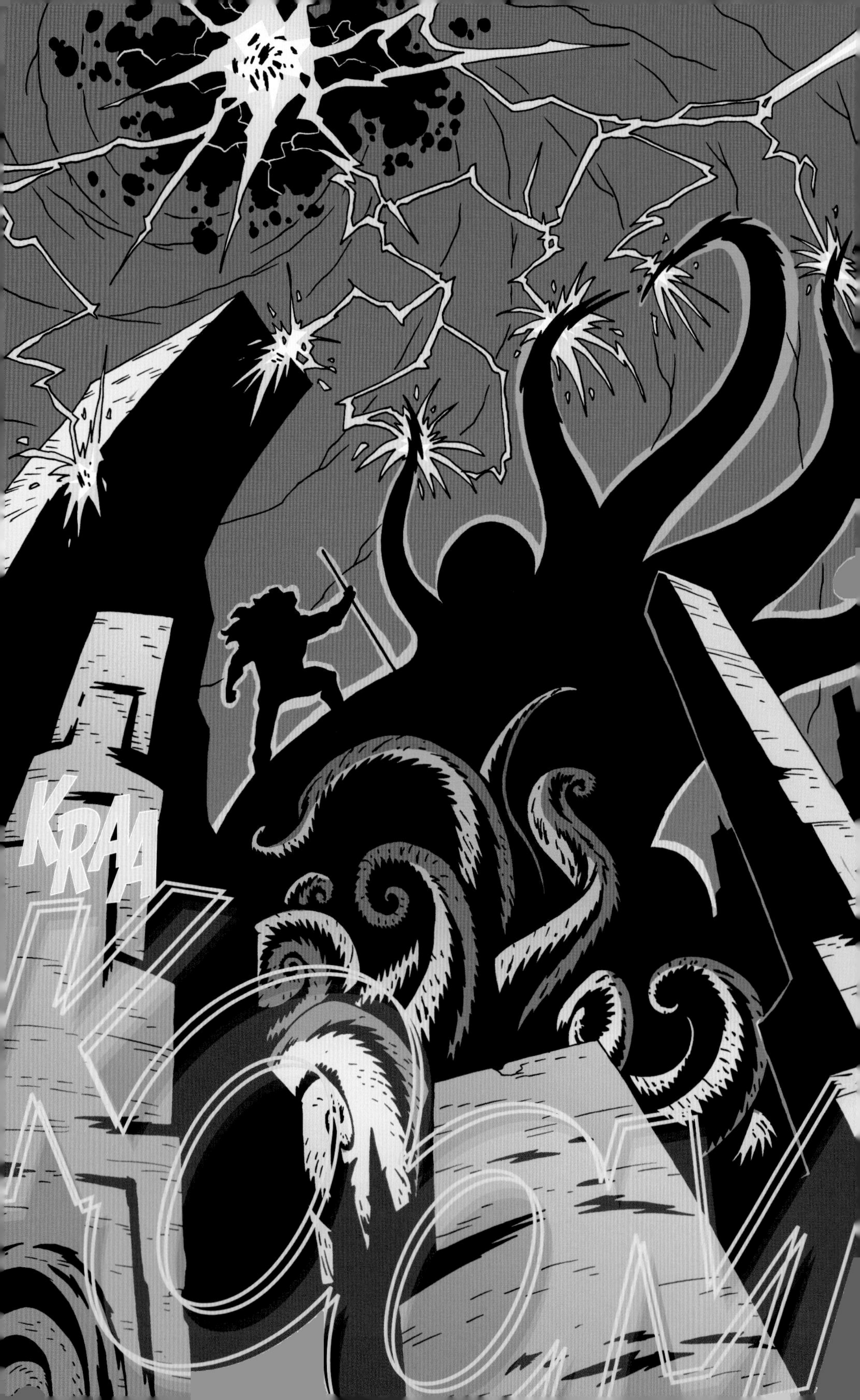
KRAAA
KOOOM

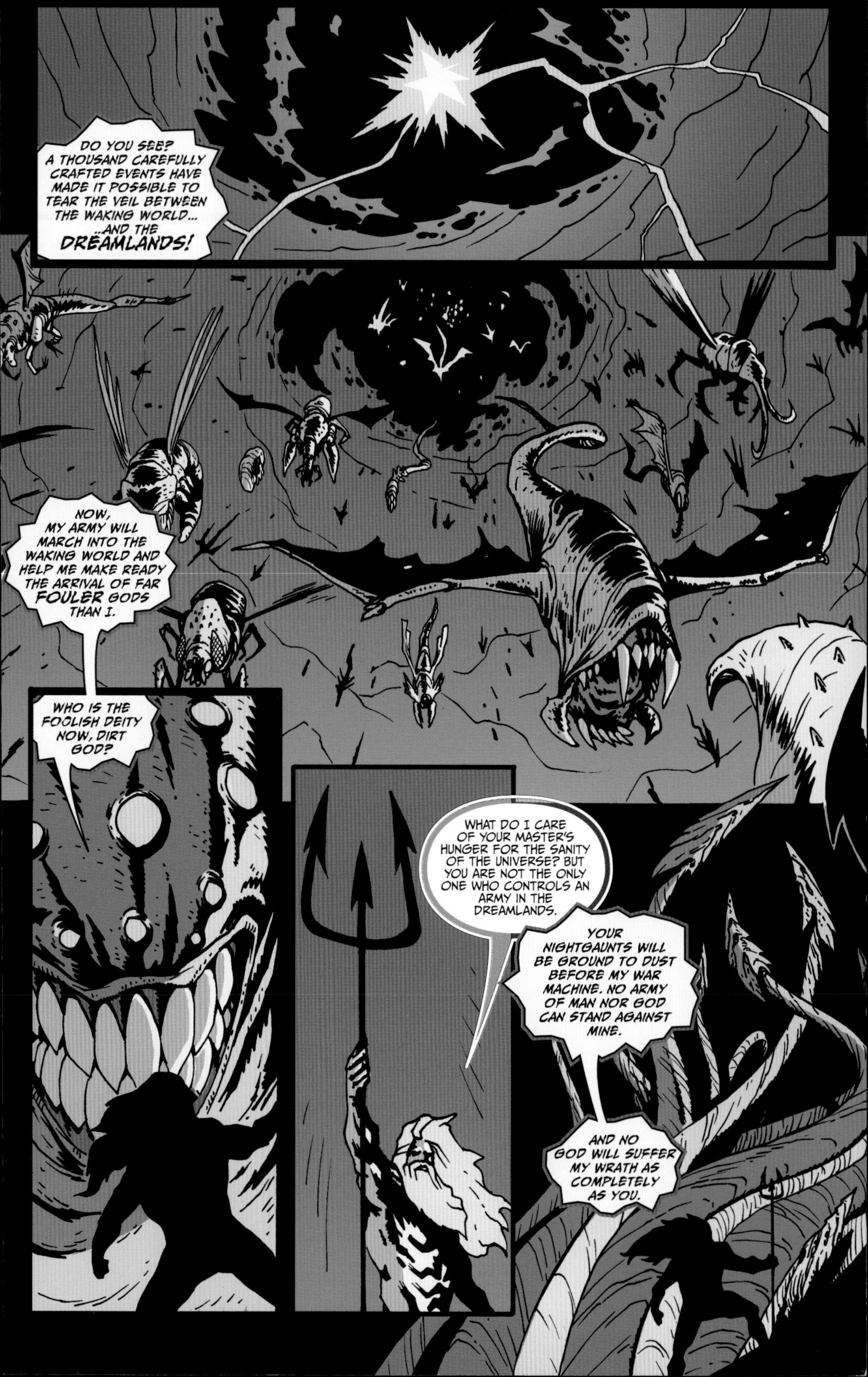
DO YOU SEE? A THOUSAND CAREFULLY CRAFTED EVENTS HAVE MADE IT POSSIBLE TO TEAR THE VEIL BETWEEN THE WAKING WORLD... ...AND THE DREAMLANDS!
NOW, MY ARMY WILL MARCH INTO THE WAKING WORLD AND HELP ME MAKE READY THE ARRIVAL OF FAR FOULER GODS THAN I.
WHO IS THE FOOLISH DEITY NOW, DIRT GOD?
WHAT DO I CARE OF YOUR MASTER'S HUNGER FOR THE SANITY OF THE UNIVERSE? BUT YOU ARE NOT THE ONLY ONE WHO CONTROLS AN ARMY IN THE DREAMLANDS.
YOUR NIGHTGAUNTS WILL BE GROUND TO DUST BEFORE MY WAR MACHINE. NO ARMY OF MAN NOR GOD CAN STAND AGAINST MINE.
AND NO GOD WILL SUFFER MY WRATH AS COMPLETELY AS YOU.

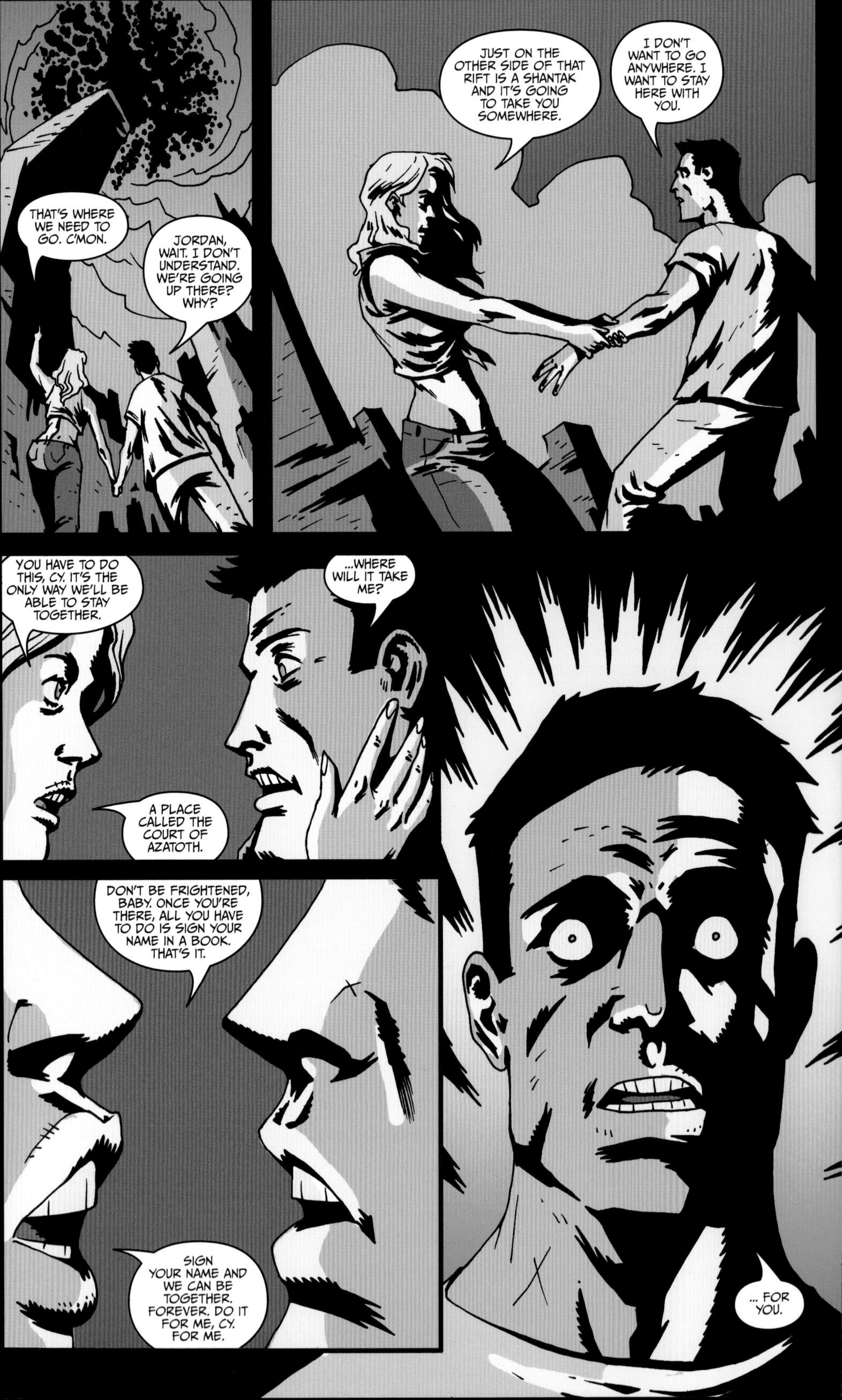
THAT'S WHERE WE NEED TO GO. C'MON.
JORDAN, WAIT. I DON'T UNDERSTAND. WE'RE GOING UP THERE? WHY?
JUST ON THE OTHER SIDE OF THAT RIFT IS A SHANTAK AND IT'S GOING TO TAKE YOU SOMEWHERE.
I DON'T WANT TO GO ANYWHERE. I WANT TO STAY HERE WITH YOU.
YOU HAVE TO DO THIS, CY. IT'S THE ONLY WAY WE'LL BE ABLE TO STAY TOGETHER.
...WHERE WILL IT TAKE ME?
A PLACE CALLED THE COURT OF AZATOTH.
DON'T BE FRIGHTENED, BABY. ONCE YOU'RE THERE, ALL YOU HAVE TO DO IS SIGN YOUR NAME IN A BOOK. THAT'S IT.
SIGN YOUR NAME AND WE CAN BE TOGETHER. FOREVER. DO IT FOR ME, CY. FOR ME.
... FOR YOU.

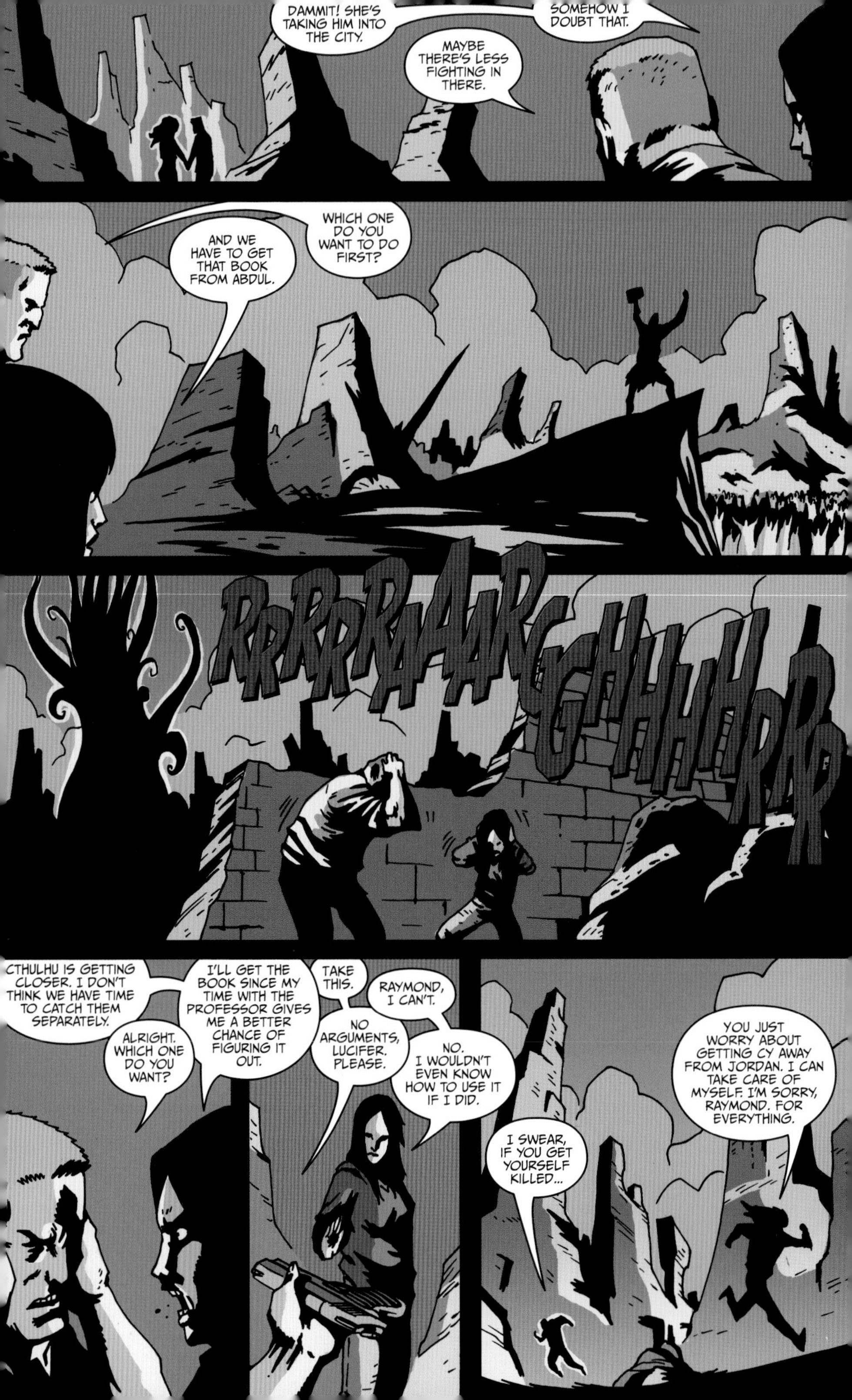
DAMMIT! SHE'S TAKING HIM INTO THE CITY.
MAYBE THERE'S LESS FIGHTING IN THERE.
SOMEHOW I DOUBT THAT.
AND WE HAVE TO GET THAT BOOK FROM ABDUL.
WHICH ONE DO YOU WANT TO DO FIRST?
RRRRRAAARGHHHHRRR
CTHULHU IS GETTING CLOSER. I DON'T THINK WE HAVE TIME TO CATCH THEM SEPARATELY.
ALRIGHT. WHICH ONE DO YOU WANT?
I'LL GET THE BOOK SINCE MY TIME WITH THE PROFESSOR GIVES ME A BETTER CHANCE OF FIGURING IT OUT.
TAKE THIS.
RAYMOND, I CAN'T.
NO ARGUMENTS, LUCIFER. PLEASE.
NO. I WOULDN'T EVEN KNOW HOW TO USE IT IF I DID.
I SWEAR, IF YOU GET YOURSELF KILLED...
YOU JUST WORRY ABOUT GETTING CY AWAY FROM JORDAN. I CAN TAKE CARE OF MYSELF. I'M SORRY, RAYMOND. FOR EVERYTHING.

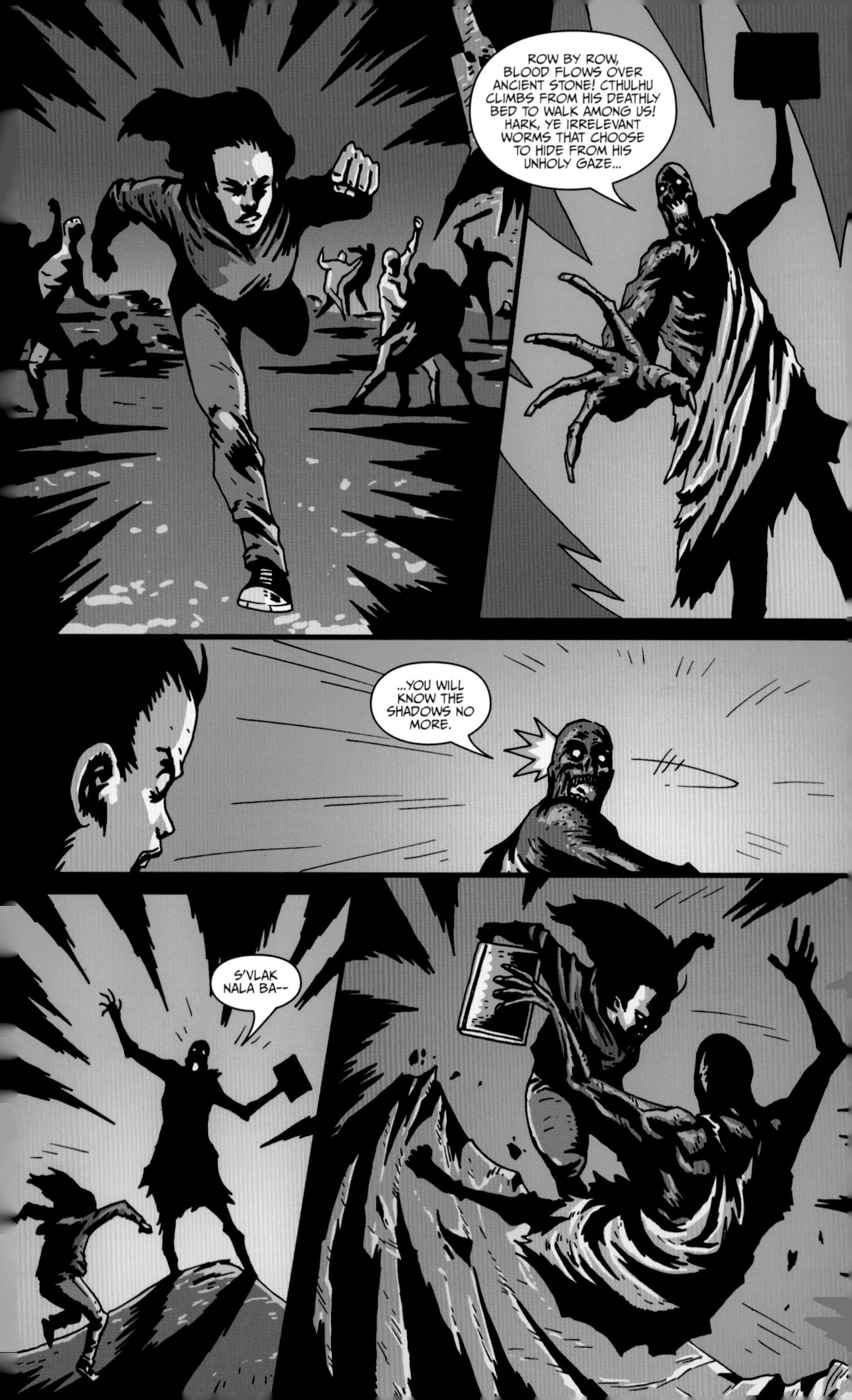
ROW BY ROW, BLOOD FLOWS OVER ANCIENT STONE! CTHULHU CLIMBS FROM HIS DEATHLY BED TO WALK AMONG US! HARK, YE IRRELEVANT WORMS THAT CHOOSE TO HIDE FROM HIS UNHOLY GAZE...
...YOU WILL KNOW THE SHADOWS NO MORE.
S'VLAK NALA BA--

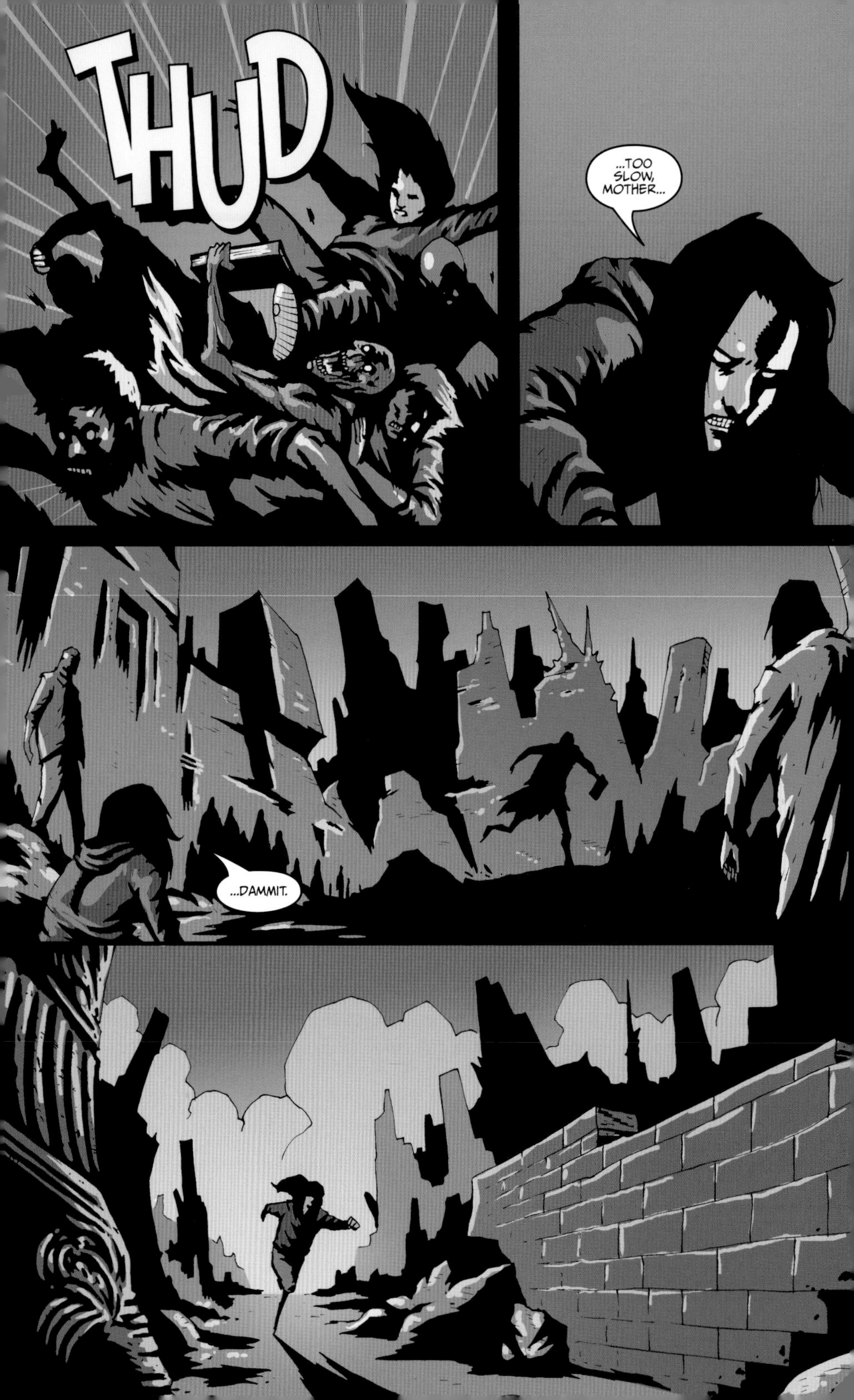
THUD
...TOO SLOW, MOTHER...
...DAMMIT.

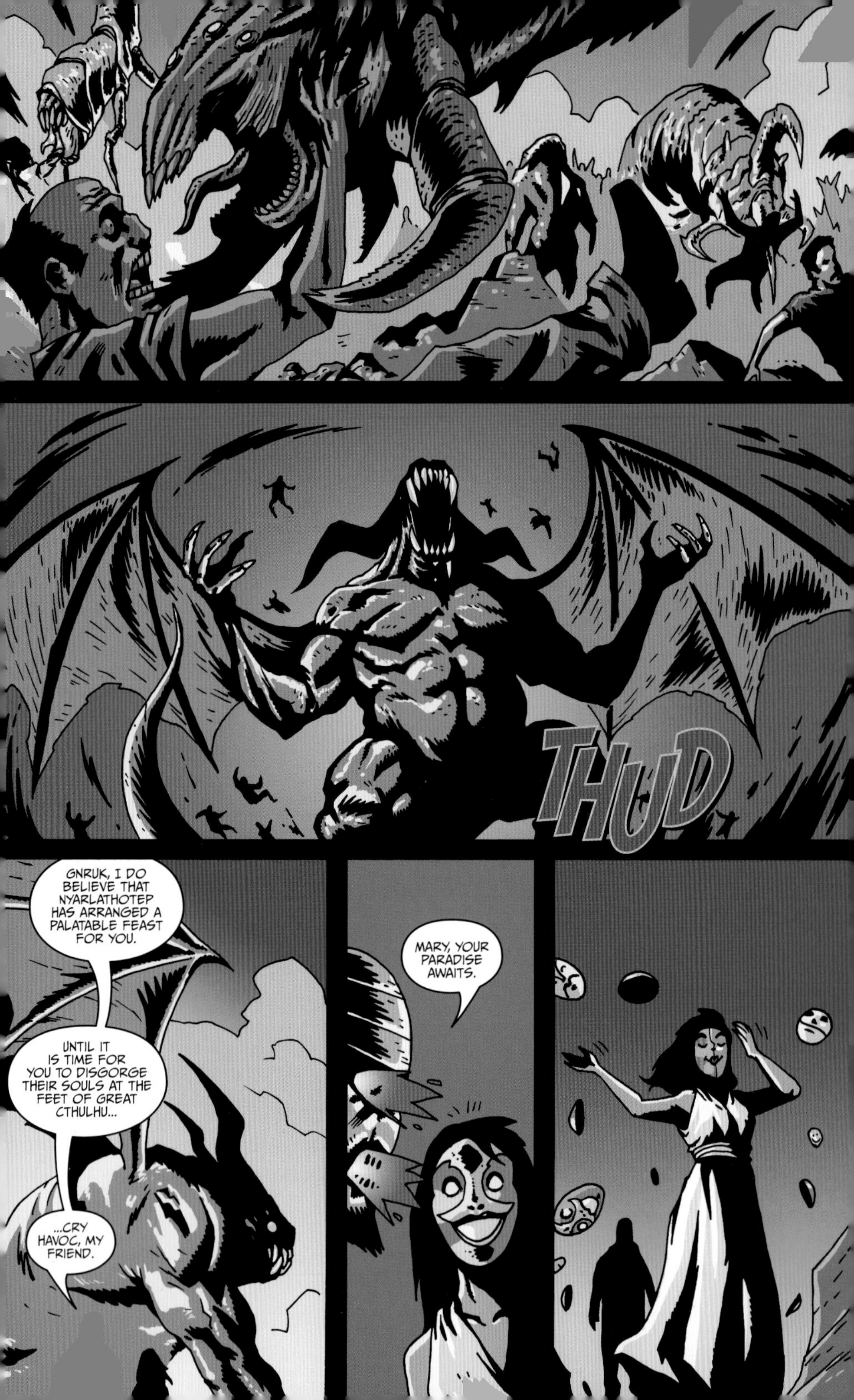
THUD
GNRUK, I DO BELIEVE THAT NYARLATHOTEP HAS ARRANGED A PALATABLE FEAST FOR YOU.
UNTIL IT IS TIME FOR YOU TO DISGORGE THEIR SOULS AT THE FEET OF GREAT CTHULHU...
...CRY HAVOC, MY FRIEND.
MARY, YOUR PARADISE AWAITS.

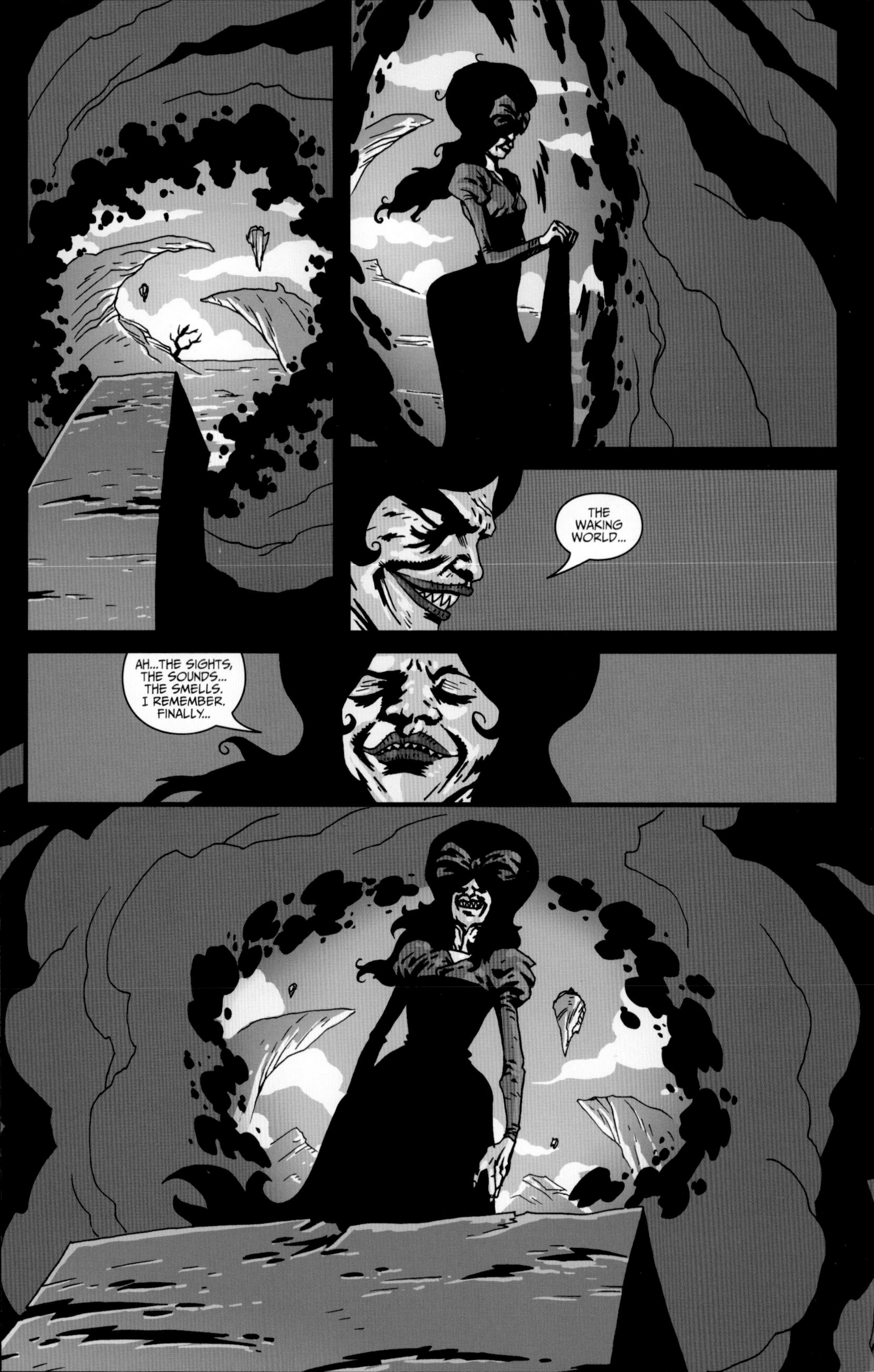
THE WAKING WORLD...
AH...THE SIGHTS, THE SOUNDS... THE SMELLS. I REMEMBER. FINALLY...

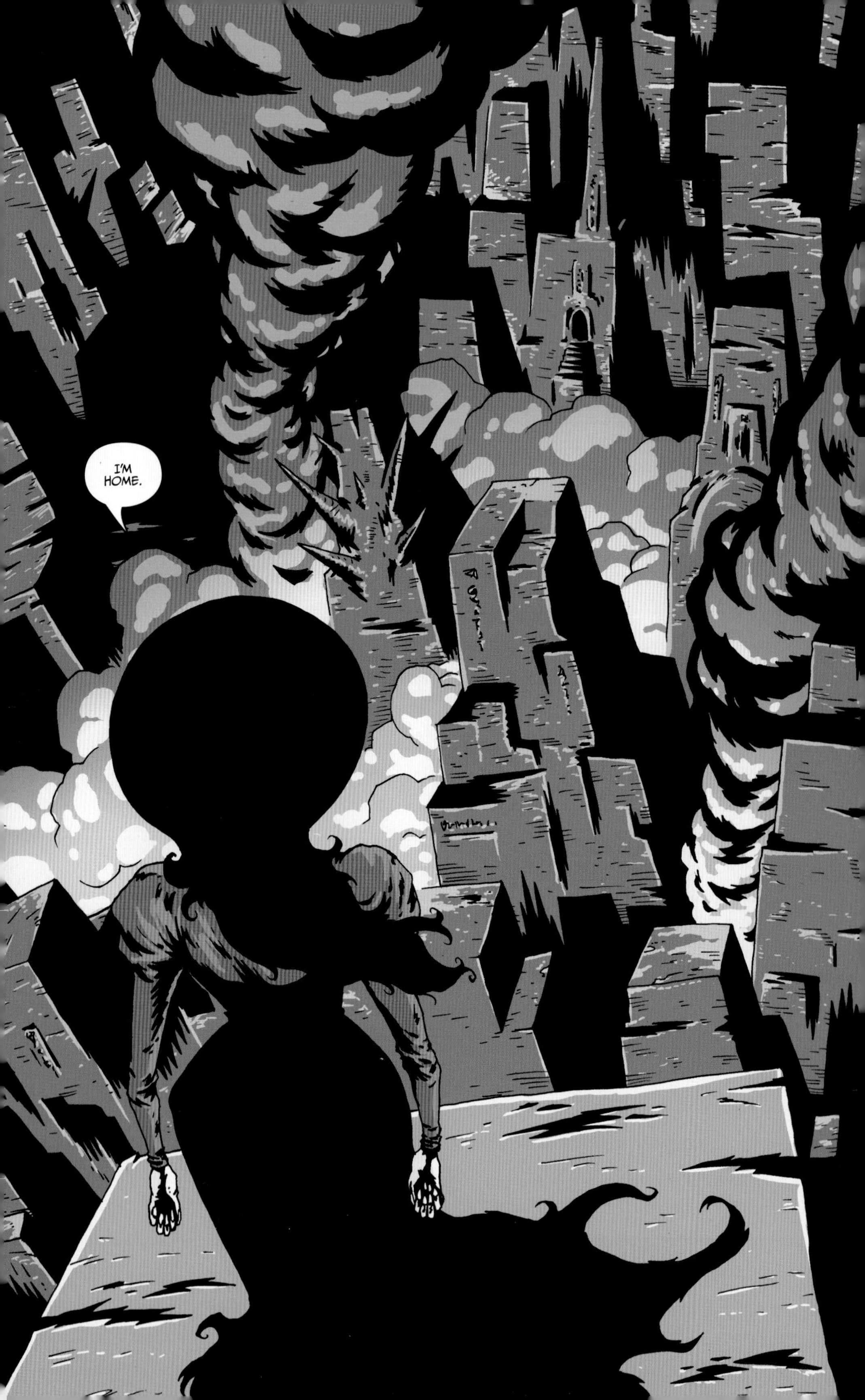
I'M HOME.

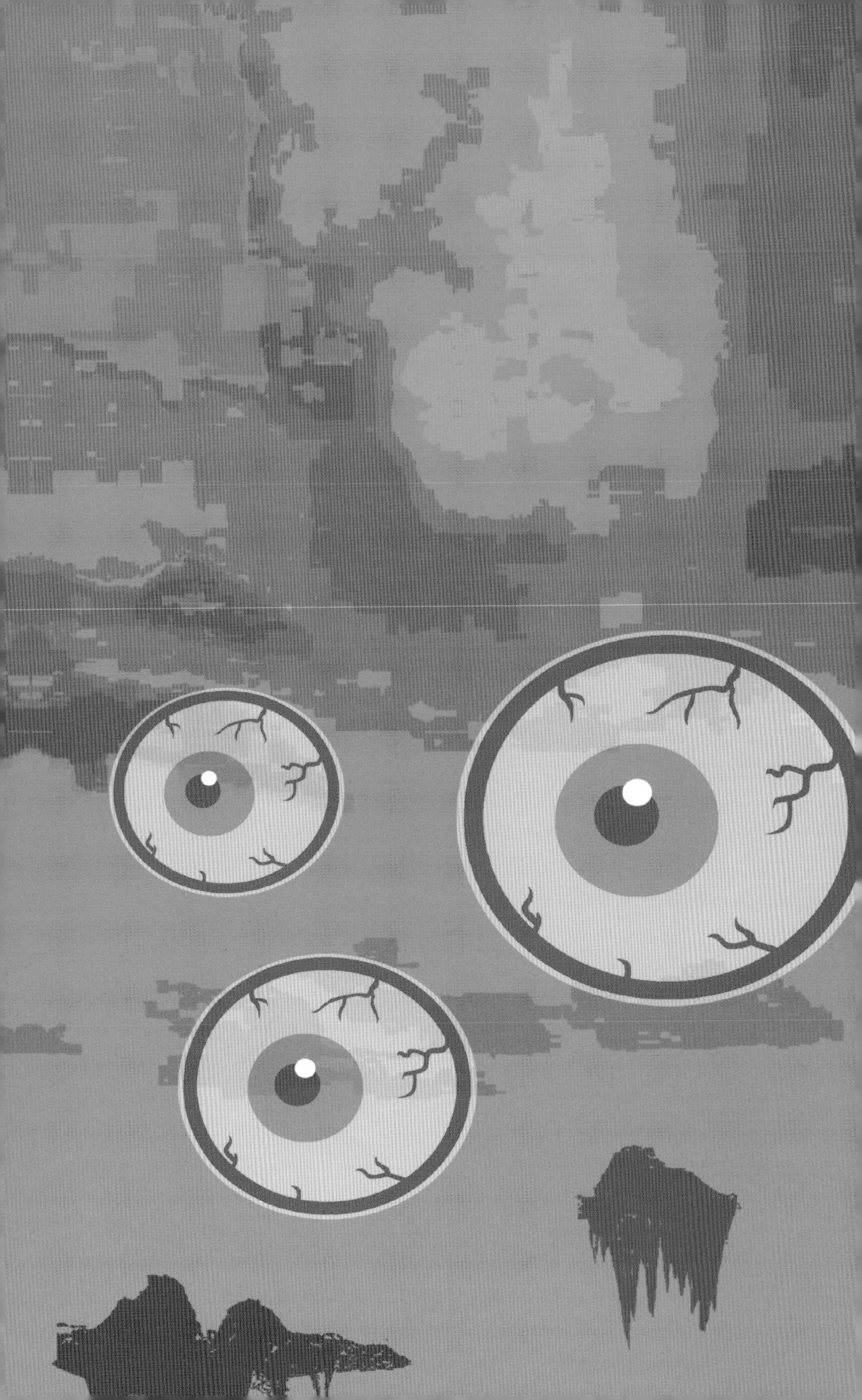

CHAPTER 2

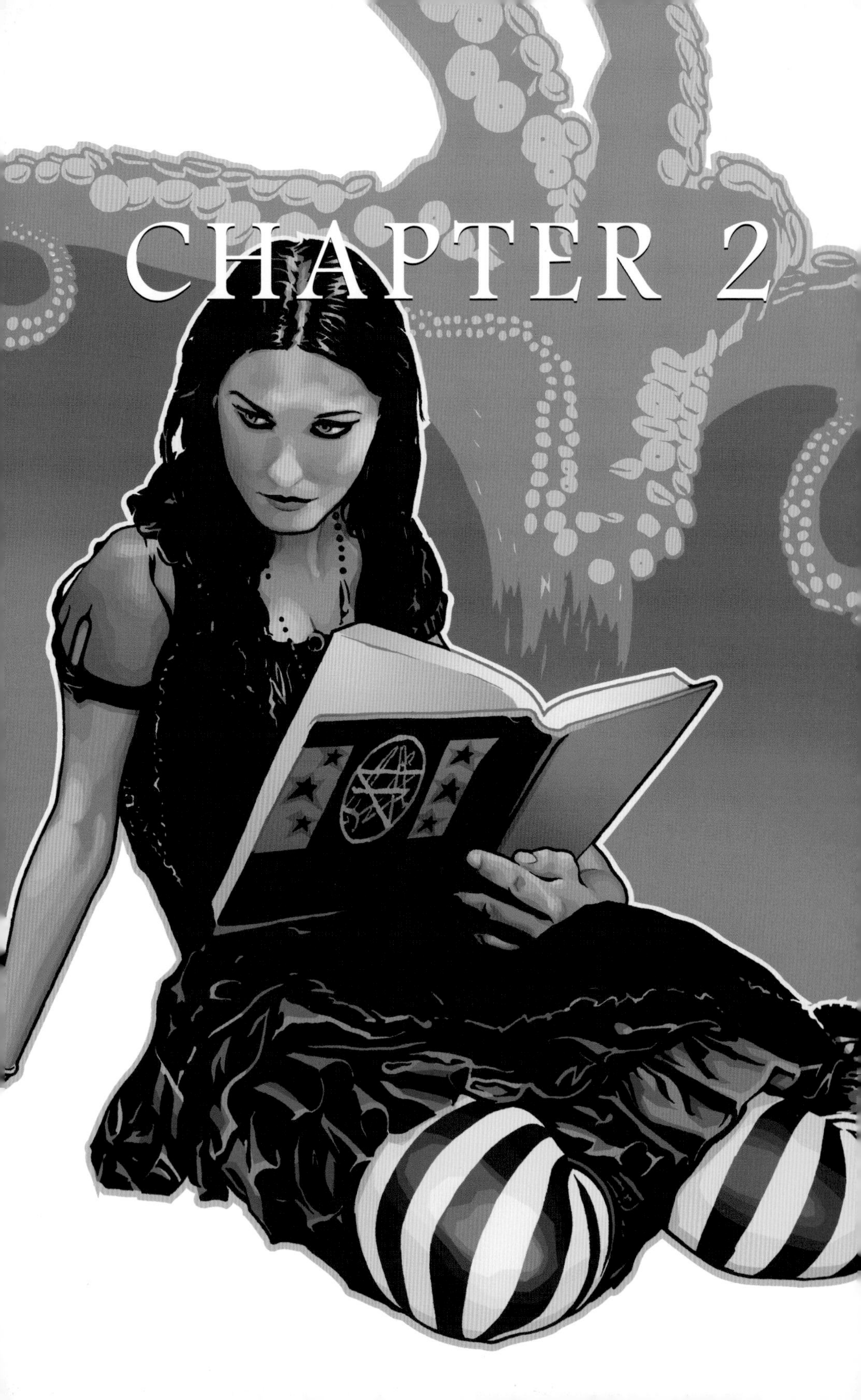

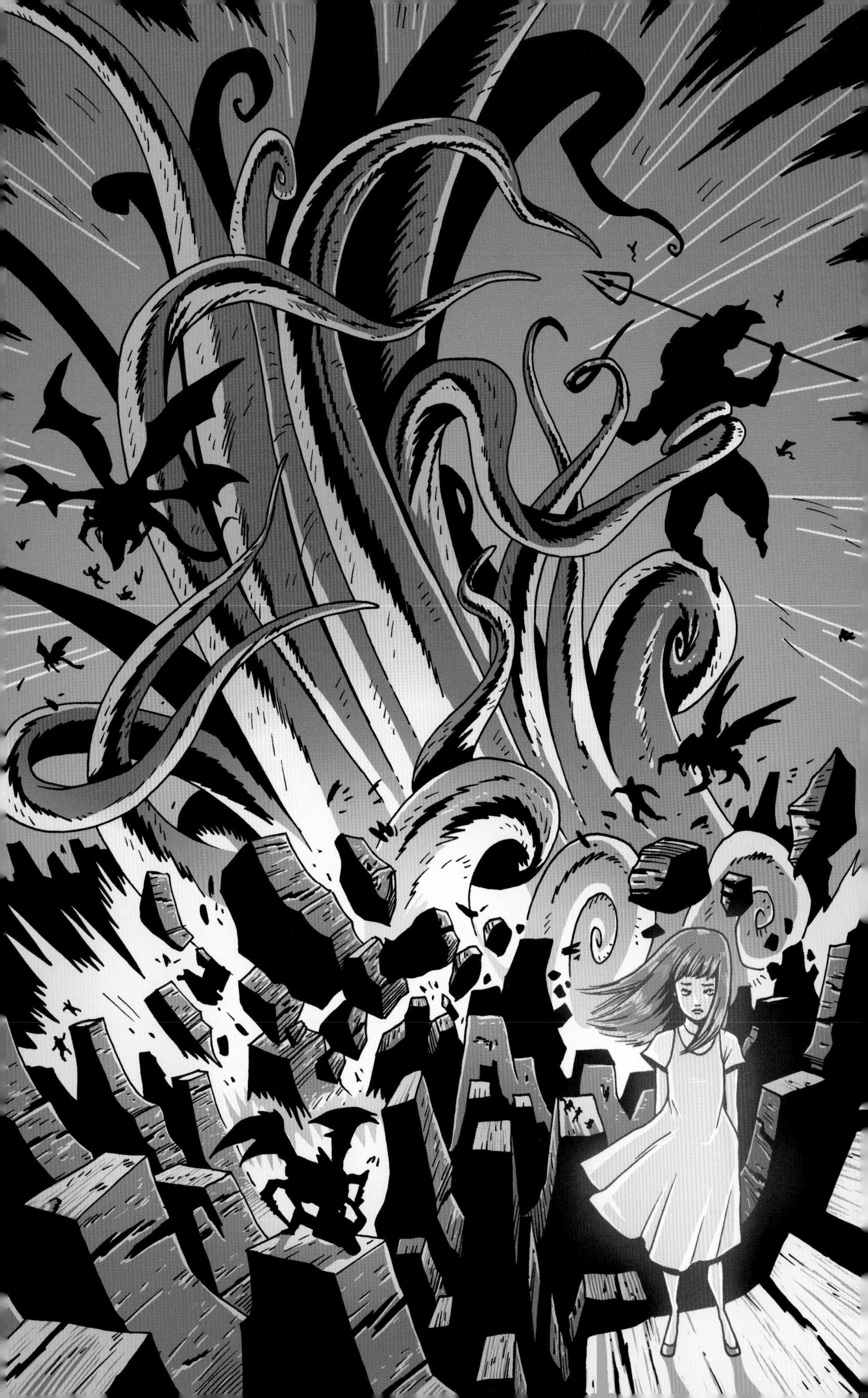

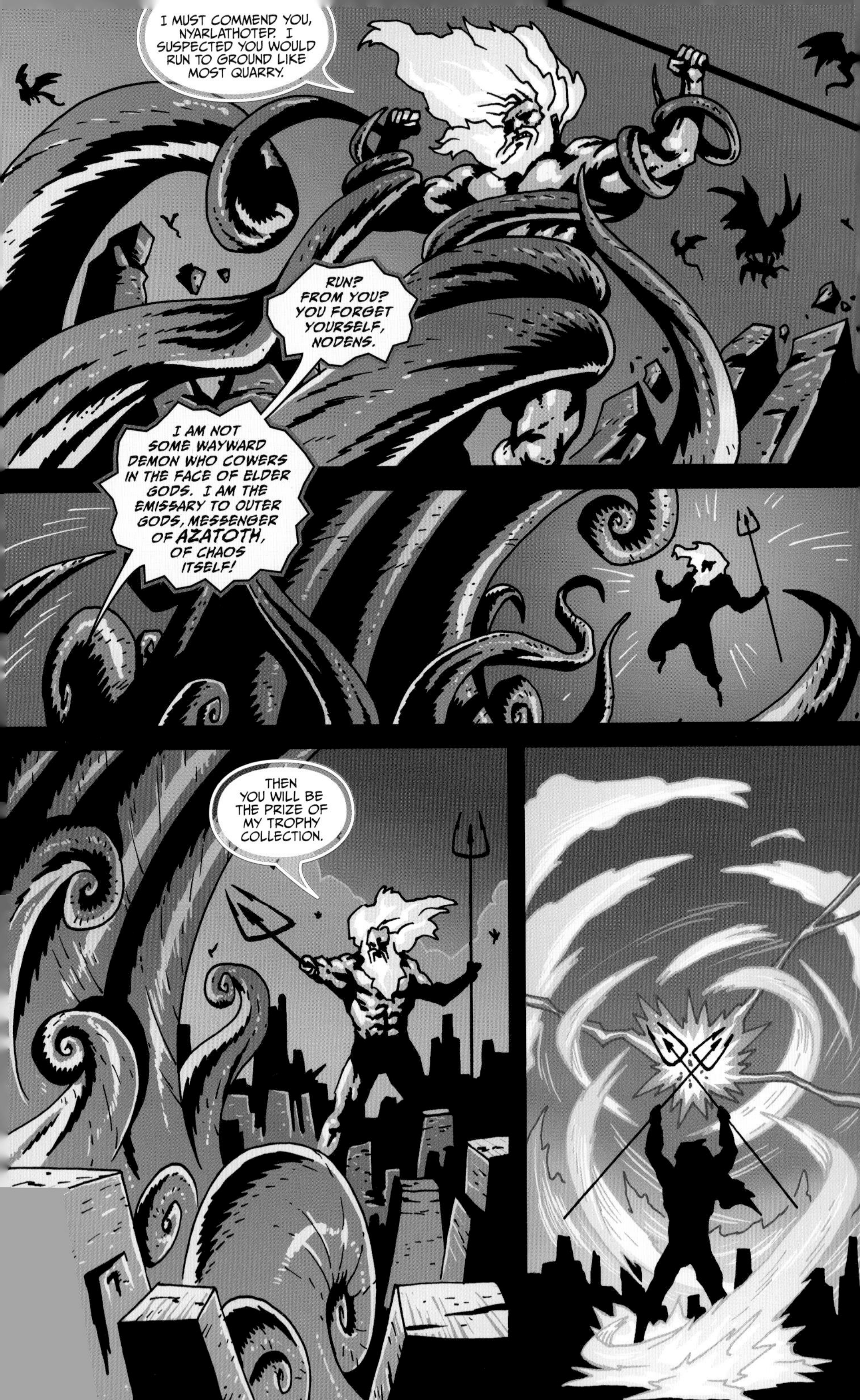
I MUST COMMEND YOU, NYARLATHOTEP. I SUSPECTED YOU WOULD RUN TO GROUND LIKE MOST QUARRY.
RUN? FROM YOU? YOU FORGET YOURSELF, NODENS.
I AM NOT SOME WAYWARD DEMON WHO COWERS IN THE FACE OF ELDER GODS. I AM THE EMISSARY TO OUTER GODS, MESSENGER OF AZATOTH, OF CHAOS ITSELF!
THEN YOU WILL BE THE PRIZE OF MY TROPHY COLLECTION.

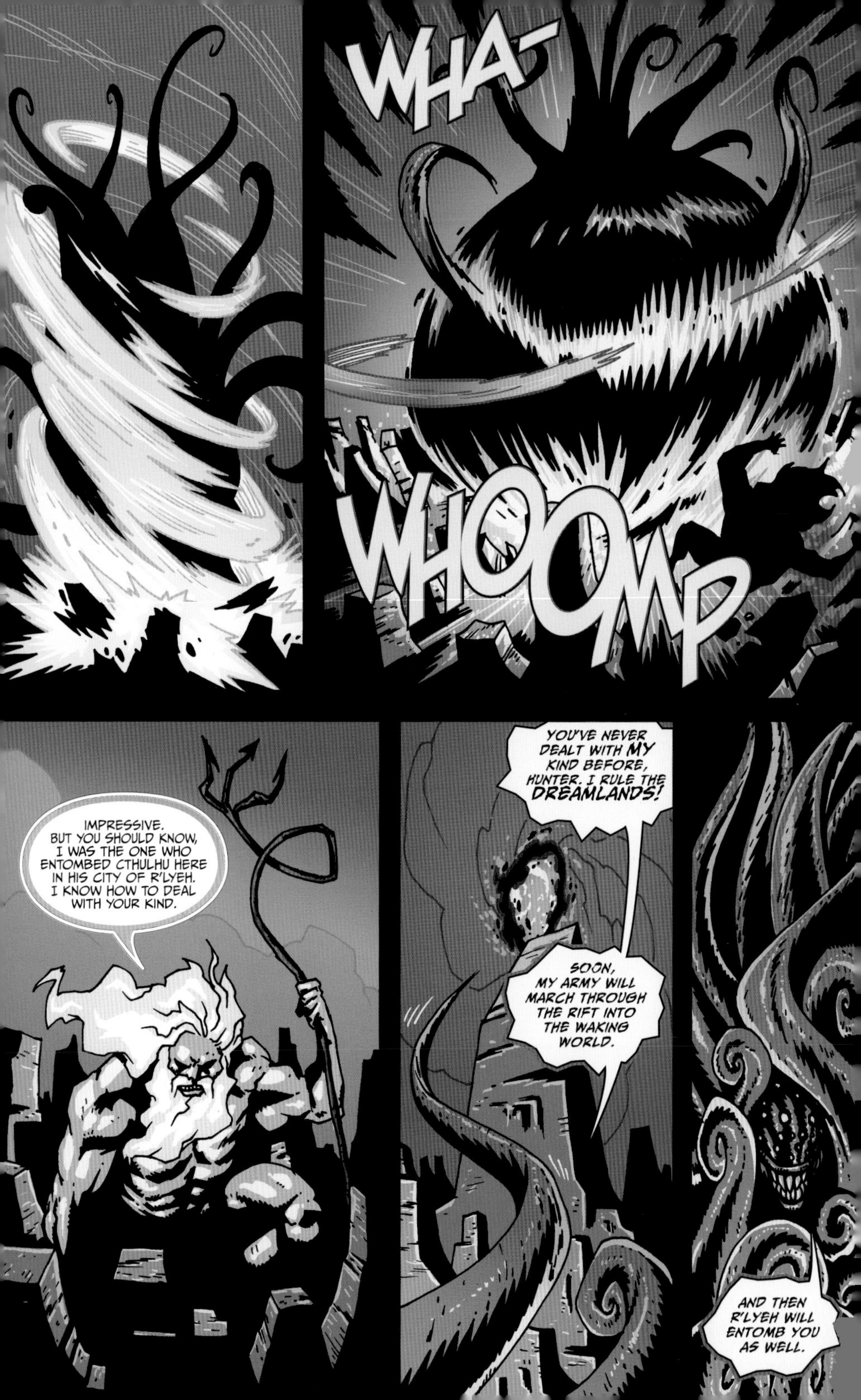
WHA-
WHOOMP
IMPRESSIVE. BUT YOU SHOULD KNOW, I WAS THE ONE WHO ENTOMBED CTHULHU HERE IN HIS CITY OF R'LYEH. I KNOW HOW TO DEAL WITH YOUR KIND.
YOU'VE NEVER DEALT WITH MY KIND BEFORE, HUNTER. I RULE THE DREAMLANDS!
SOON, MY ARMY WILL MARCH THROUGH THE RIFT INTO THE WAKING WORLD.
AND THEN R'LYEH WILL ENTOMB YOU AS WELL.

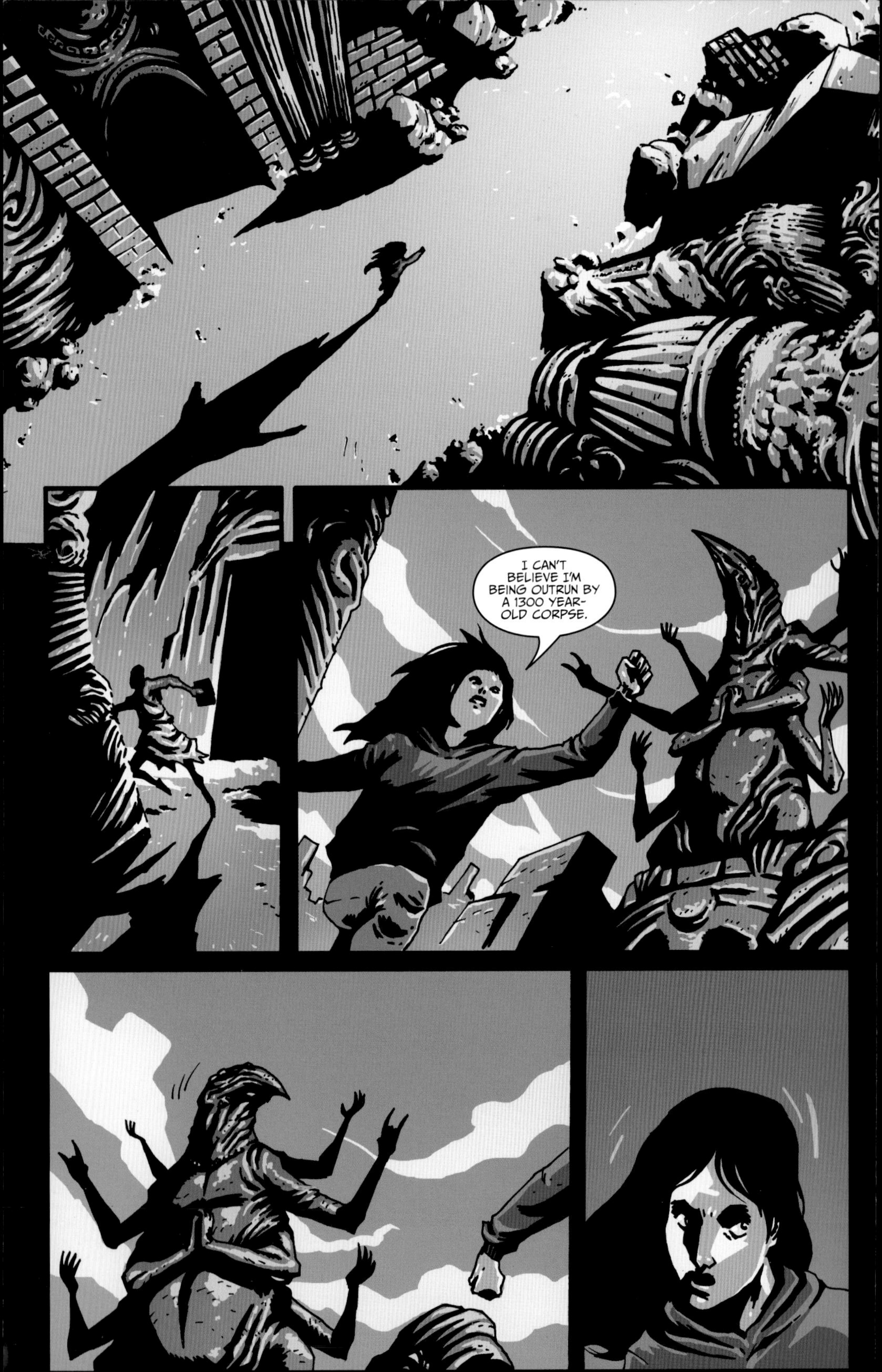
I CAN'T BELIEVE I'M BEING OUTRUN BY A 1300 YEAR-OLD CORPSE.

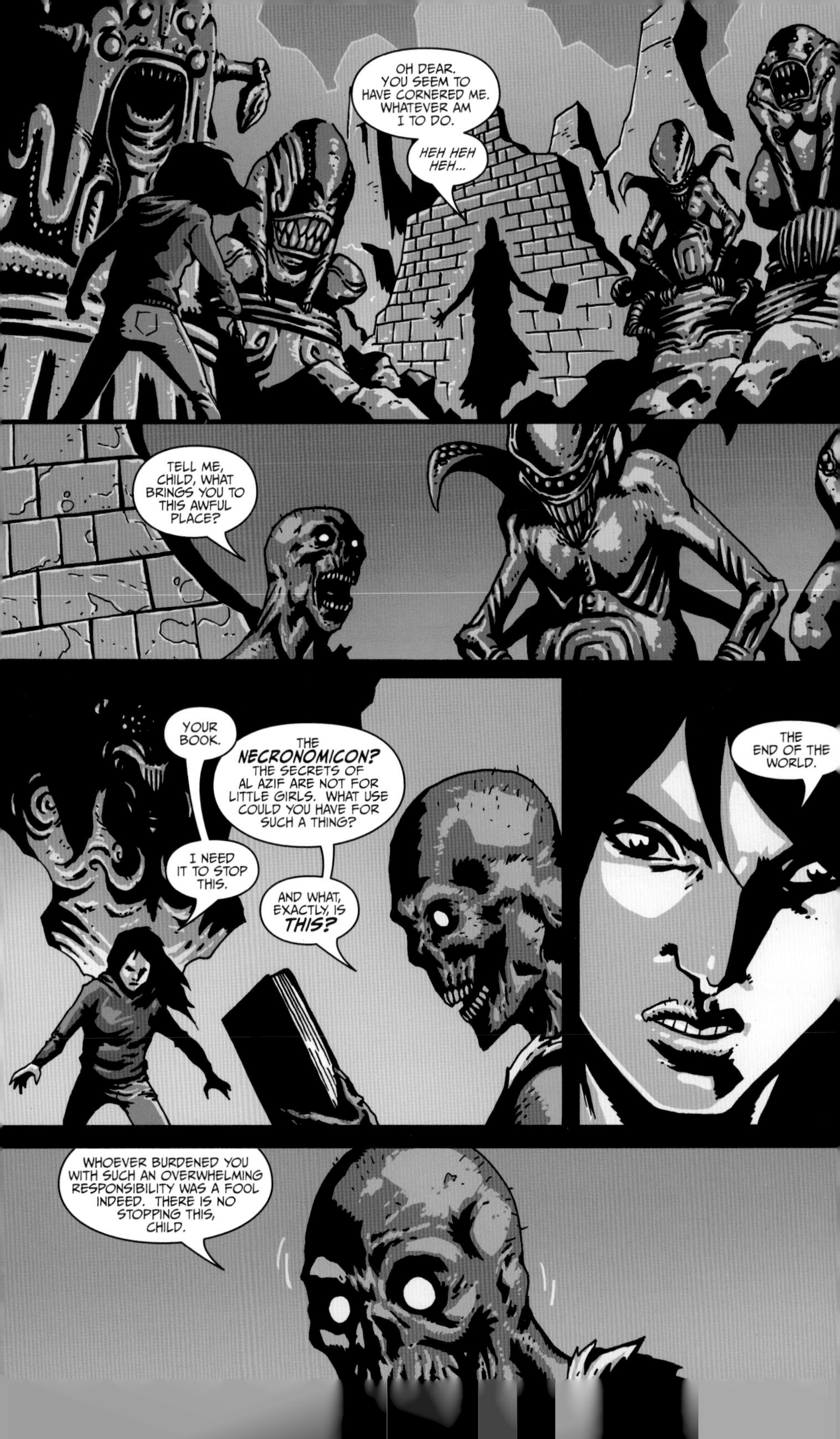
OH DEAR. YOU SEEM TO HAVE CORNERED ME. WHATEVER AM I TO DO.
HEH HEH HEH...
TELL ME, CHILD, WHAT BRINGS YOU TO THIS AWFUL PLACE?
YOUR BOOK.
THE NECRONOMICON? THE SECRETS OF AL AZIF ARE NOT FOR LITTLE GIRLS. WHAT USE COULD YOU HAVE FOR SUCH A THING?
I NEED IT TO STOP THIS.
AND WHAT, EXACTLY, IS THIS?
THE END OF THE WORLD.
WHOEVER BURDENED YOU WITH SUCH AN OVERWHELMING RESPONSIBILITY WAS A FOOL INDEED. THERE IS NO STOPPING THIS, CHILD.

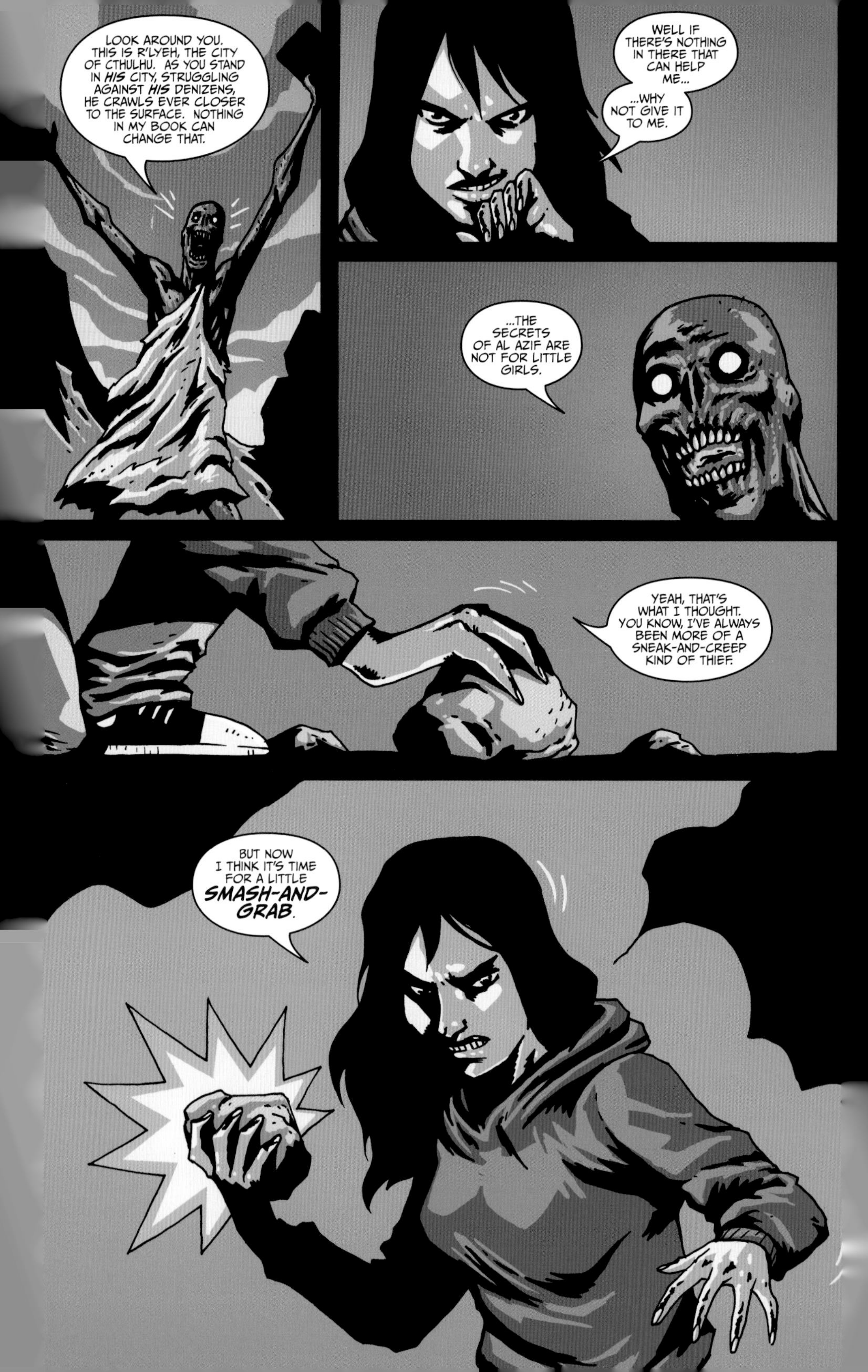
LOOK AROUND YOU. THIS IS R'LYEH, THE CITY OF CTHULHU. AS YOU STAND IN *HIS* CITY, STRUGGLING AGAINST *HIS* DENIZENS, HE CRAWLS EVER CLOSER TO THE SURFACE. NOTHING IN MY BOOK CAN CHANGE THAT.
WELL IF THERE'S NOTHING IN THERE THAT CAN HELP ME...
...WHY NOT GIVE IT TO ME.
...THE SECRETS OF AL AZIF ARE NOT FOR LITTLE GIRLS.
YEAH, THAT'S WHAT I THOUGHT. YOU KNOW, I'VE ALWAYS BEEN MORE OF A SNEAK-AND-CREEP KIND OF THIEF.
BUT NOW I THINK IT'S TIME FOR A LITTLE **SMASH-AND-GRAB**.

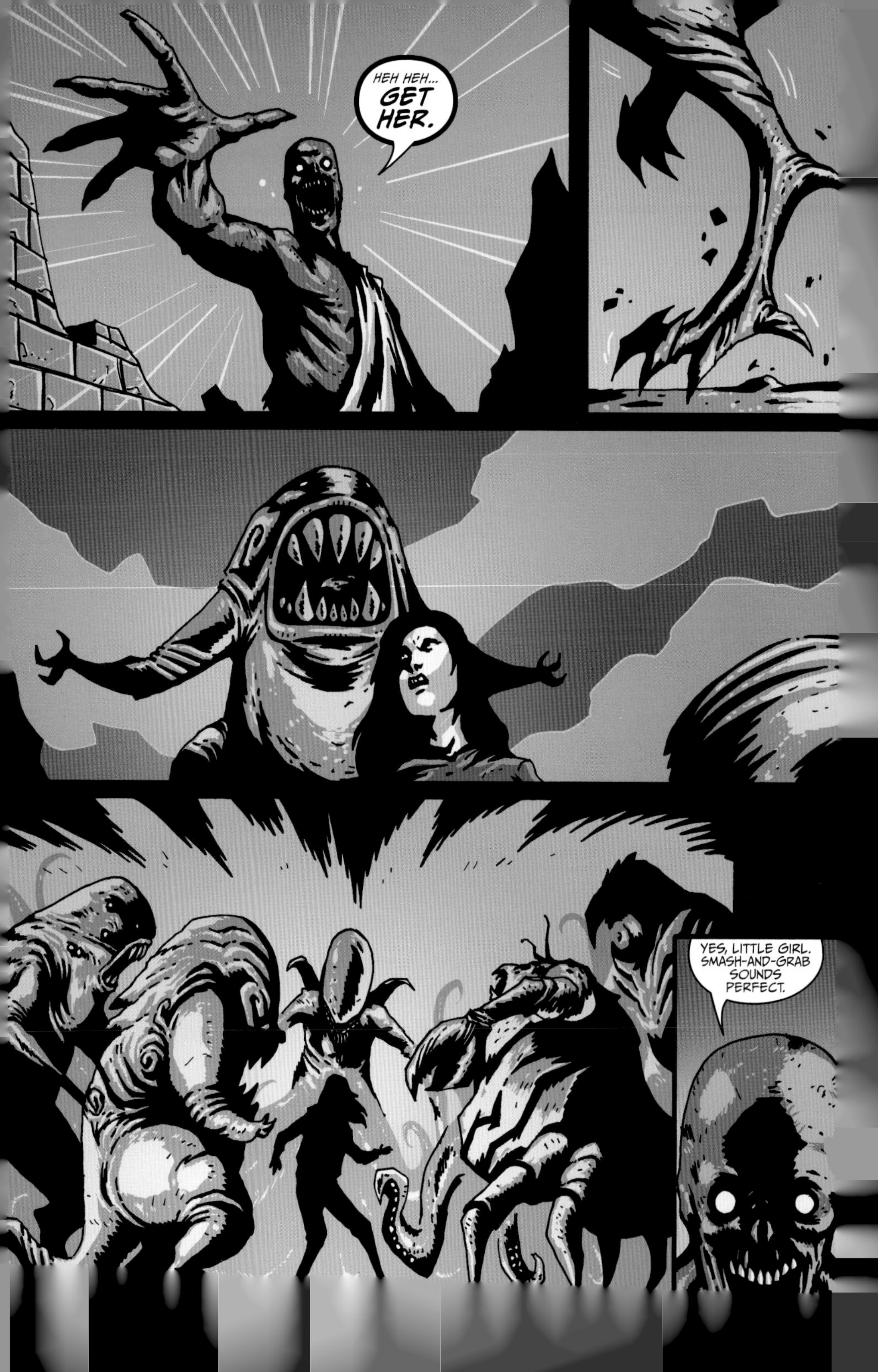
HEH HEH... GET HER.
YES, LITTLE GIRL. SMASH-AND-GRAB SOUNDS PERFECT.

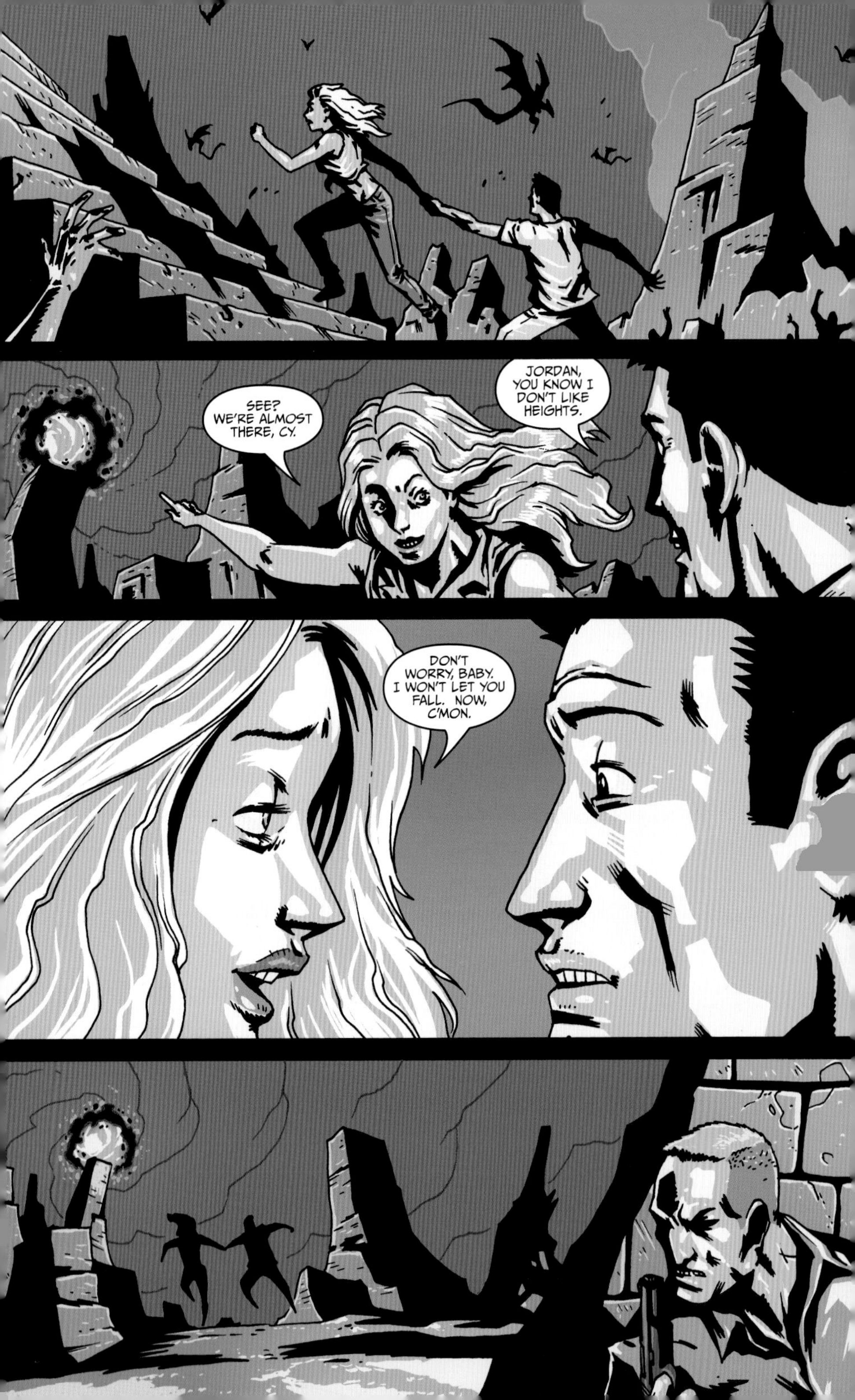
SEE? WE'RE ALMOST THERE, CY.
JORDAN, YOU KNOW I DON'T LIKE HEIGHTS.
DON'T WORRY, BABY. I WON'T LET YOU FALL. NOW, C'MON.

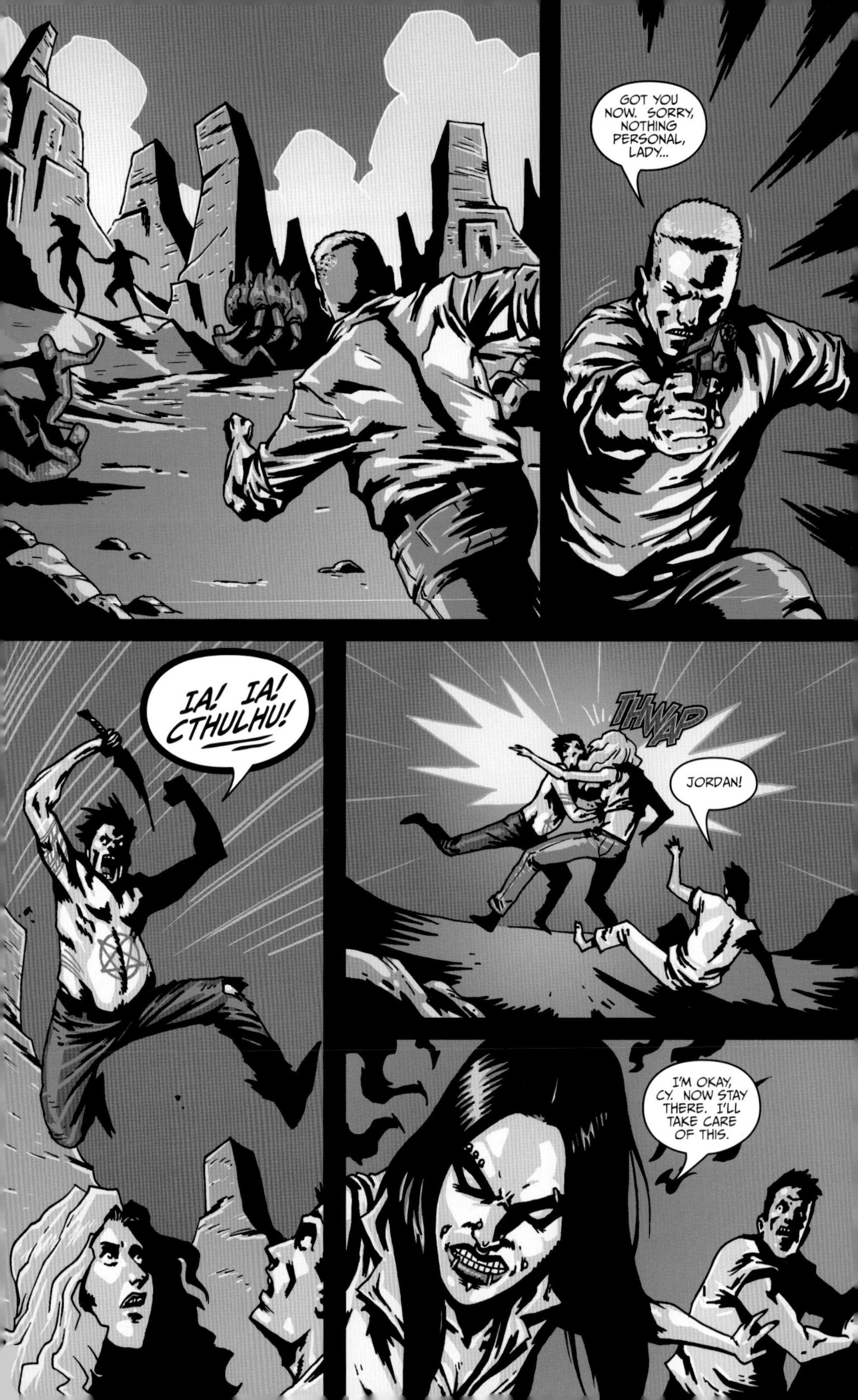
GOT YOU NOW. SORRY, NOTHING PERSONAL, LADY...
IA! IA! CTHULHU!
THWAP
JORDAN!
I'M OKAY, CY. NOW STAY THERE. I'LL TAKE CARE OF THIS.

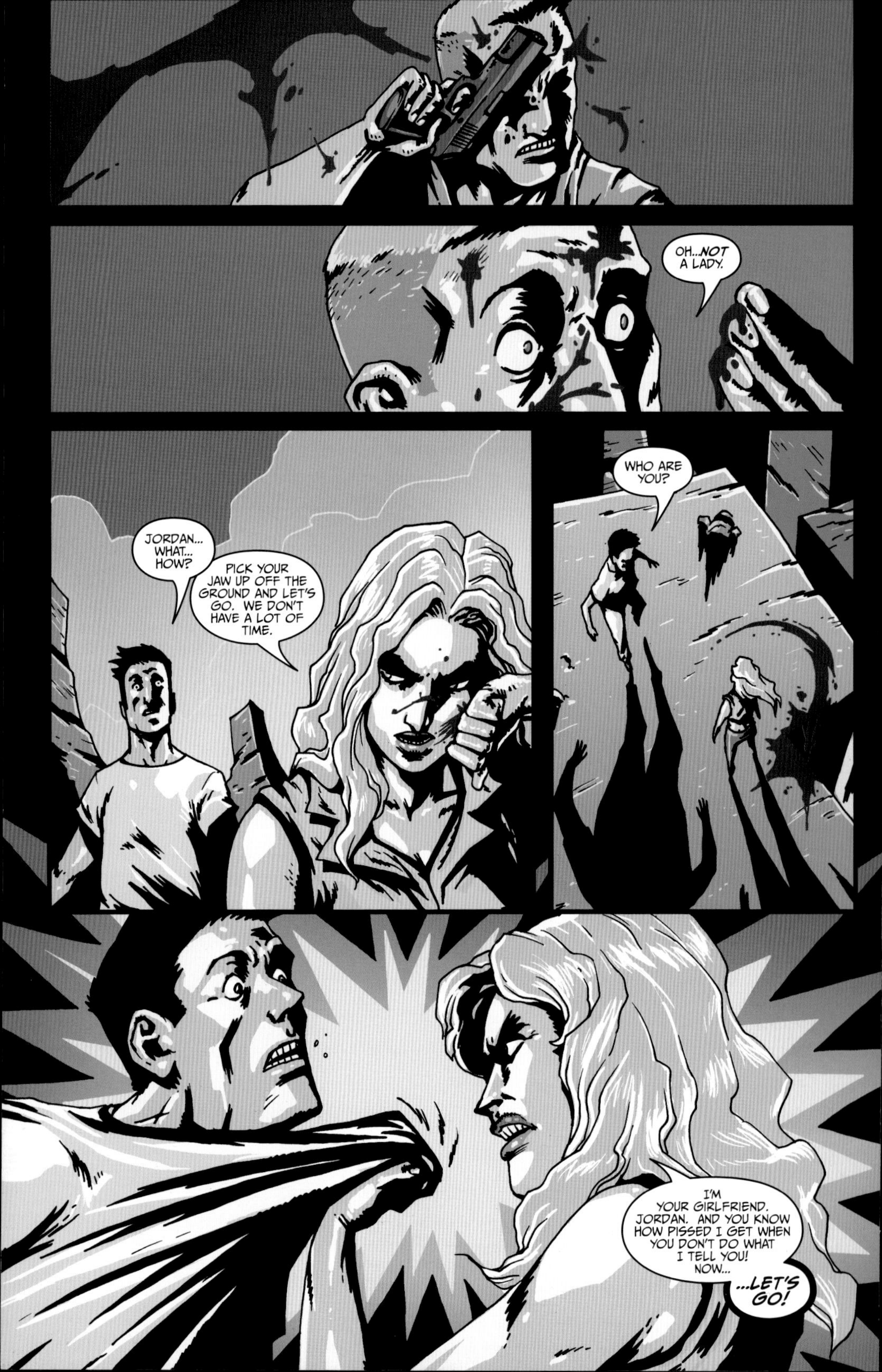
OH...NOT A LADY.
JORDAN... WHAT... HOW?
PICK YOUR JAW UP OFF THE GROUND AND LET'S GO. WE DON'T HAVE A LOT OF TIME.
WHO ARE YOU?
I'M YOUR GIRLFRIEND. JORDAN. AND YOU KNOW HOW PISSED I GET WHEN YOU DON'T DO WHAT I TELL YOU! NOW...
...LET'S GO!

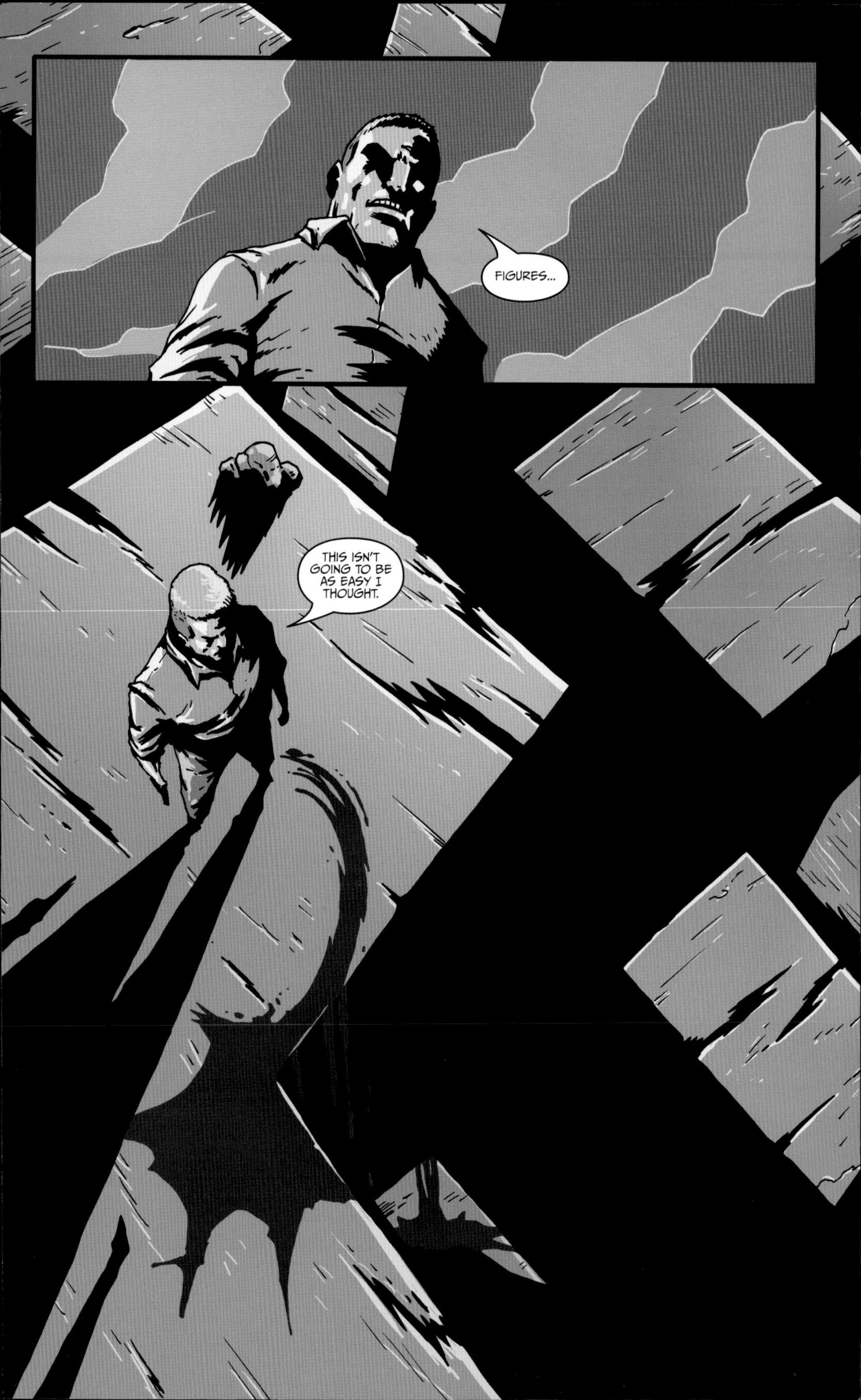
FIGURES...
THIS ISN'T GOING TO BE AS EASY I THOUGHT.

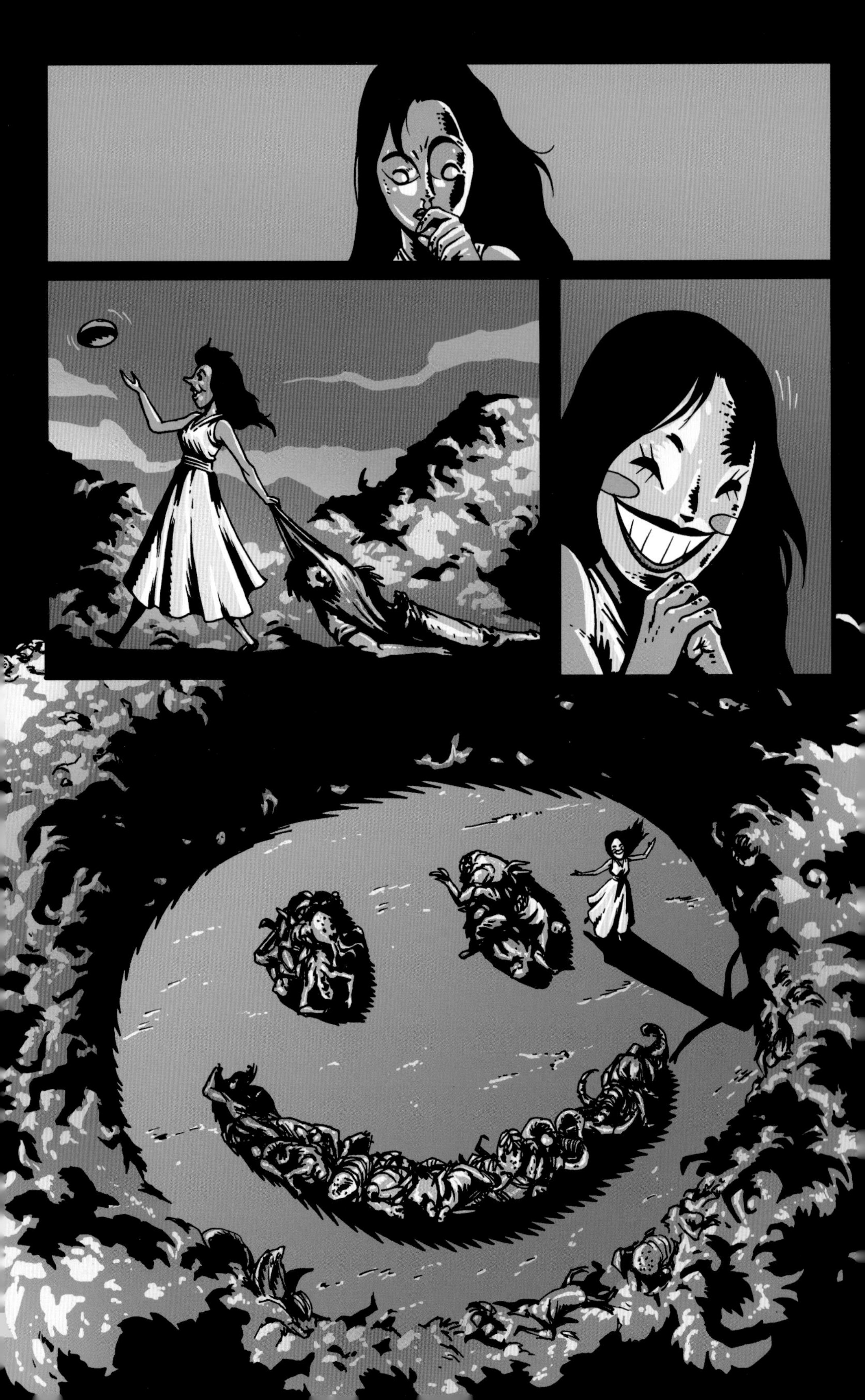

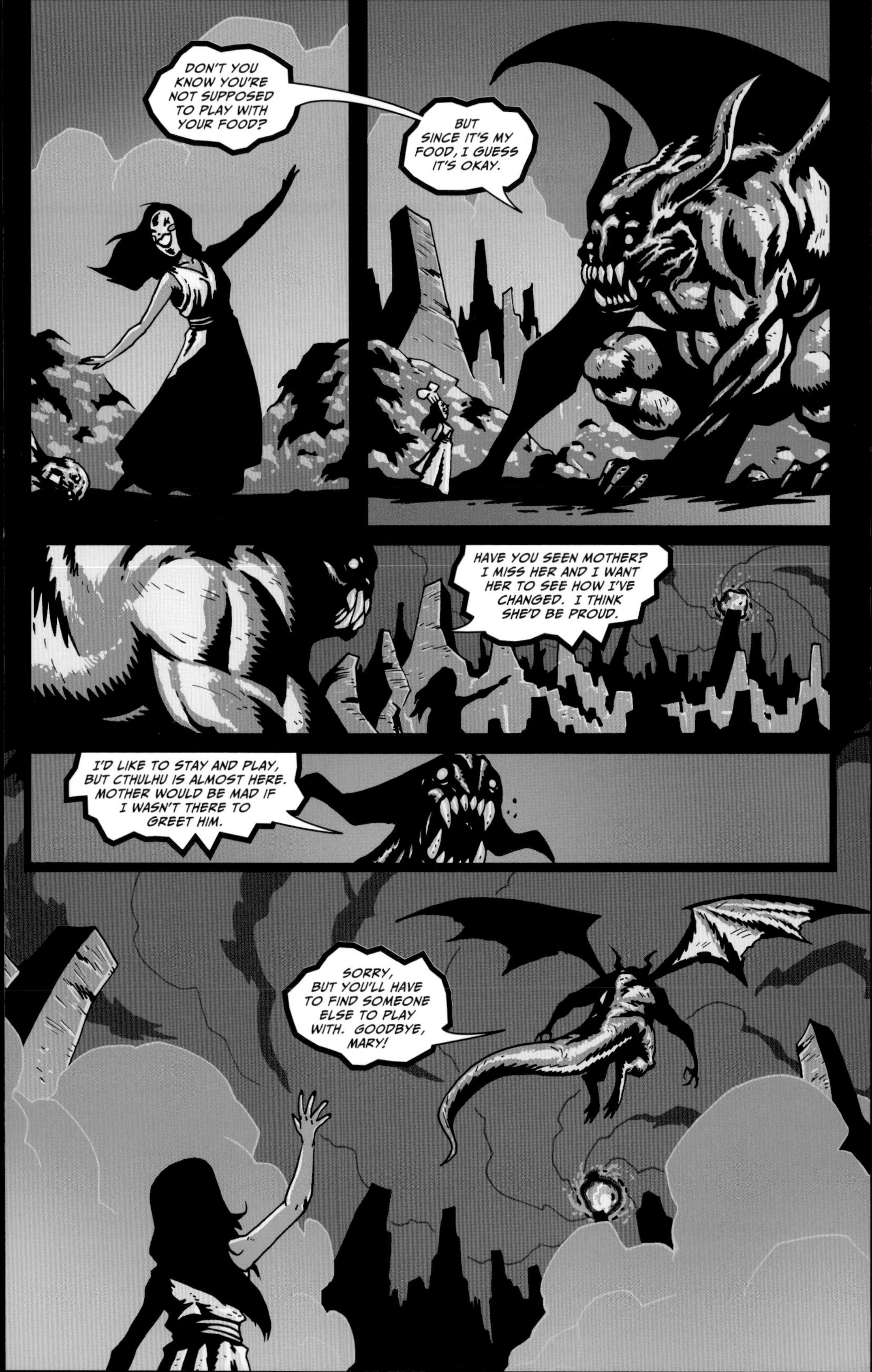
DON'T YOU KNOW YOU'RE NOT SUPPOSED TO PLAY WITH YOUR FOOD?
BUT SINCE IT'S MY FOOD, I GUESS IT'S OKAY.
HAVE YOU SEEN MOTHER? I MISS HER AND I WANT HER TO SEE HOW I'VE CHANGED. I THINK SHE'D BE PROUD.
I'D LIKE TO STAY AND PLAY, BUT CTHULHU IS ALMOST HERE. MOTHER WOULD BE MAD IF I WASN'T THERE TO GREET HIM.
SORRY, BUT YOU'LL HAVE TO FIND SOMEONE ELSE TO PLAY WITH. GOODBYE, MARY!

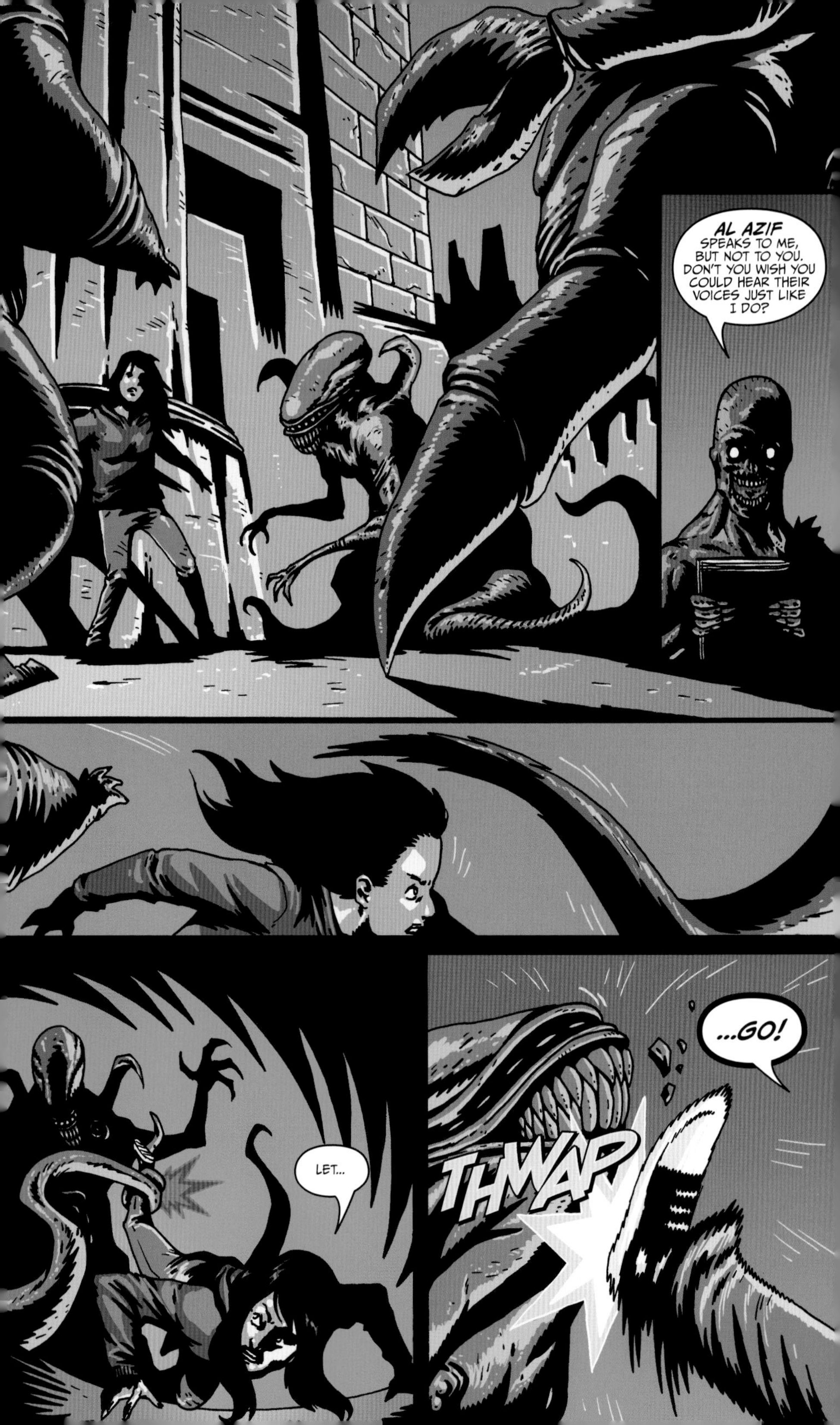
AL AZIF SPEAKS TO ME, BUT NOT TO YOU. DON'T YOU WISH YOU COULD HEAR THEIR VOICES JUST LIKE I DO?
LET...
THWAP
...GO!

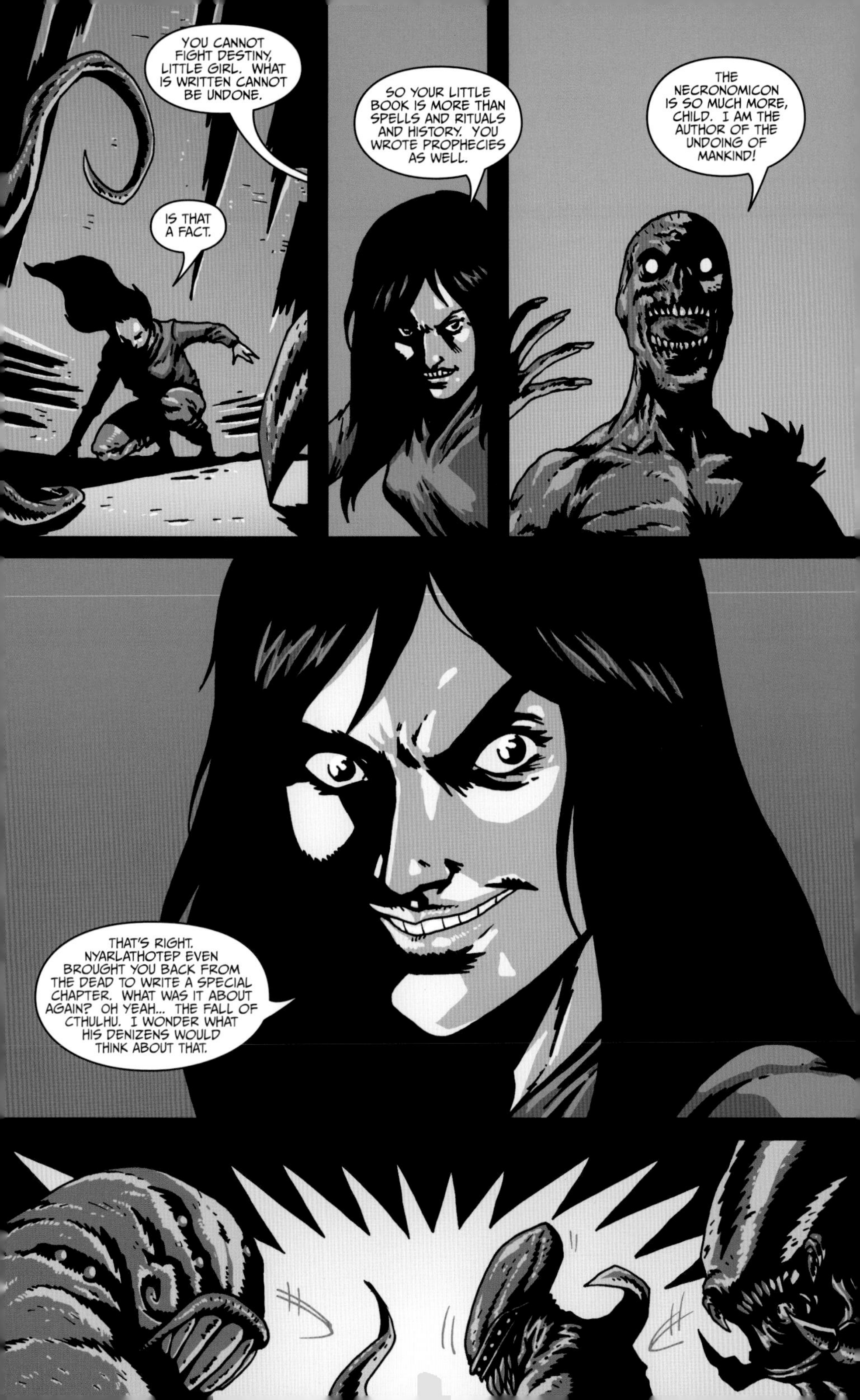
YOU CANNOT FIGHT DESTINY, LITTLE GIRL. WHAT IS WRITTEN CANNOT BE UNDONE.
IS THAT A FACT.
SO YOUR LITTLE BOOK IS MORE THAN SPELLS AND RITUALS AND HISTORY. YOU WROTE PROPHECIES AS WELL.
THE NECRONOMICON IS SO MUCH MORE, CHILD. I AM THE AUTHOR OF THE UNDOING OF MANKIND!
THAT'S RIGHT. NYARLATHOTEP EVEN BROUGHT YOU BACK FROM THE DEAD TO WRITE A SPECIAL CHAPTER. WHAT WAS IT ABOUT AGAIN? OH YEAH... THE FALL OF CTHULHU. I WONDER WHAT HIS DENIZENS WOULD THINK ABOUT THAT.

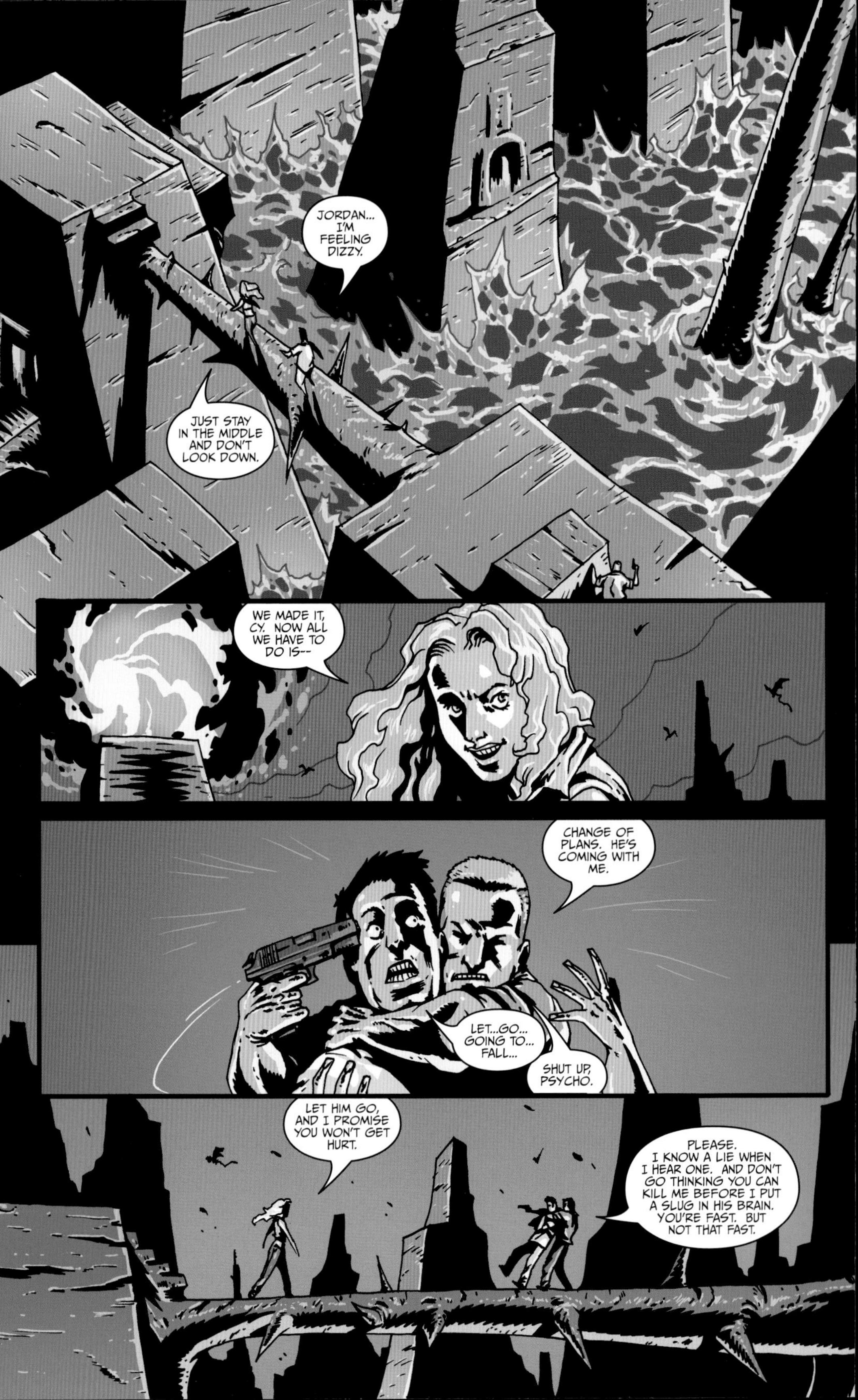
JORDAN... I'M FEELING DIZZY.
JUST STAY IN THE MIDDLE AND DON'T LOOK DOWN.
WE MADE IT, CY. NOW ALL WE HAVE TO DO IS--
CHANGE OF PLANS. HE'S COMING WITH ME.
LET...GO... GOING TO... FALL...
SHUT UP, PSYCHO.
LET HIM GO, AND I PROMISE YOU WON'T GET HURT.
PLEASE. I KNOW A LIE WHEN I HEAR ONE. AND DON'T GO THINKING YOU CAN KILL ME BEFORE I PUT A SLUG IN HIS BRAIN. YOU'RE FAST. BUT NOT THAT FAST.

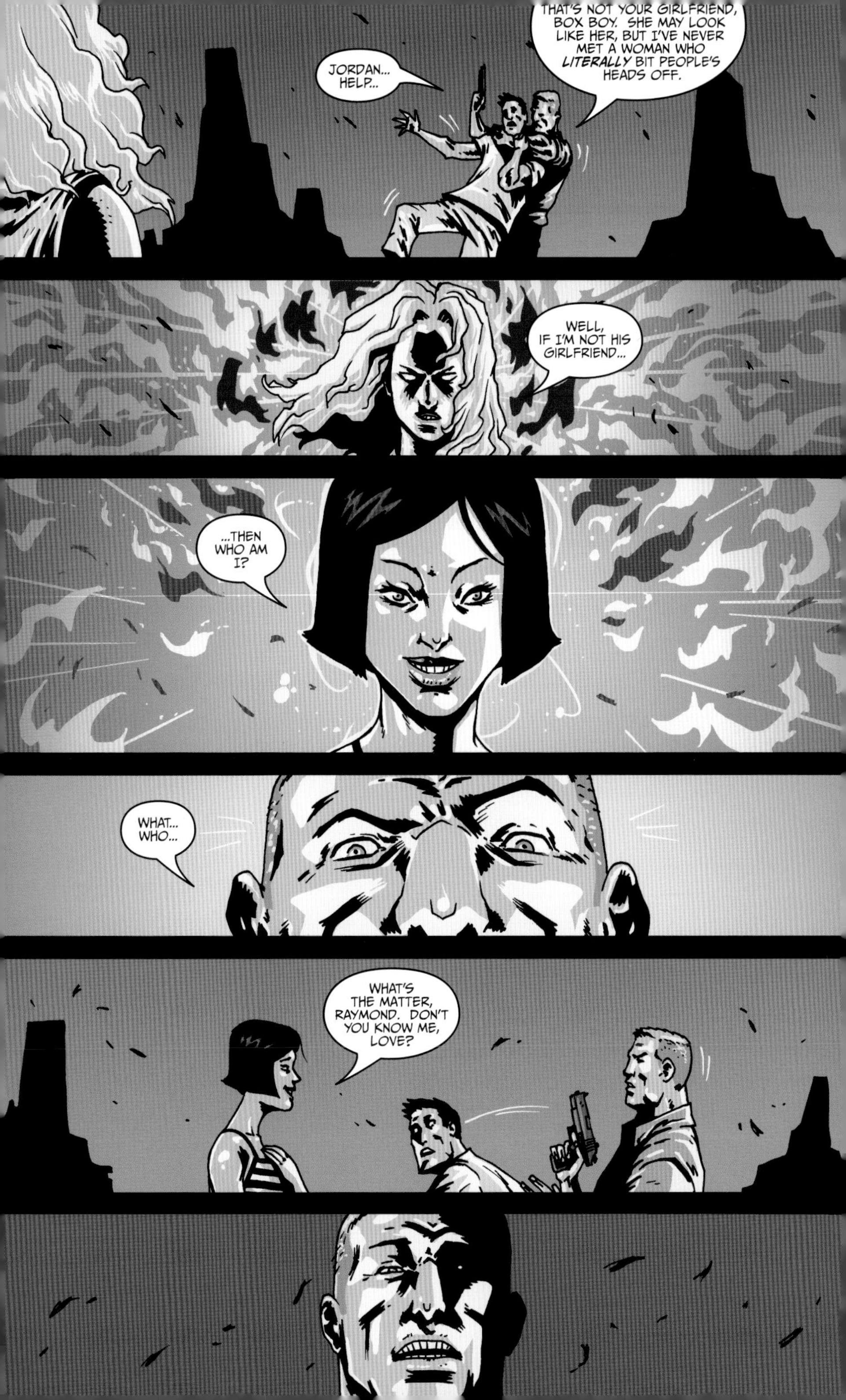
JORDAN... HELP...
THAT'S NOT YOUR GIRLFRIEND, BOX BOY. SHE MAY LOOK LIKE HER, BUT I'VE NEVER MET A WOMAN WHO *LITERALLY* BIT PEOPLE'S HEADS OFF.
WELL, IF I'M NOT HIS GIRLFRIEND...
...THEN WHO AM I?
WHAT... WHO...
WHAT'S THE MATTER, RAYMOND. DON'T YOU KNOW ME, LOVE?

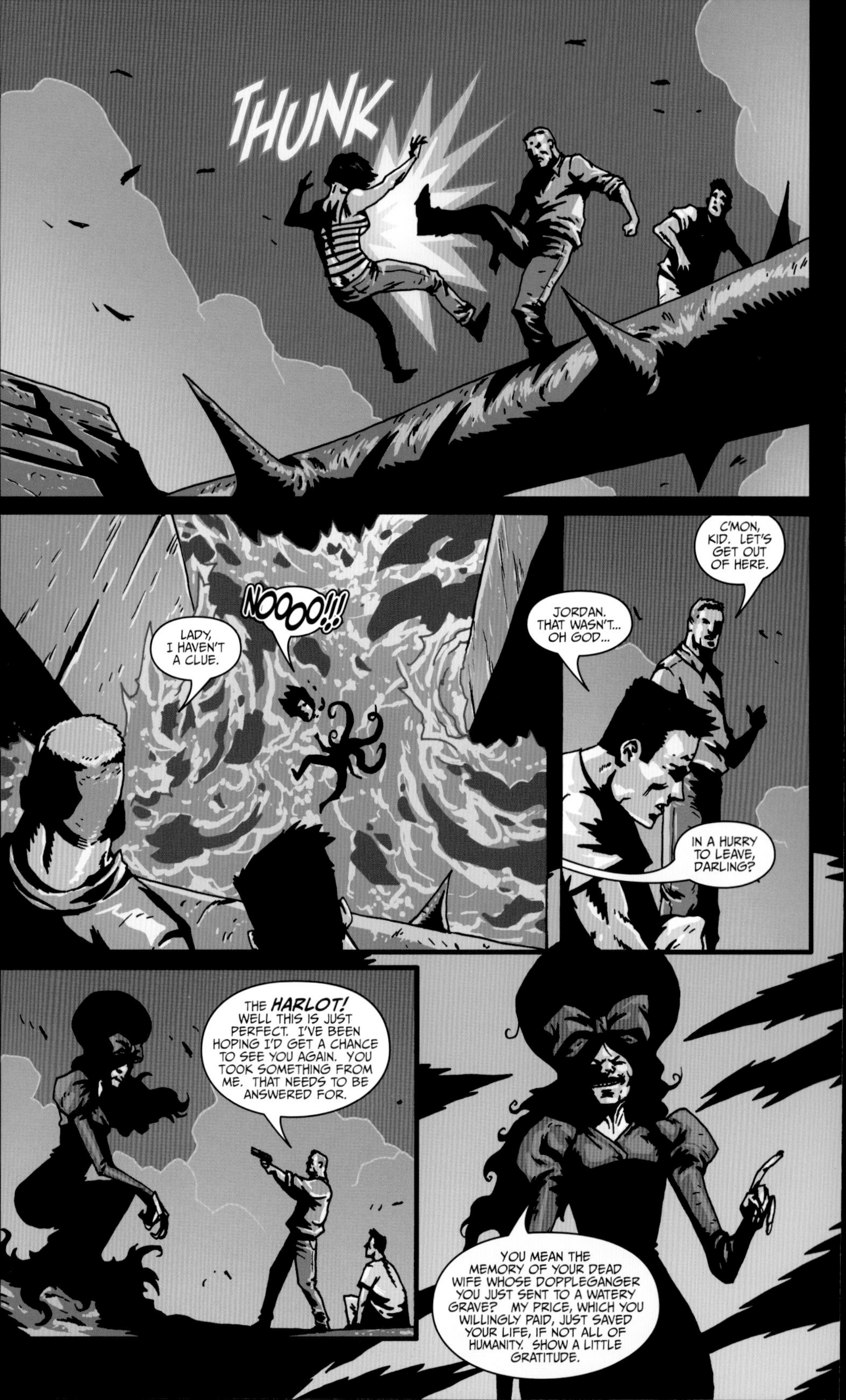
THUNK
LADY, I HAVEN'T A CLUE.
NOOOO!!!
C'MON, KID. LET'S GET OUT OF HERE.
JORDAN. THAT WASN'T... OH GOD...
IN A HURRY TO LEAVE, DARLING?
THE HARLOT! WELL THIS IS JUST PERFECT. I'VE BEEN HOPING I'D GET A CHANCE TO SEE YOU AGAIN. YOU TOOK SOMETHING FROM ME. THAT NEEDS TO BE ANSWERED FOR.
YOU MEAN THE MEMORY OF YOUR DEAD WIFE WHOSE DOPPLEGANGER YOU JUST SENT TO A WATERY GRAVE? MY PRICE, WHICH YOU WILLINGLY PAID, JUST SAVED YOUR LIFE, IF NOT ALL OF HUMANITY. SHOW A LITTLE GRATITUDE.

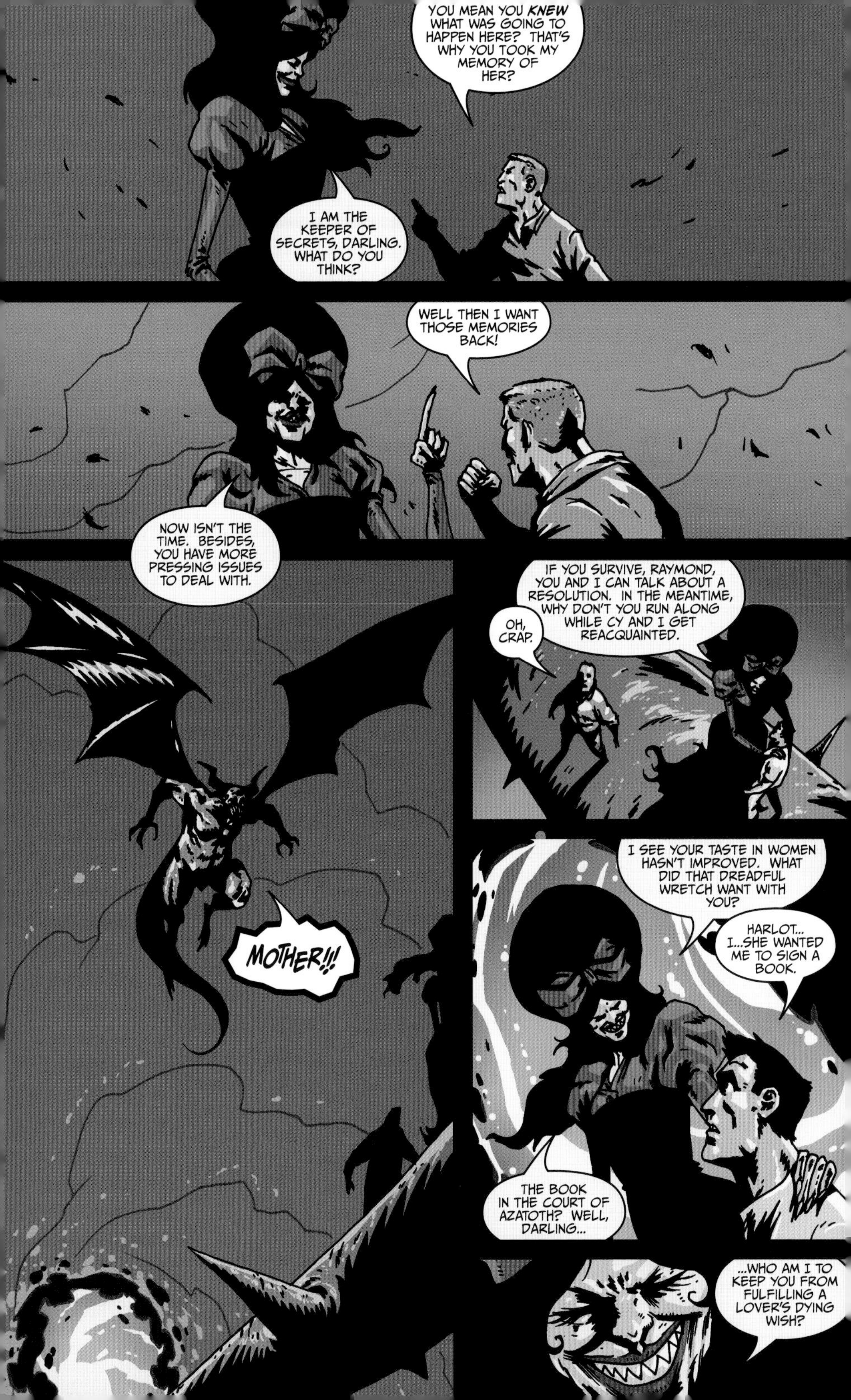
YOU MEAN YOU KNEW WHAT WAS GOING TO HAPPEN HERE? THAT'S WHY YOU TOOK MY MEMORY OF HER?
I AM THE KEEPER OF SECRETS, DARLING. WHAT DO YOU THINK?
WELL THEN I WANT THOSE MEMORIES BACK!
NOW ISN'T THE TIME. BESIDES, YOU HAVE MORE PRESSING ISSUES TO DEAL WITH.
MOTHER!!!
IF YOU SURVIVE, RAYMOND, YOU AND I CAN TALK ABOUT A RESOLUTION. IN THE MEANTIME, WHY DON'T YOU RUN ALONG WHILE CY AND I GET REACQUAINTED.
OH, CRAP.
I SEE YOUR TASTE IN WOMEN HASN'T IMPROVED. WHAT DID THAT DREADFUL WRETCH WANT WITH YOU?
HARLOT... I...SHE WANTED ME TO SIGN A BOOK.
THE BOOK IN THE COURT OF AZATOTH? WELL, DARLING...
...WHO AM I TO KEEP YOU FROM FULFILLING A LOVER'S DYING WISH?

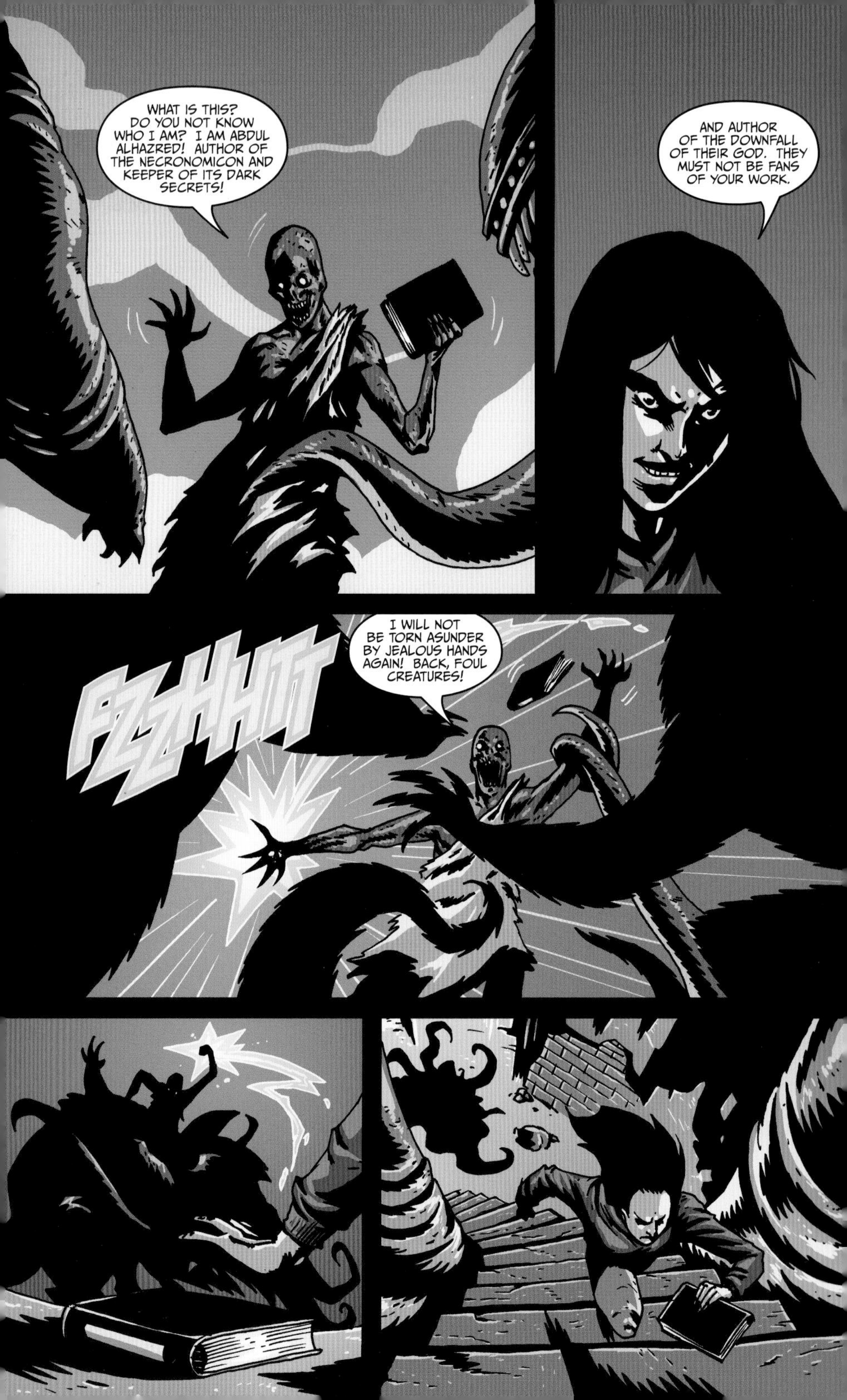
WHAT IS THIS? DO YOU NOT KNOW WHO I AM? I AM ABDUL ALHAZRED! AUTHOR OF THE NECRONOMICON AND KEEPER OF ITS DARK SECRETS!
AND AUTHOR OF THE DOWNFALL OF THEIR GOD. THEY MUST NOT BE FANS OF YOUR WORK.
FZZHHHTT
I WILL NOT BE TORN ASUNDER BY JEALOUS HANDS AGAIN! BACK, FOUL CREATURES!

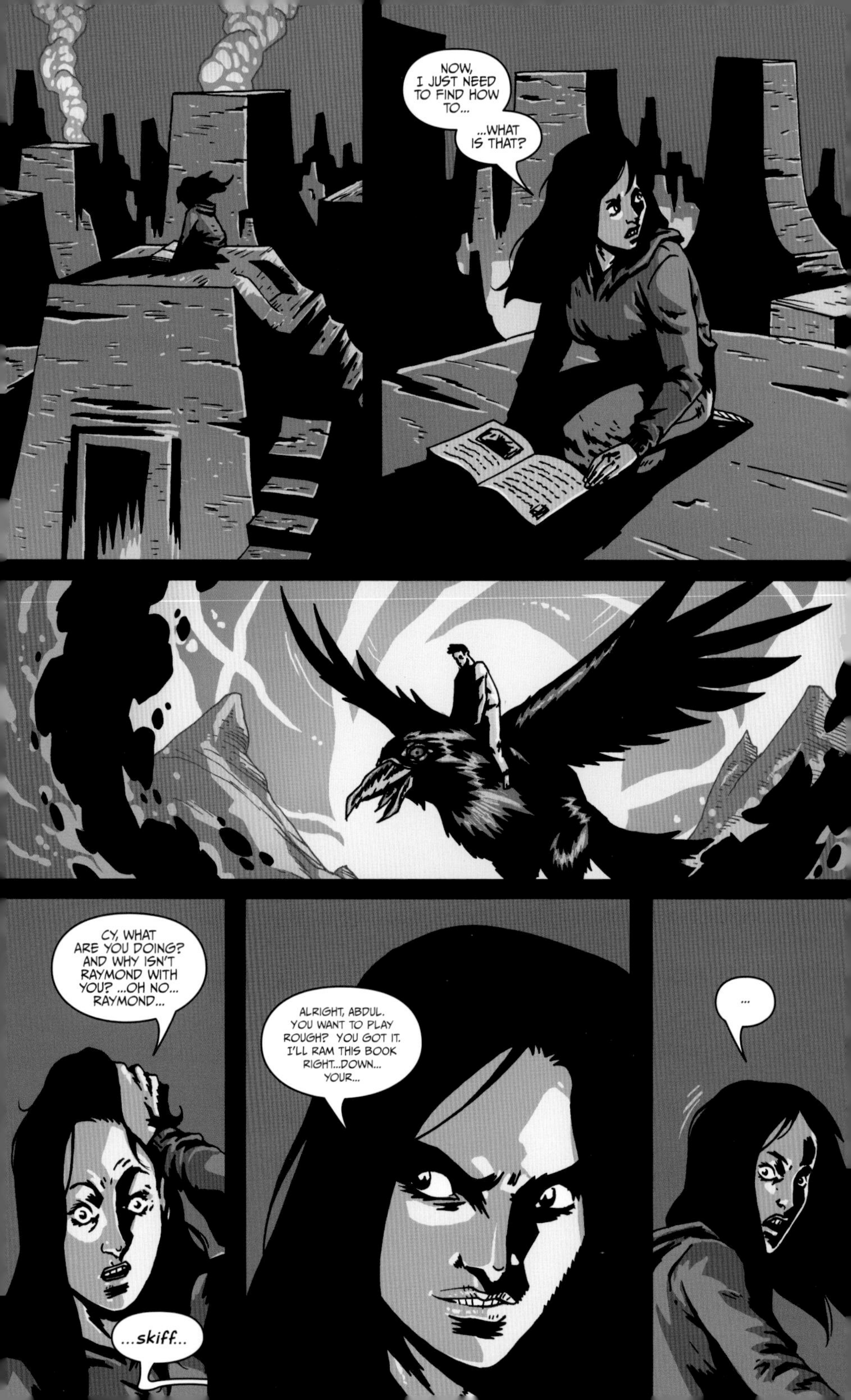
NOW, I JUST NEED TO FIND HOW TO...
...WHAT IS THAT?
CY, WHAT ARE YOU DOING? AND WHY ISN'T RAYMOND WITH YOU? ...OH NO... RAYMOND...
...skiff...
ALRIGHT, ABDUL. YOU WANT TO PLAY ROUGH? YOU GOT IT. I'LL RAM THIS BOOK RIGHT...DOWN... YOUR...
...

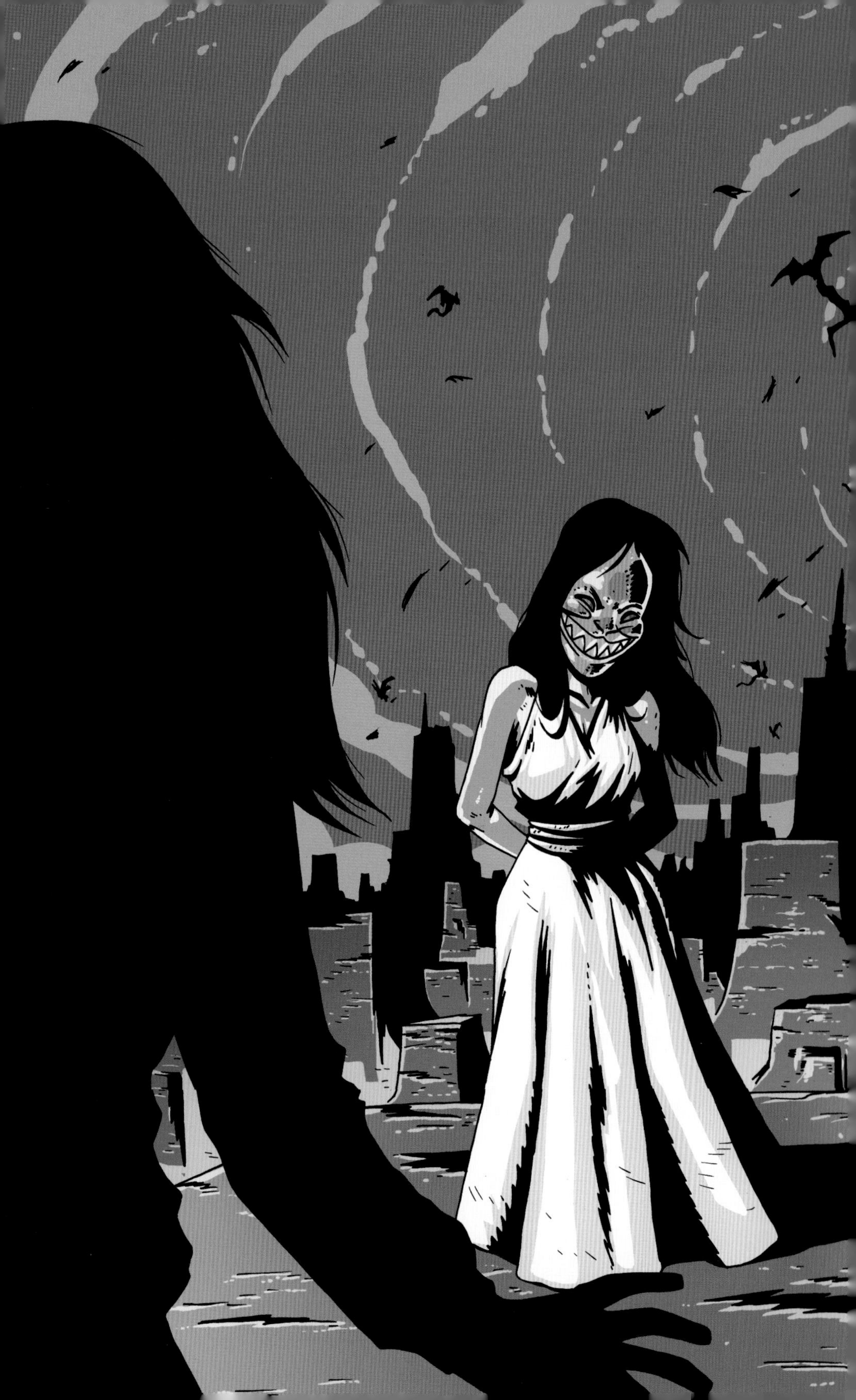

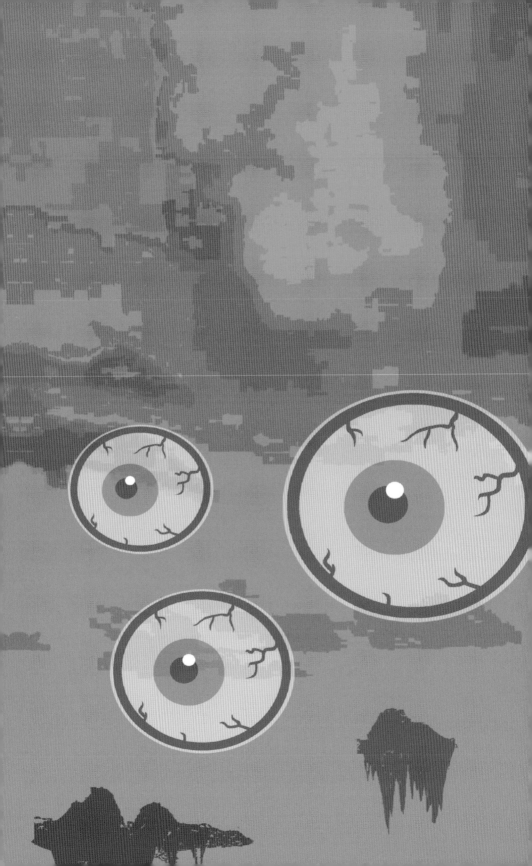

CHAPTER 3

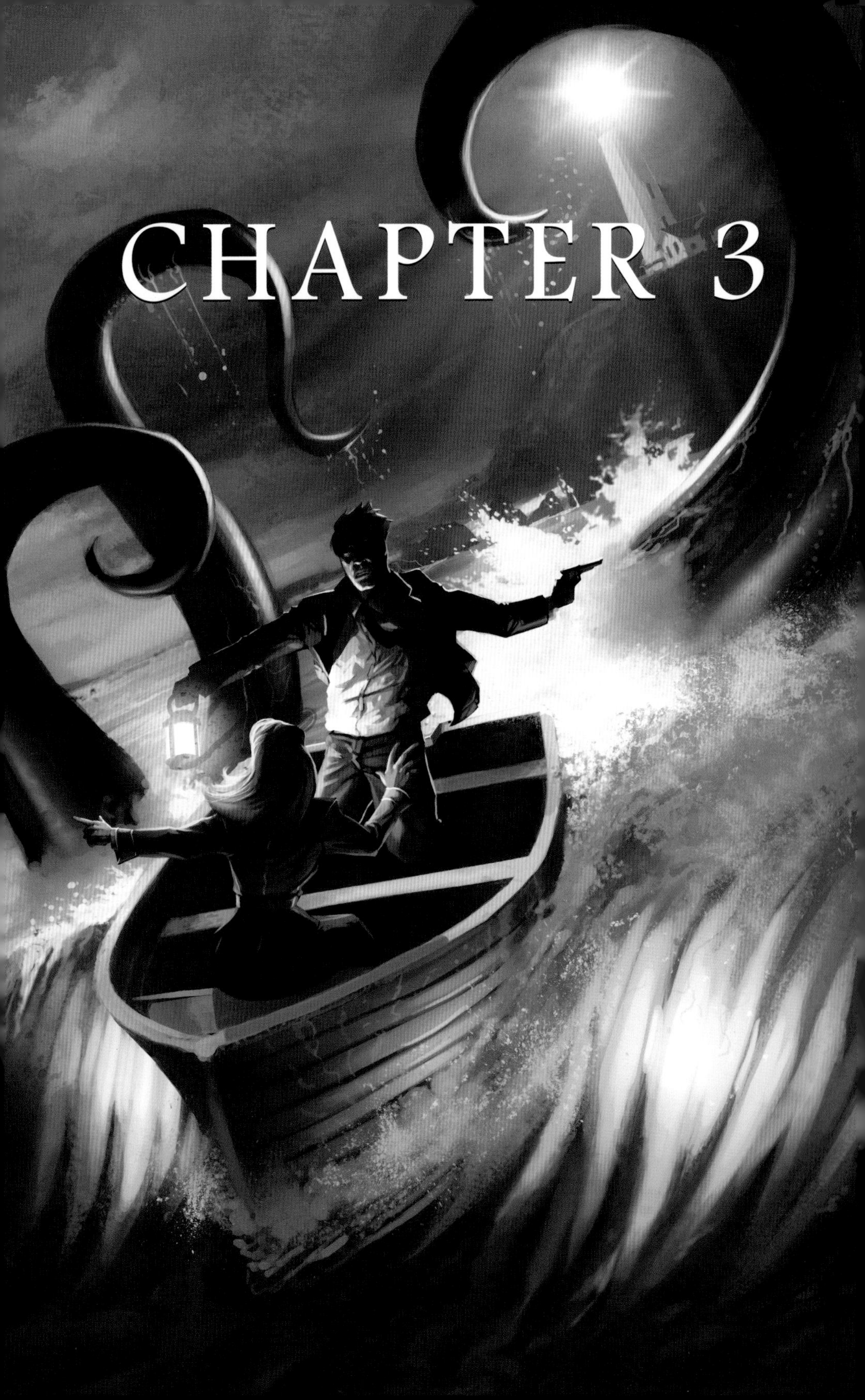

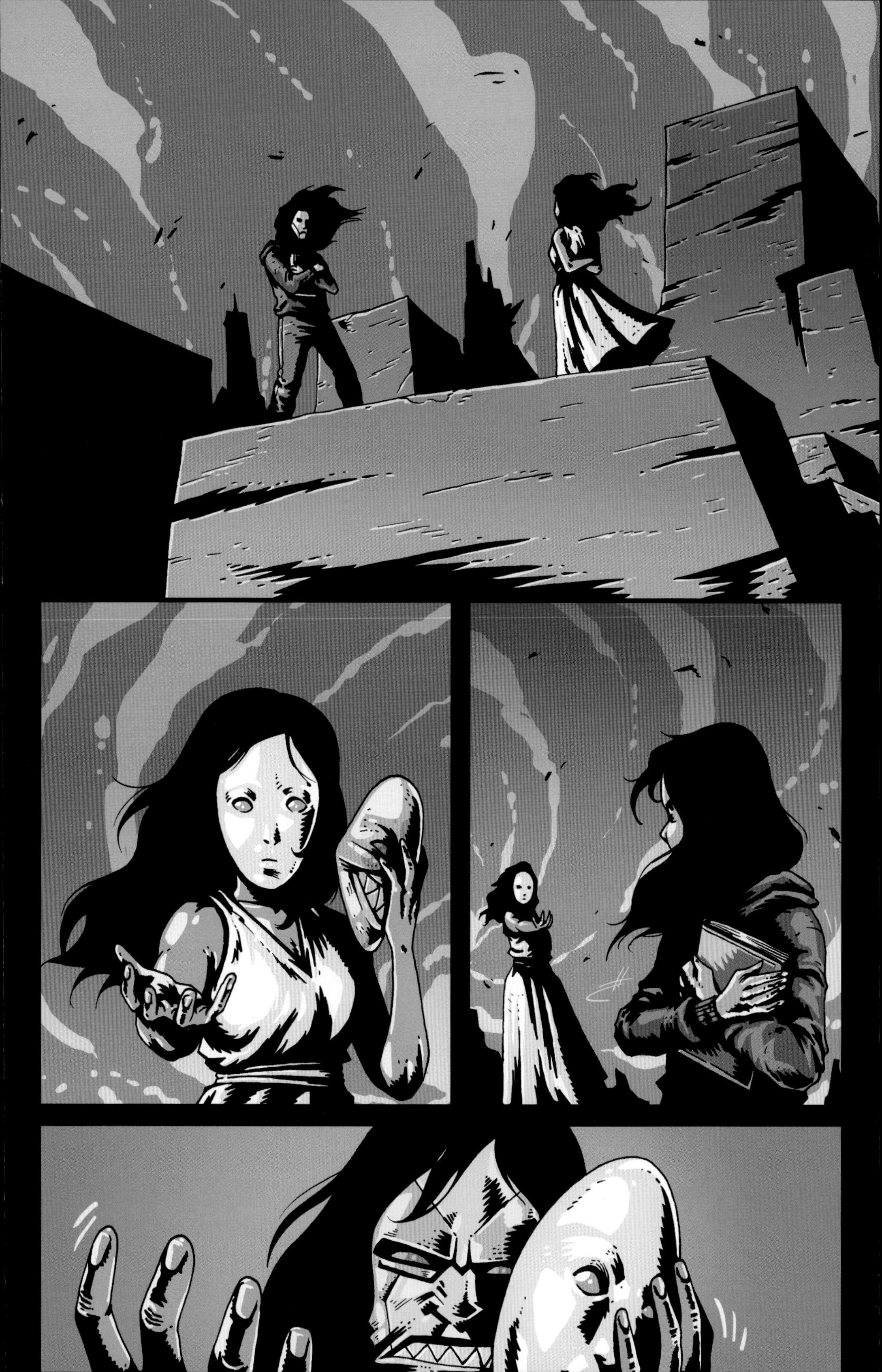

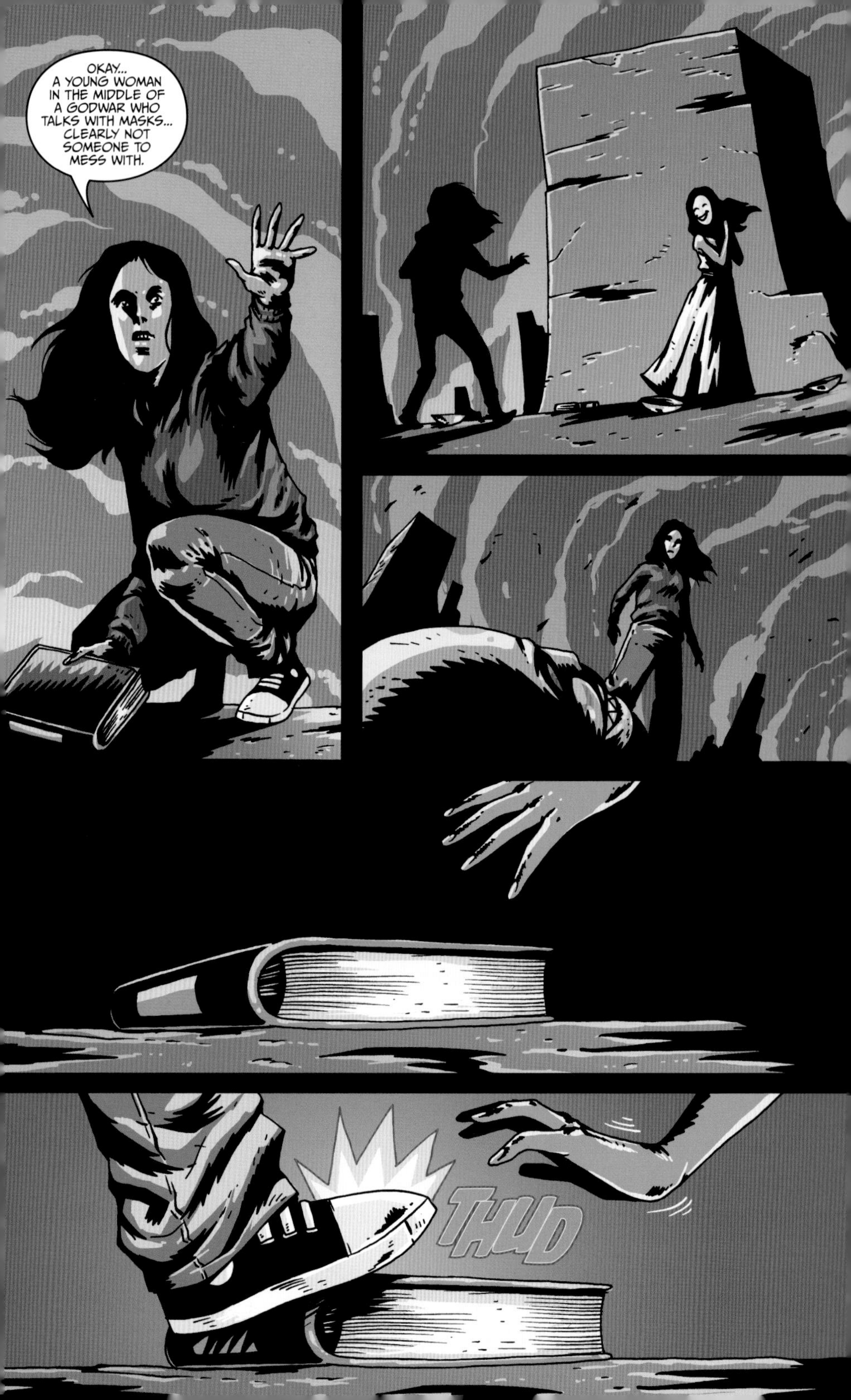
OKAY... A YOUNG WOMAN IN THE MIDDLE OF A GODWAR WHO TALKS WITH MASKS... CLEARLY NOT SOMEONE TO MESS WITH.
THUD

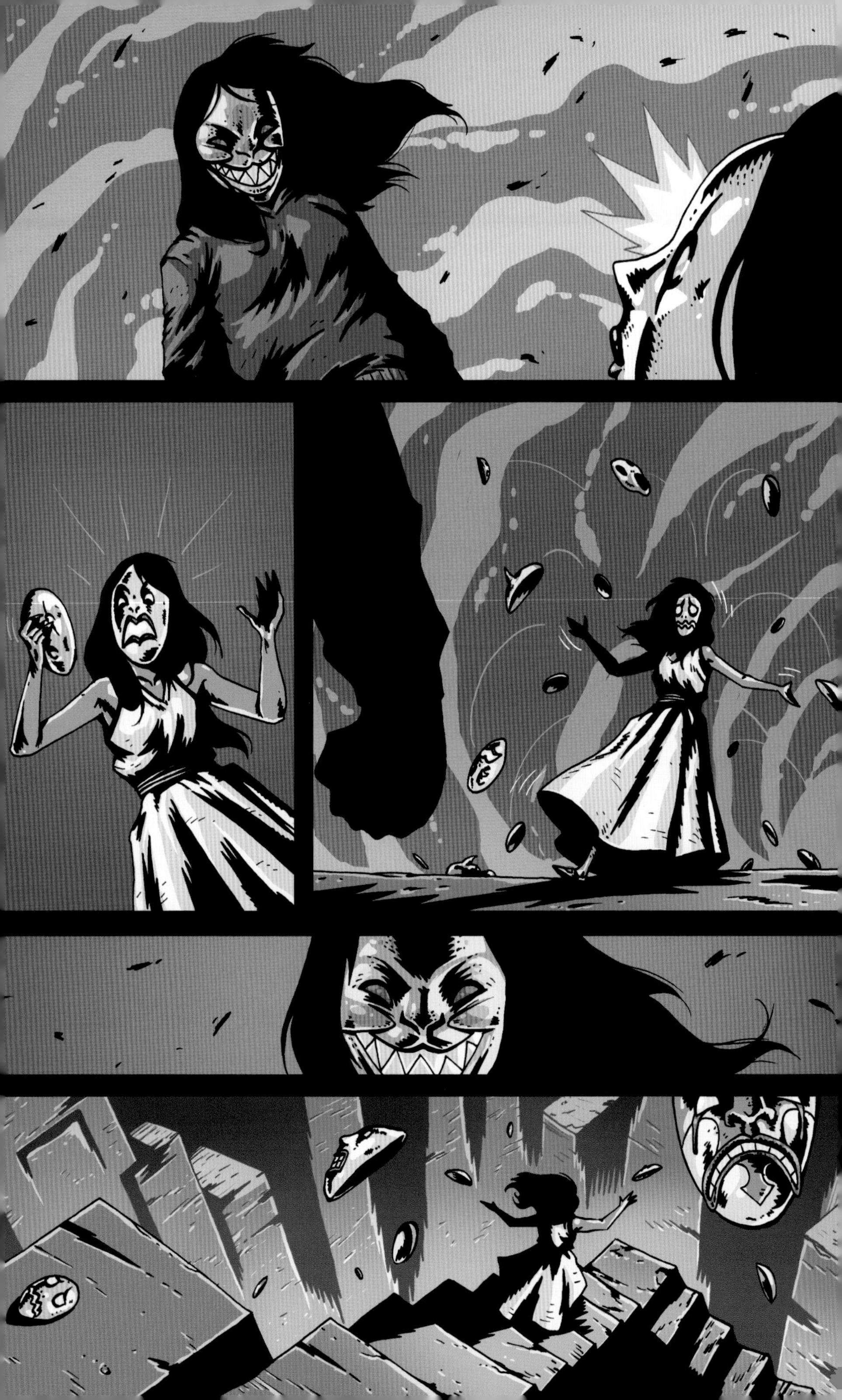

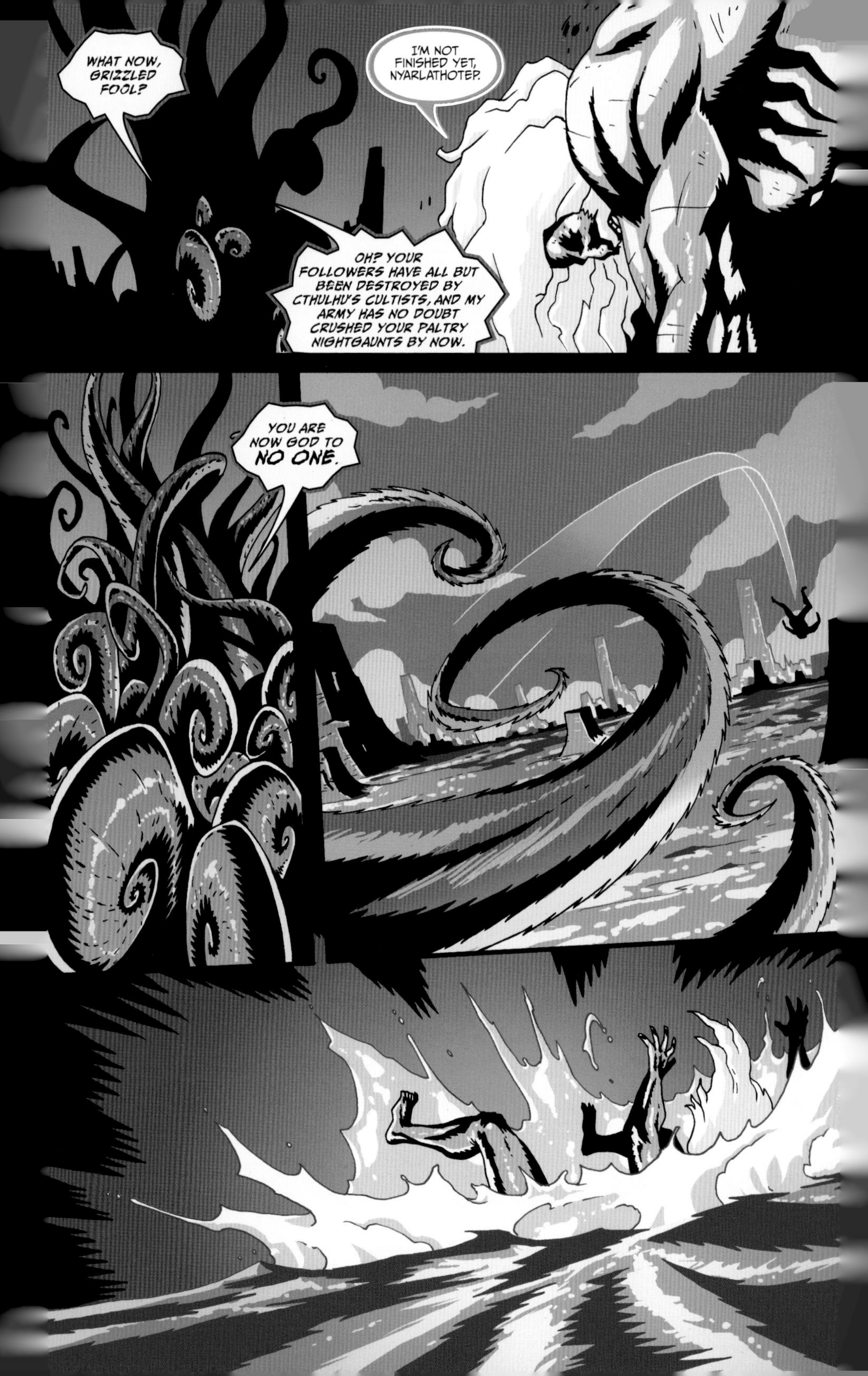
WHAT NOW, GRIZZLED FOOL?
I'M NOT FINISHED YET, NYARLATHOTEP.
OH? YOUR FOLLOWERS HAVE ALL BUT BEEN DESTROYED BY CTHULHU'S CULTISTS, AND MY ARMY HAS NO DOUBT CRUSHED YOUR PALTRY NIGHTGAUNTS BY NOW.
YOU ARE NOW GOD TO NO ONE.

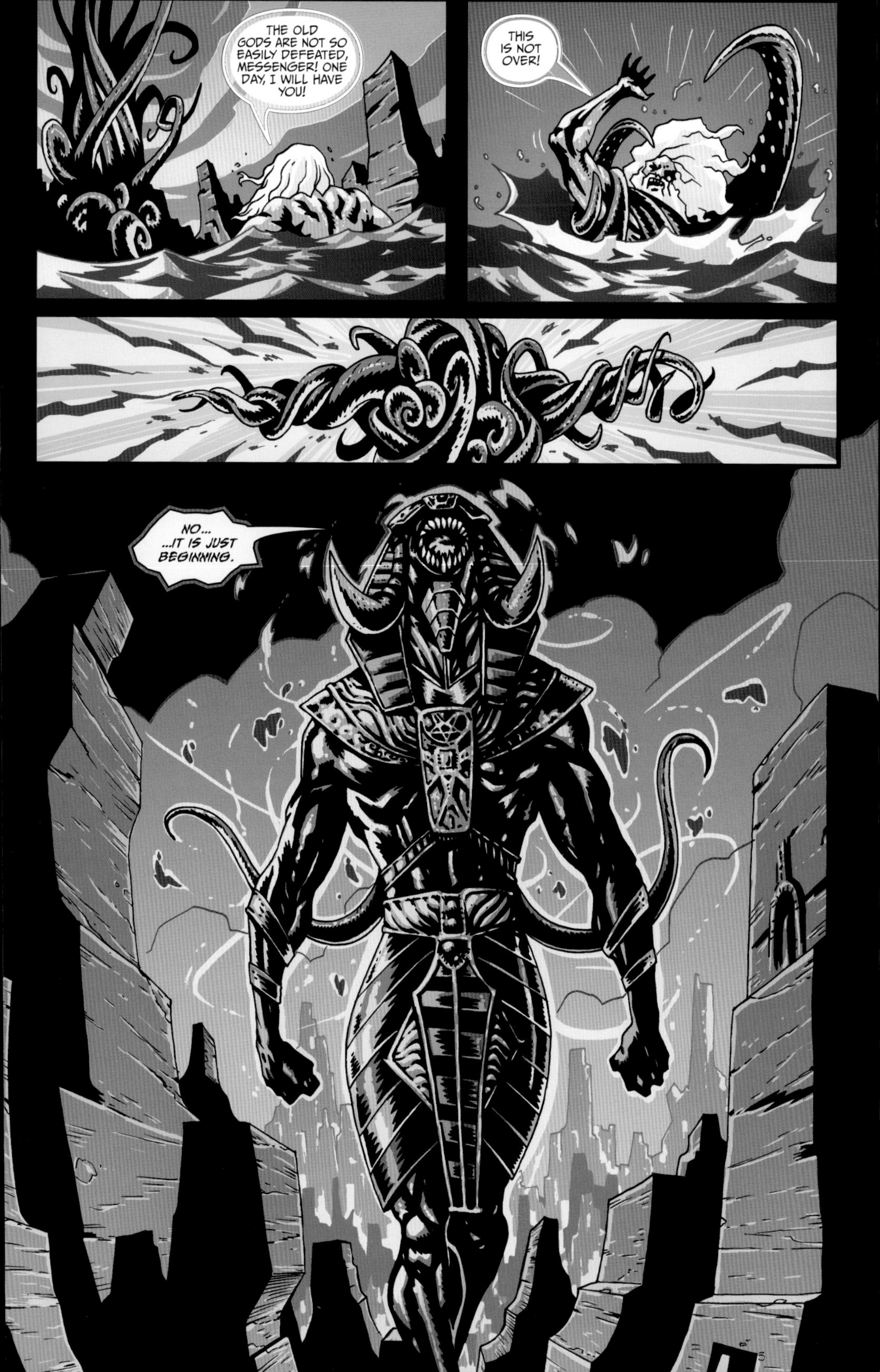
THE OLD GODS ARE NOT SO EASILY DEFEATED, MESSENGER! ONE DAY, I WILL HAVE YOU!
THIS IS NOT OVER!
NO... ...IT IS JUST BEGINNING.

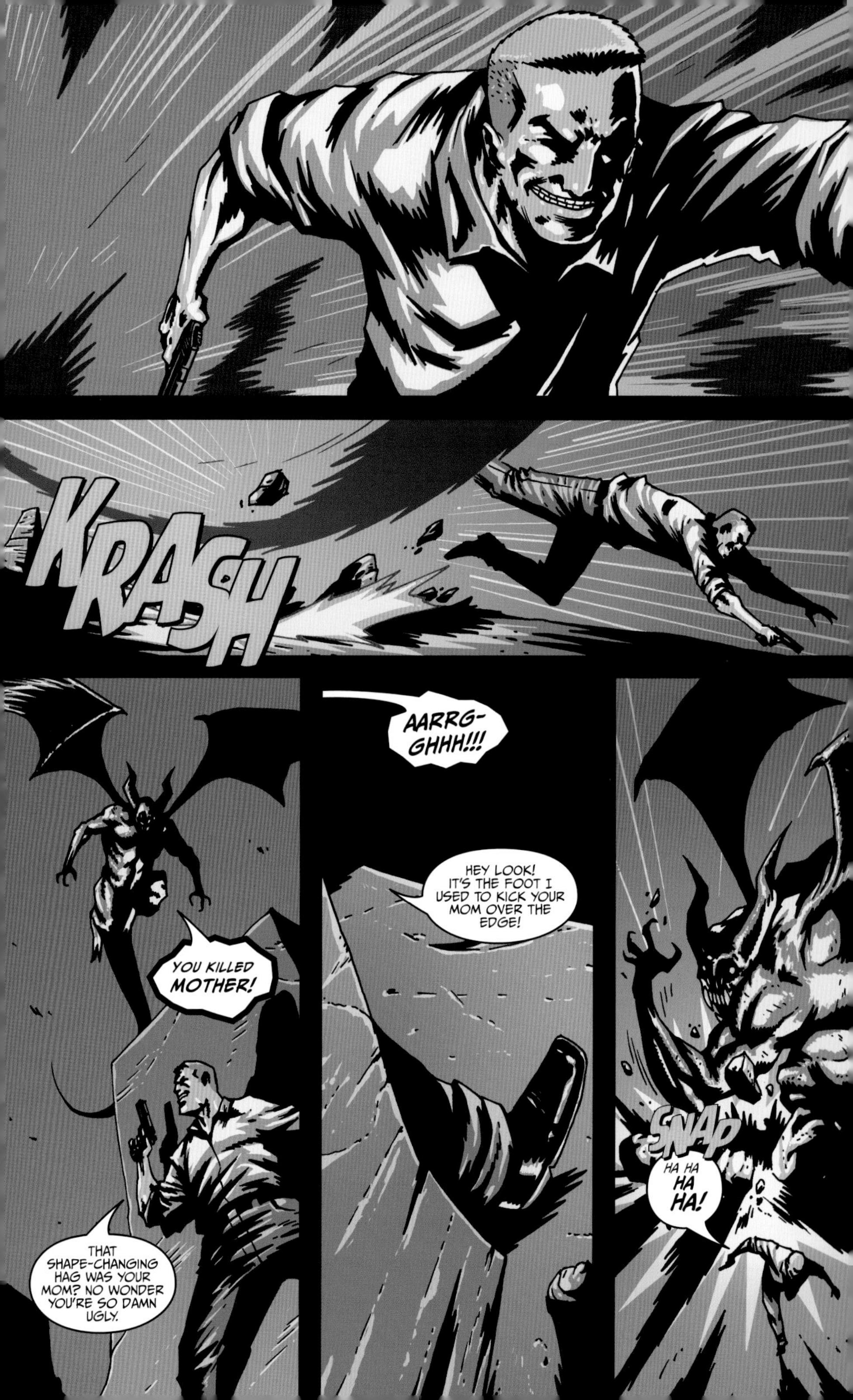
KRASH
YOU KILLED MOTHER!
THAT SHAPE-CHANGING HAG WAS YOUR MOM? NO WONDER YOU'RE SO DAMN UGLY.
AARRG-GHHH!!!
HEY LOOK! IT'S THE FOOT I USED TO KICK YOUR MOM OVER THE EDGE!
SNAP
HA HA HA HA!

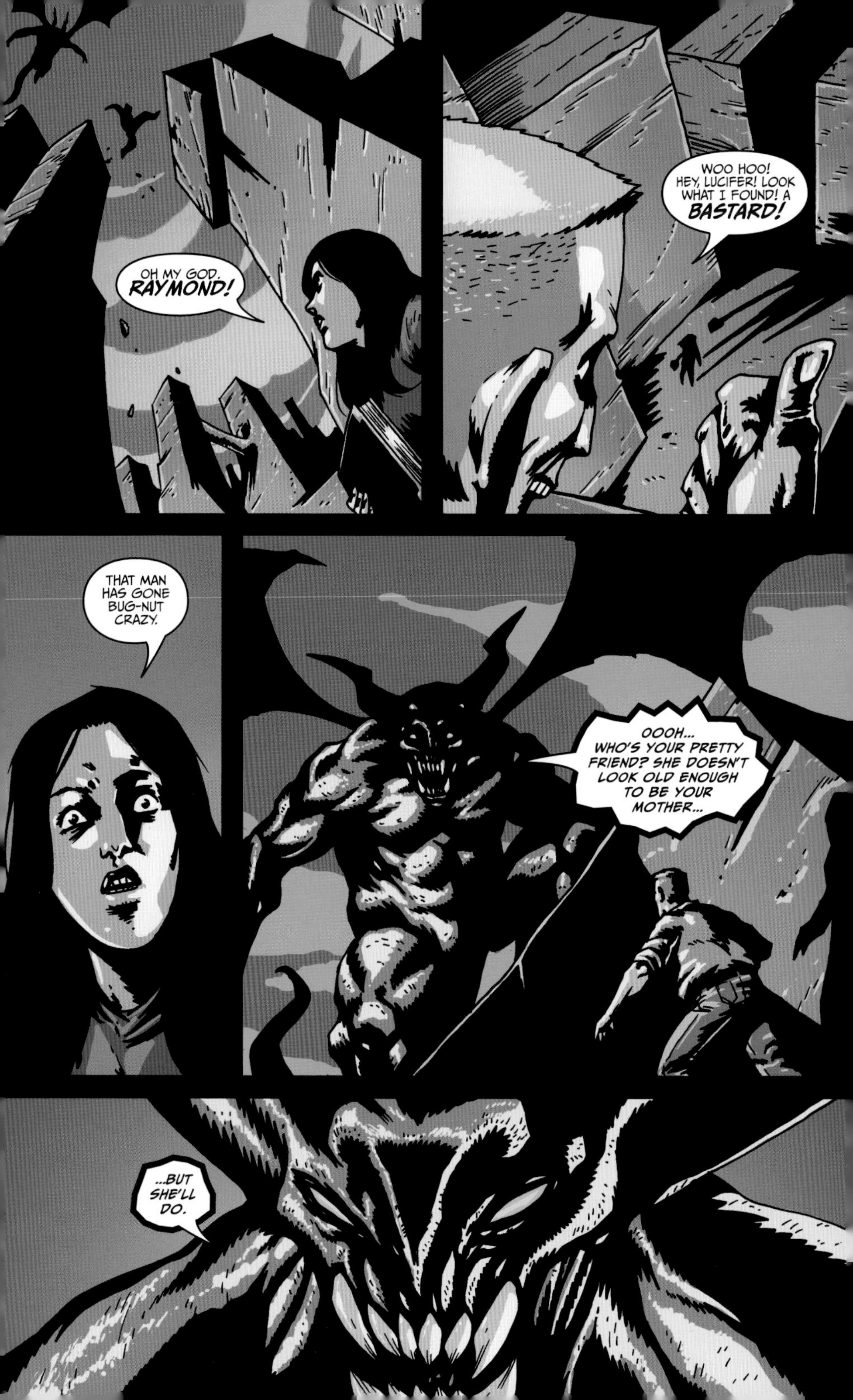
OH MY GOD. RAYMOND!
WOO HOO! HEY, LUCIFER! LOOK WHAT I FOUND! A BASTARD!
THAT MAN HAS GONE BUG-NUT CRAZY.
OOOH... WHO'S YOUR PRETTY FRIEND? SHE DOESN'T LOOK OLD ENOUGH TO BE YOUR MOTHER...
...BUT SHE'LL DO.

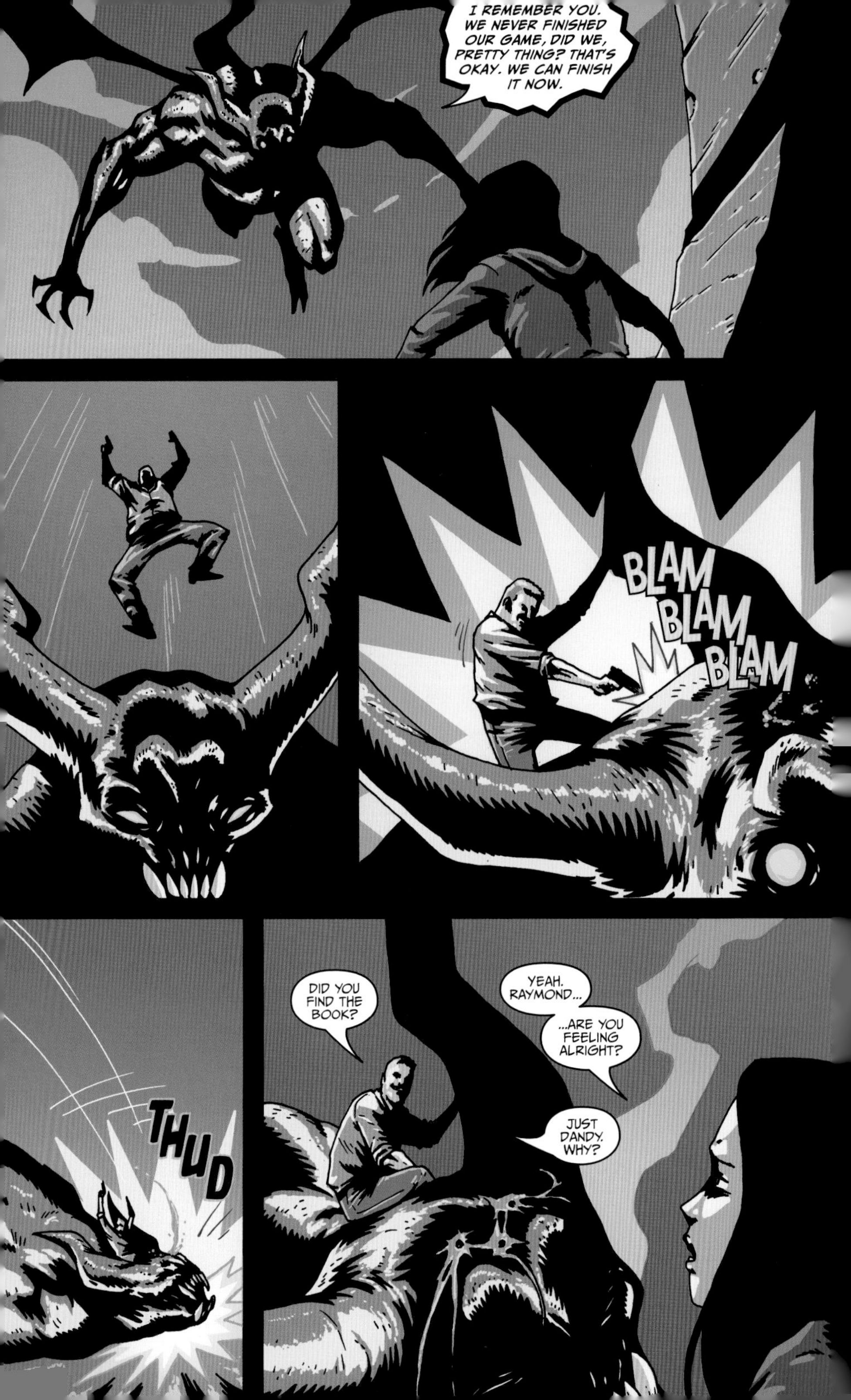
I REMEMBER YOU. WE NEVER FINISHED OUR GAME, DID WE, PRETTY THING? THAT'S OKAY. WE CAN FINISH IT NOW.
BLAM
BLAM
BLAM
THUD
DID YOU FIND THE BOOK?
YEAH. RAYMOND...
...ARE YOU FEELING ALRIGHT?
JUST DANDY. WHY?

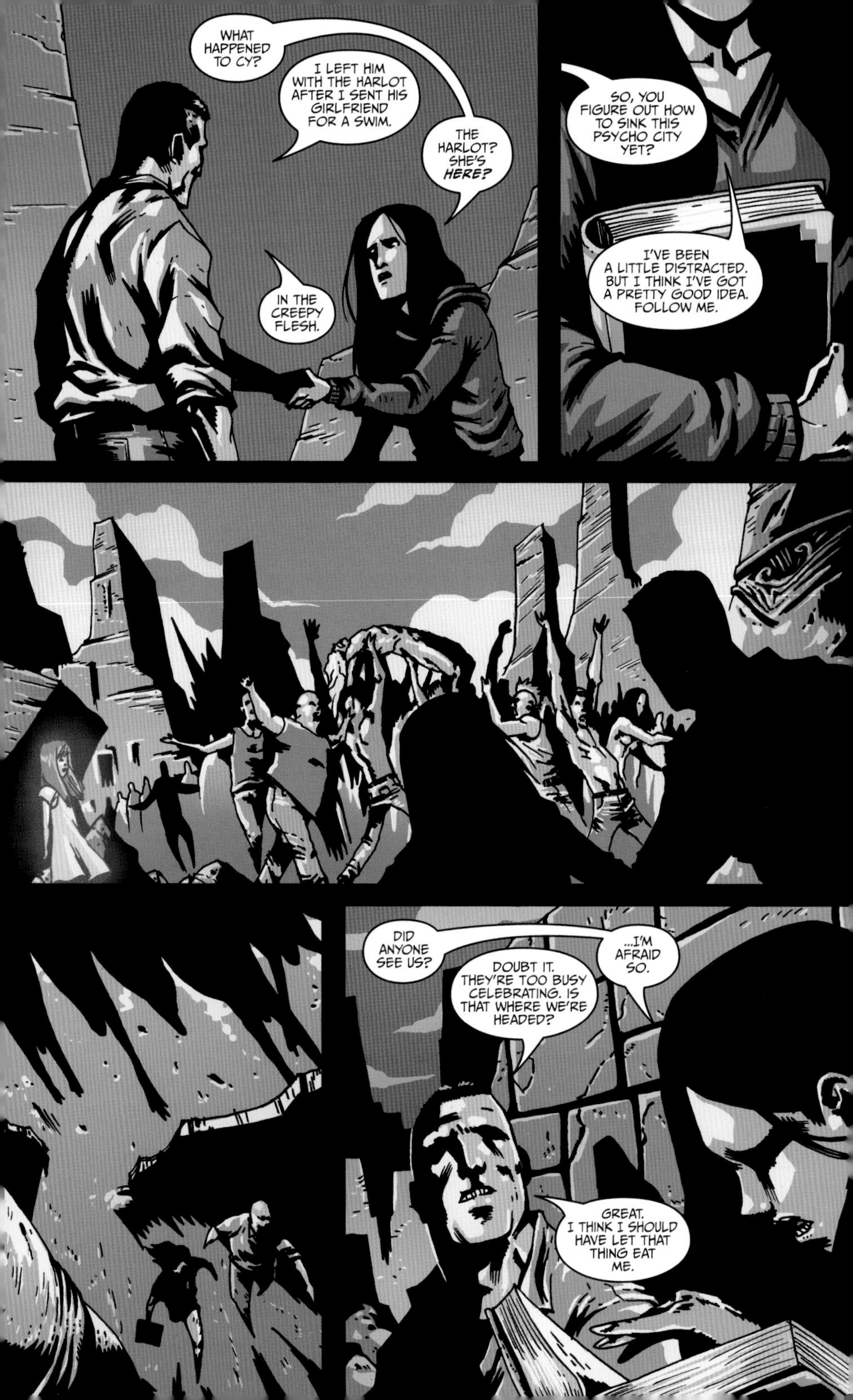
WHAT HAPPENED TO CY?
I LEFT HIM WITH THE HARLOT AFTER I SENT HIS GIRLFRIEND FOR A SWIM.
THE HARLOT? SHE'S *HERE?*
IN THE CREEPY FLESH.
SO, YOU FIGURE OUT HOW TO SINK THIS PSYCHO CITY YET?
I'VE BEEN A LITTLE DISTRACTED. BUT I THINK I'VE GOT A PRETTY GOOD IDEA. FOLLOW ME.
DID ANYONE SEE US?
DOUBT IT. THEY'RE TOO BUSY CELEBRATING. IS THAT WHERE WE'RE HEADED?
...I'M AFRAID SO.
GREAT. I THINK I SHOULD HAVE LET THAT THING EAT ME.

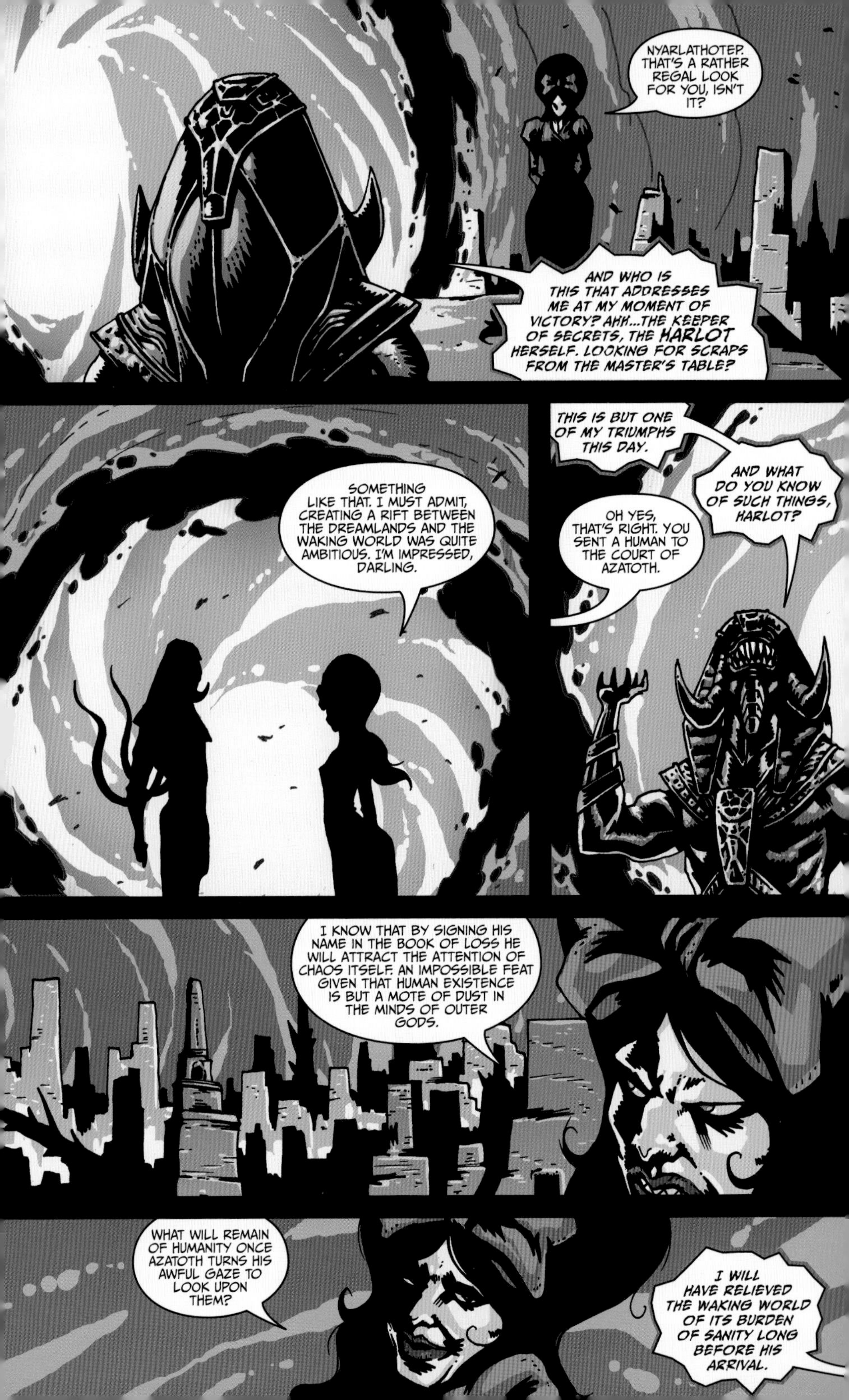
NYARLATHOTEP. THAT'S A RATHER REGAL LOOK FOR YOU, ISN'T IT?
AND WHO IS THIS THAT ADDRESSES ME AT MY MOMENT OF VICTORY? AHH...THE KEEPER OF SECRETS, THE HARLOT HERSELF. LOOKING FOR SCRAPS FROM THE MASTER'S TABLE?
SOMETHING LIKE THAT. I MUST ADMIT, CREATING A RIFT BETWEEN THE DREAMLANDS AND THE WAKING WORLD WAS QUITE AMBITIOUS. I'M IMPRESSED, DARLING.
THIS IS BUT ONE OF MY TRIUMPHS THIS DAY.
OH YES, THAT'S RIGHT. YOU SENT A HUMAN TO THE COURT OF AZATOTH.
AND WHAT DO YOU KNOW OF SUCH THINGS, HARLOT?
I KNOW THAT BY SIGNING HIS NAME IN THE BOOK OF LOSS HE WILL ATTRACT THE ATTENTION OF CHAOS ITSELF. AN IMPOSSIBLE FEAT GIVEN THAT HUMAN EXISTENCE IS BUT A MOTE OF DUST IN THE MINDS OF OUTER GODS.
WHAT WILL REMAIN OF HUMANITY ONCE AZATOTH TURNS HIS AWFUL GAZE TO LOOK UPON THEM?
I WILL HAVE RELIEVED THE WAKING WORLD OF ITS BURDEN OF SANITY LONG BEFORE HIS ARRIVAL.

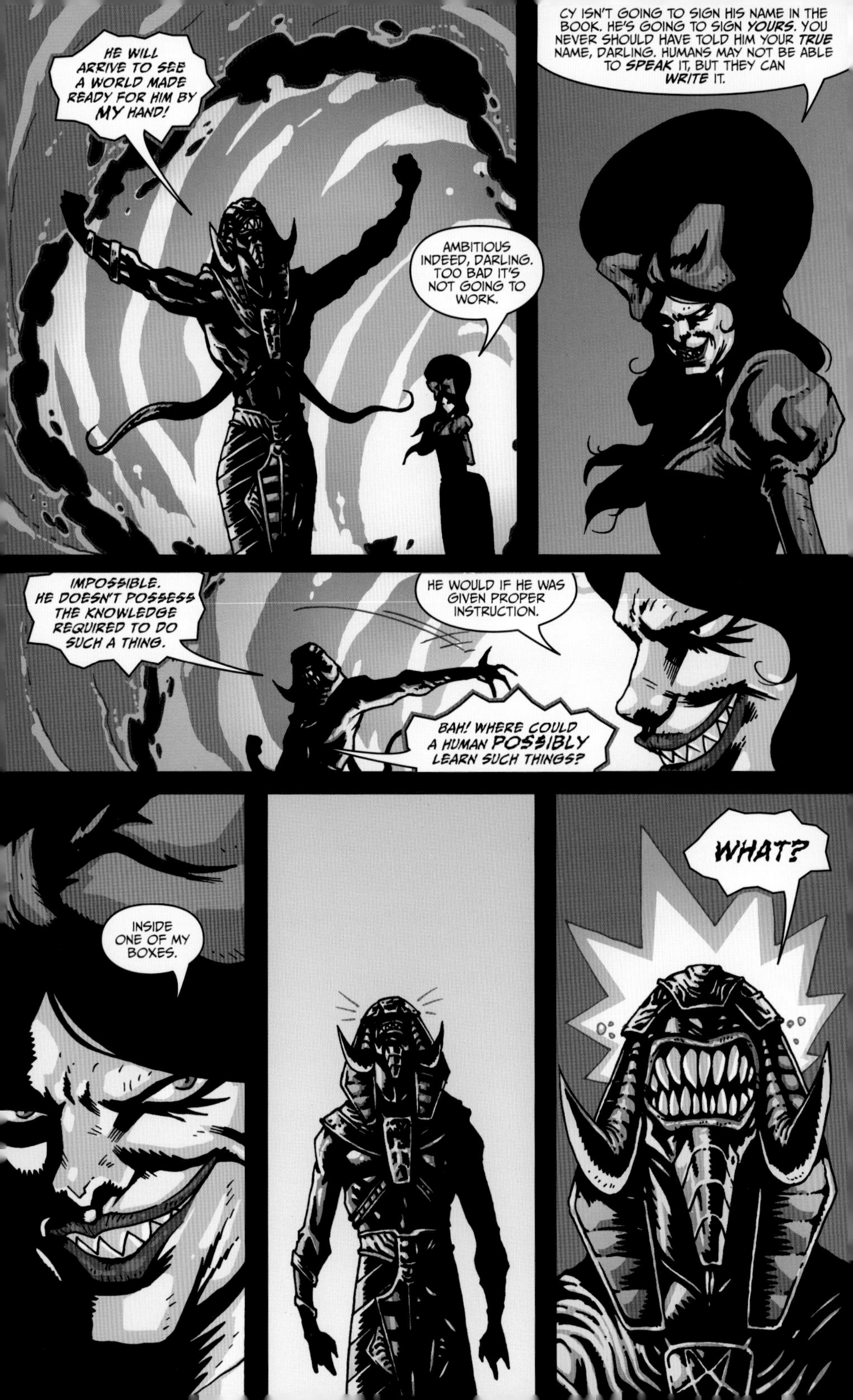
HE WILL ARRIVE TO SEE A WORLD MADE READY FOR HIM BY MY HAND!
AMBITIOUS INDEED, DARLING. TOO BAD IT'S NOT GOING TO WORK.
CY ISN'T GOING TO SIGN HIS NAME IN THE BOOK. HE'S GOING TO SIGN YOURS. YOU NEVER SHOULD HAVE TOLD HIM YOUR TRUE NAME, DARLING. HUMANS MAY NOT BE ABLE TO SPEAK IT, BUT THEY CAN WRITE IT.
IMPOSSIBLE. HE DOESN'T POSSESS THE KNOWLEDGE REQUIRED TO DO SUCH A THING.
HE WOULD IF HE WAS GIVEN PROPER INSTRUCTION.
BAH! WHERE COULD A HUMAN POSSIBLY LEARN SUCH THINGS?
INSIDE ONE OF MY BOXES.
WHAT?

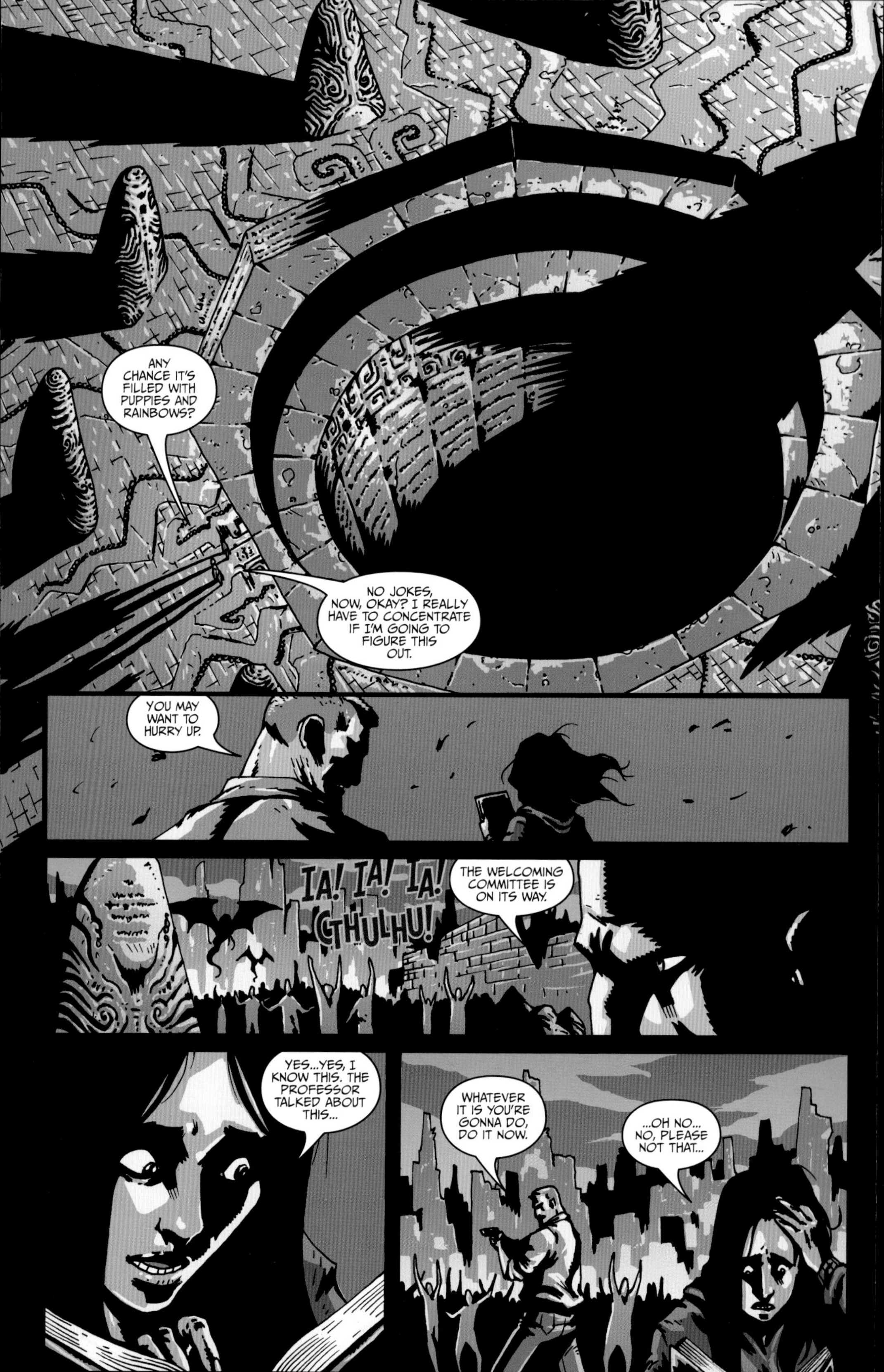
ANY CHANCE IT'S FILLED WITH PUPPIES AND RAINBOWS?
NO JOKES, NOW, OKAY? I REALLY HAVE TO CONCENTRATE IF I'M GOING TO FIGURE THIS OUT.
YOU MAY WANT TO HURRY UP.
IA! IA! IA! CTHULHU!
THE WELCOMING COMMITTEE IS ON ITS WAY.
YES...YES, I KNOW THIS. THE PROFESSOR TALKED ABOUT THIS...
WHATEVER IT IS YOU'RE GONNA DO, DO IT NOW.
...OH NO... NO, PLEASE NOT THAT...

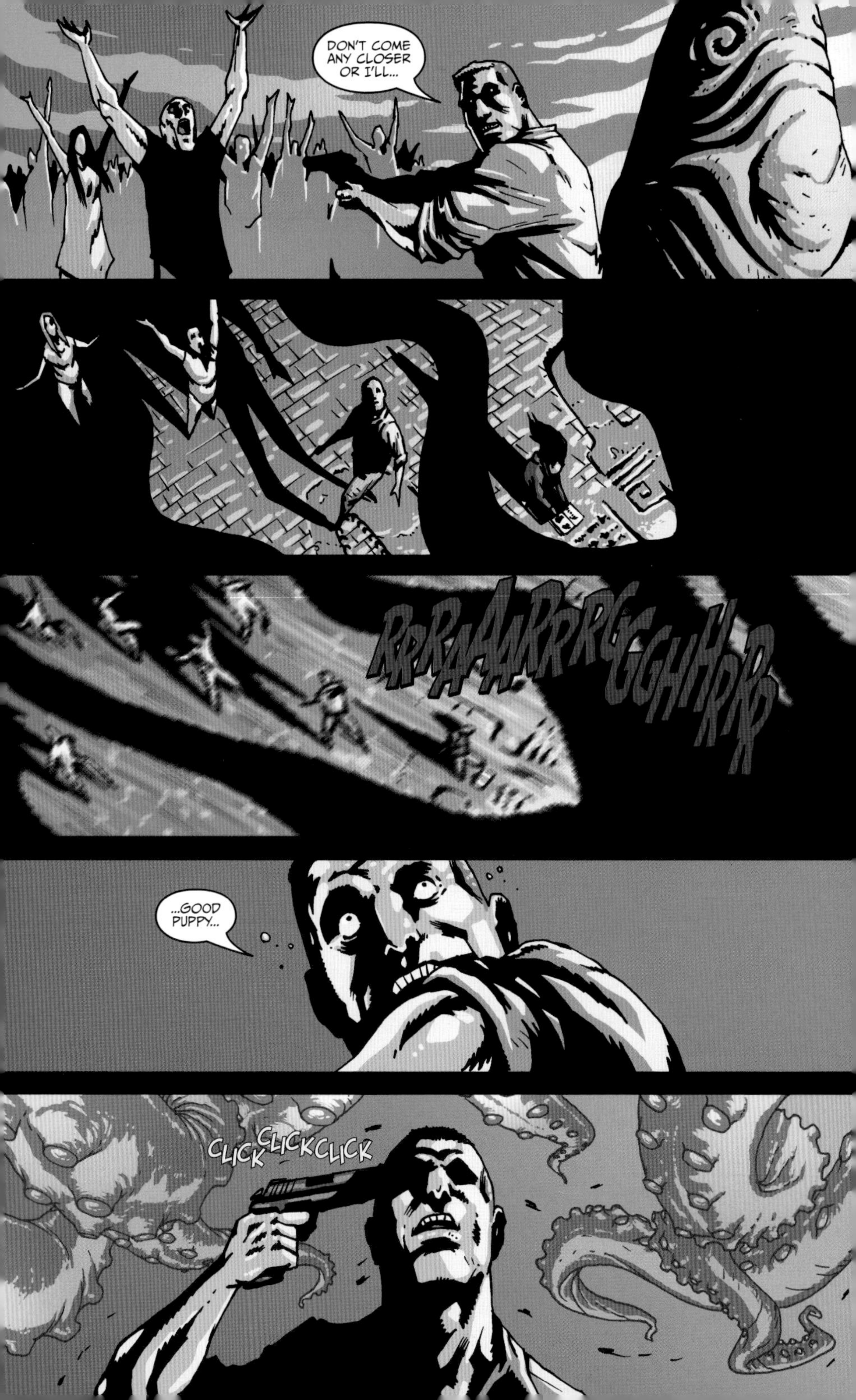
DON'T COME ANY CLOSER OR I'LL...
RRRAAARRRGGHHRRR
...GOOD PUPPY...
CLICKCLICKCLICK

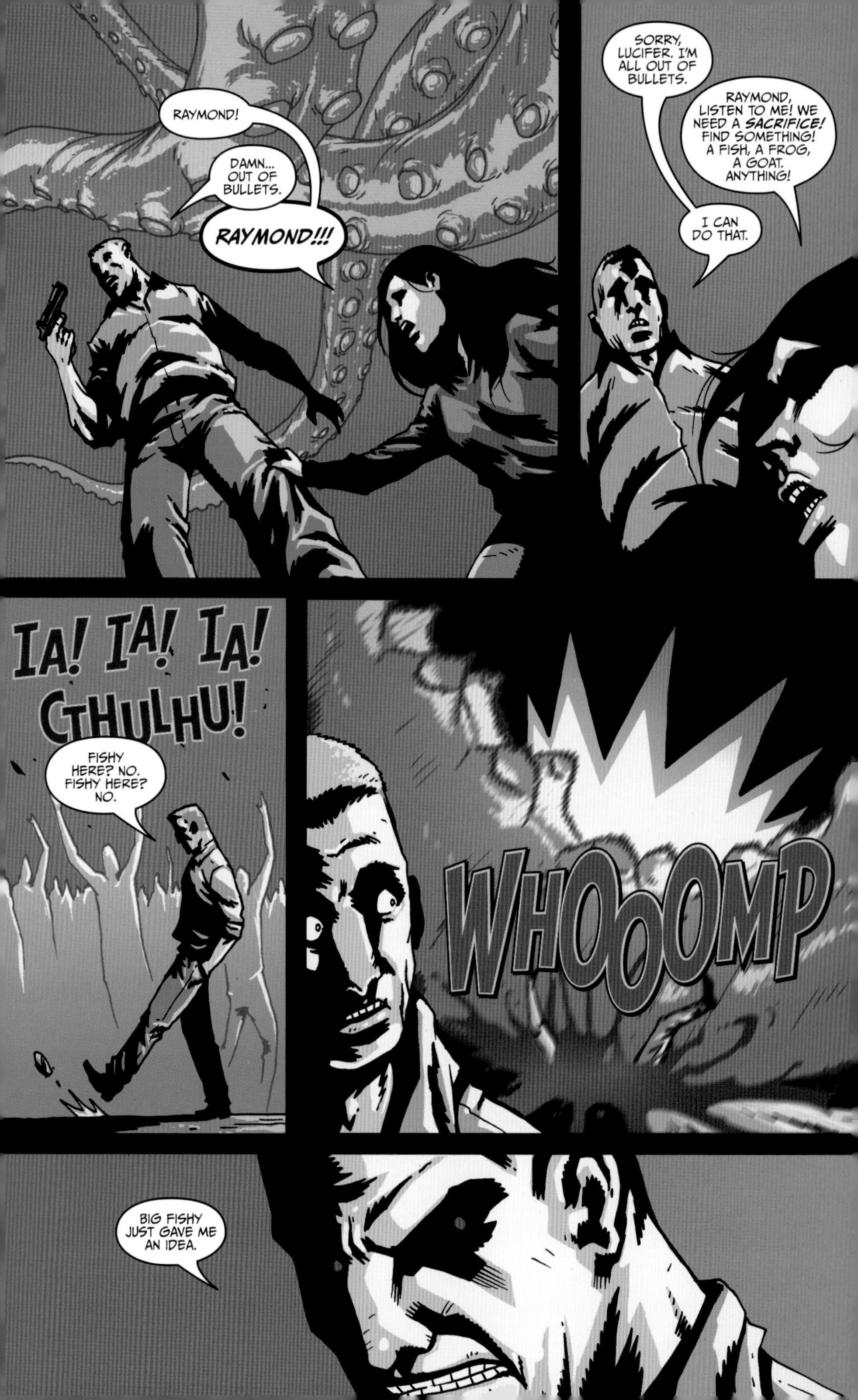
RAYMOND!
DAMN... OUT OF BULLETS.
RAYMOND!!!
SORRY, LUCIFER. I'M ALL OUT OF BULLETS.
RAYMOND, LISTEN TO ME! WE NEED A SACRIFICE! FIND SOMETHING! A FISH, A FROG, A GOAT. ANYTHING!
I CAN DO THAT.
IA! IA! IA! CTHULHU!
FISHY HERE? NO. FISHY HERE? NO.
WHOOOOMP
BIG FISHY JUST GAVE ME AN IDEA.

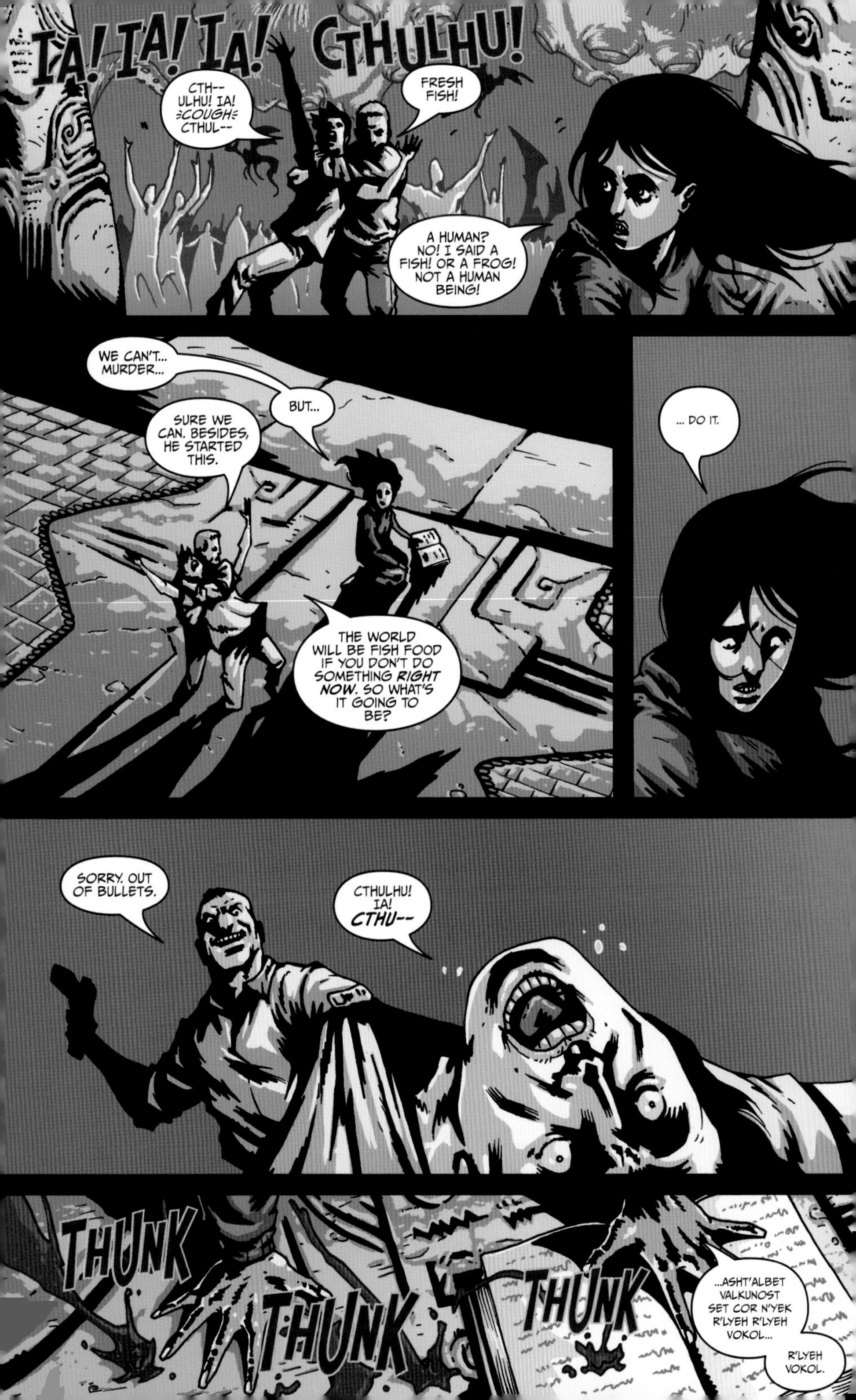
IA! IA! IA! CTHULHU!
CTH--ULHU! IA! *COUGH* CTHUL--
FRESH FISH!
A HUMAN? NO! I SAID A FISH! OR A FROG! NOT A HUMAN BEING!
WE CAN'T... MURDER...
BUT...
SURE WE CAN. BESIDES, HE STARTED THIS.
THE WORLD WILL BE FISH FOOD IF YOU DON'T DO SOMETHING RIGHT NOW. SO WHAT'S IT GOING TO BE?
... DO IT.
SORRY. OUT OF BULLETS.
CTHULHU! IA! CTHU--
THUNK
THUNK
THUNK
...ASHT'ALBET VALKUNOST SET COR N'YEK R'LYEH R'LYEH VOKOL...
R'LYEH VOKOL.

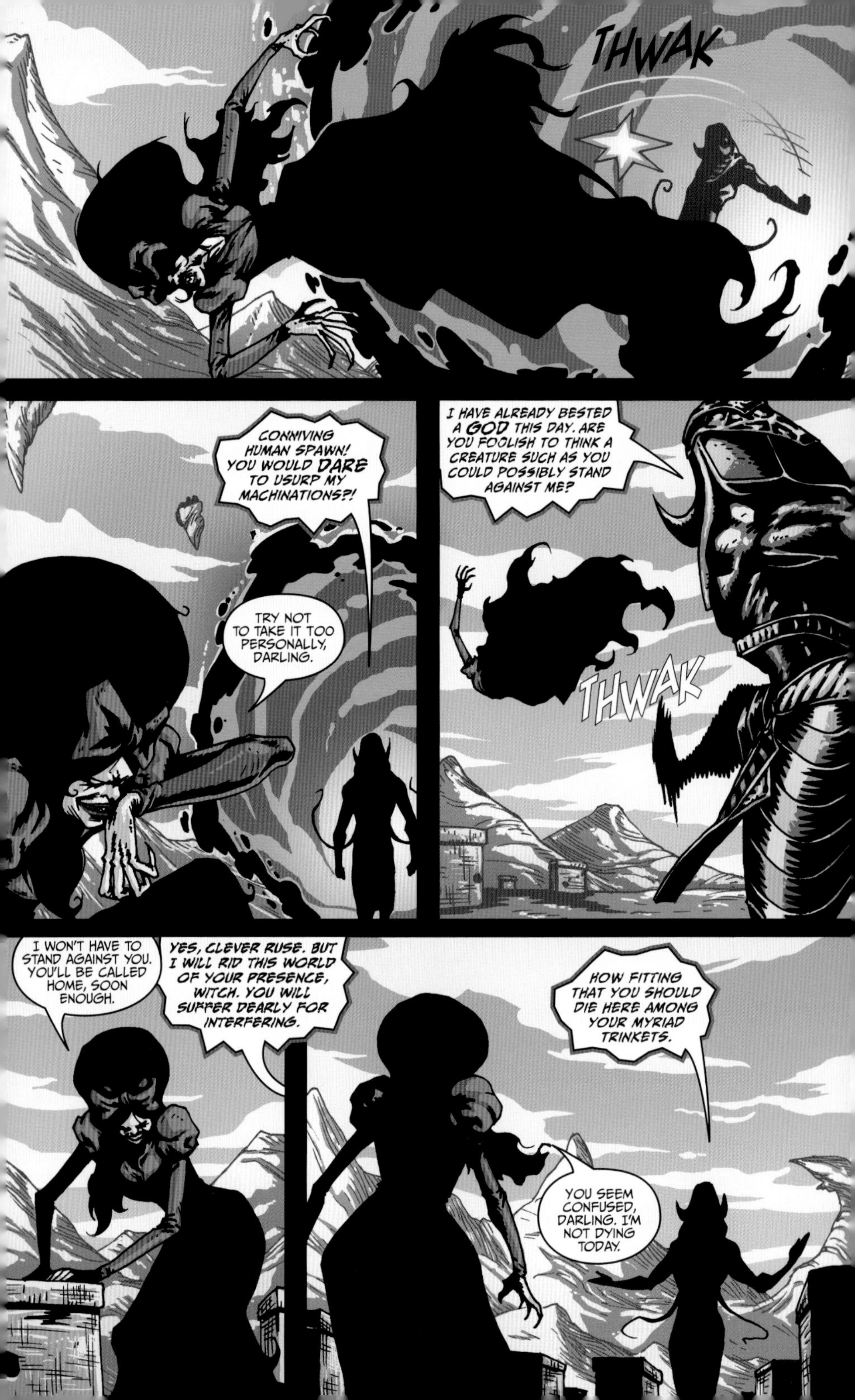
THWAK
CONNIVING HUMAN SPAWN! YOU WOULD DARE TO USURP MY MACHINATIONS?!
TRY NOT TO TAKE IT TOO PERSONALLY, DARLING.
I HAVE ALREADY BESTED A GOD THIS DAY. ARE YOU FOOLISH TO THINK A CREATURE SUCH AS YOU COULD POSSIBLY STAND AGAINST ME?
THWAK
I WON'T HAVE TO STAND AGAINST YOU. YOU'LL BE CALLED HOME, SOON ENOUGH.
YES, CLEVER RUSE. BUT I WILL RID THIS WORLD OF YOUR PRESENCE, WITCH. YOU WILL SUFFER DEARLY FOR INTERFERING.
HOW FITTING THAT YOU SHOULD DIE HERE AMONG YOUR MYRIAD TRINKETS.
YOU SEEM CONFUSED, DARLING. I'M NOT DYING TODAY.

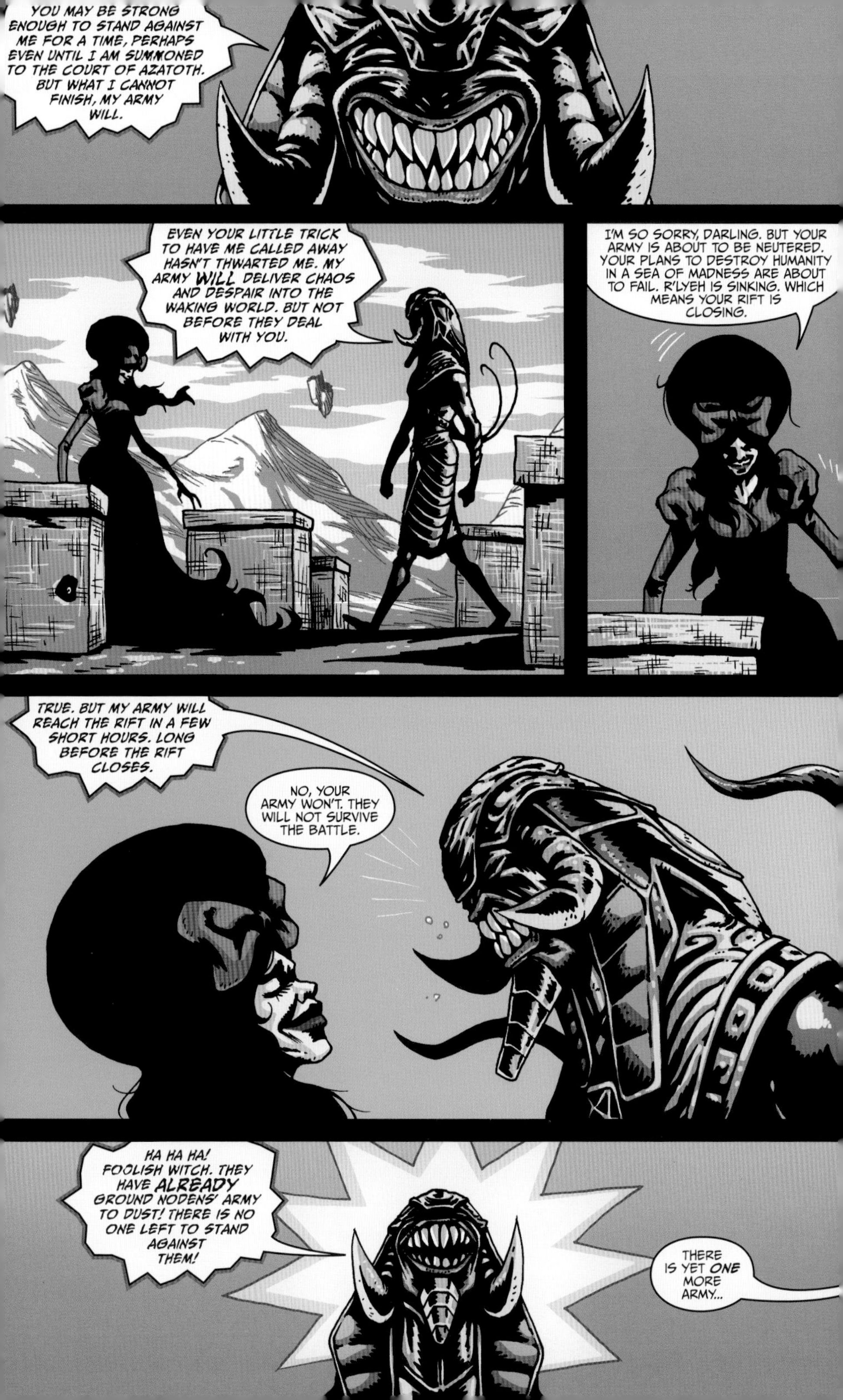
YOU MAY BE STRONG ENOUGH TO STAND AGAINST ME FOR A TIME, PERHAPS EVEN UNTIL I AM SUMMONED TO THE COURT OF AZATOTH. BUT WHAT I CANNOT FINISH, MY ARMY WILL.
EVEN YOUR LITTLE TRICK TO HAVE ME CALLED AWAY HASN'T THWARTED ME. MY ARMY WILL DELIVER CHAOS AND DESPAIR INTO THE WAKING WORLD. BUT NOT BEFORE THEY DEAL WITH YOU.
I'M SO SORRY, DARLING. BUT YOUR ARMY IS ABOUT TO BE NEUTERED. YOUR PLANS TO DESTROY HUMANITY IN A SEA OF MADNESS ARE ABOUT TO FAIL. R'LYEH IS SINKING. WHICH MEANS YOUR RIFT IS CLOSING.
TRUE. BUT MY ARMY WILL REACH THE RIFT IN A FEW SHORT HOURS. LONG BEFORE THE RIFT CLOSES.
NO, YOUR ARMY WON'T. THEY WILL NOT SURVIVE THE BATTLE.
HA HA HA! FOOLISH WITCH. THEY HAVE ALREADY GROUND NODENS' ARMY TO DUST! THERE IS NO ONE LEFT TO STAND AGAINST THEM!
THERE IS YET ONE MORE ARMY...

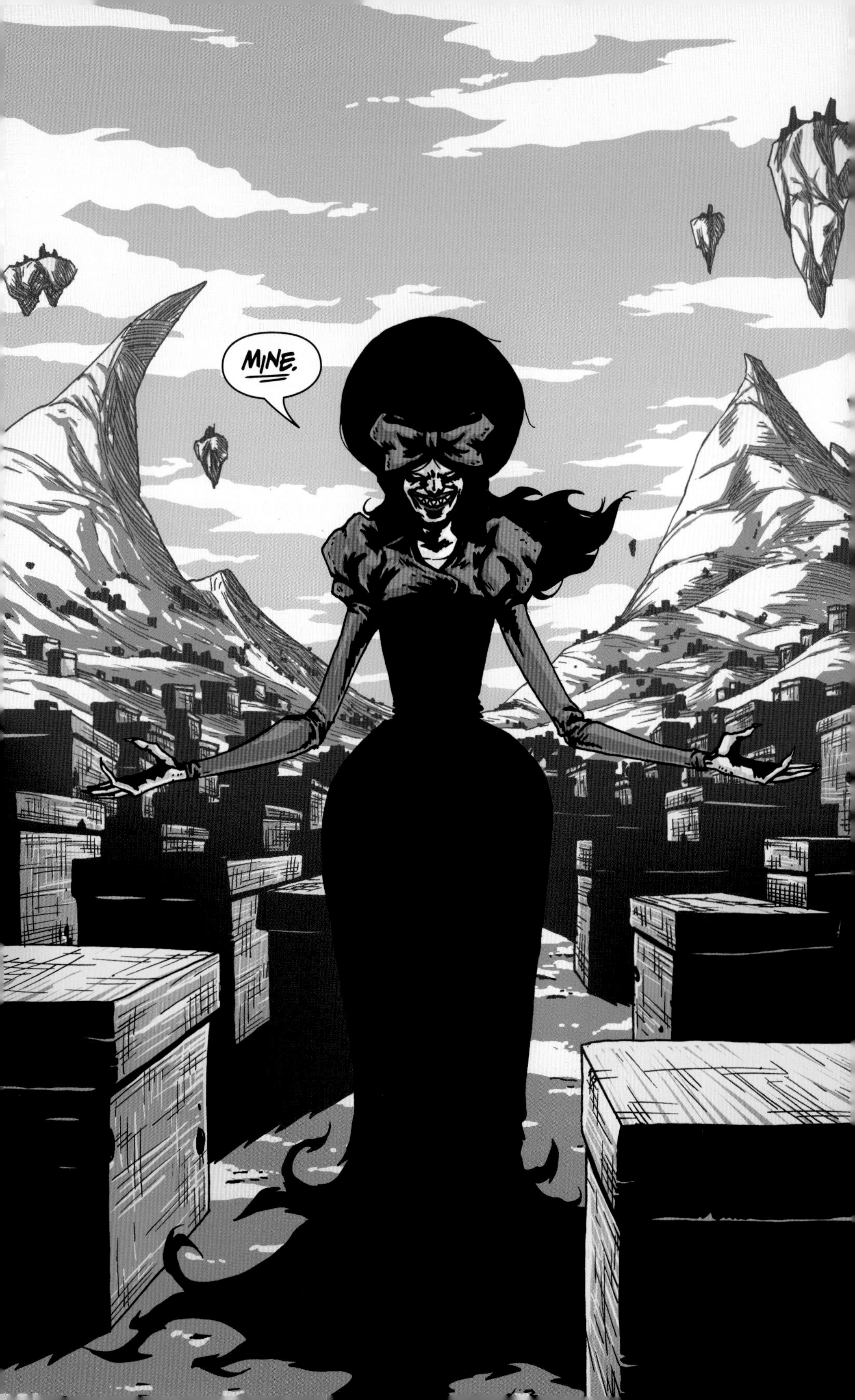
MINE.

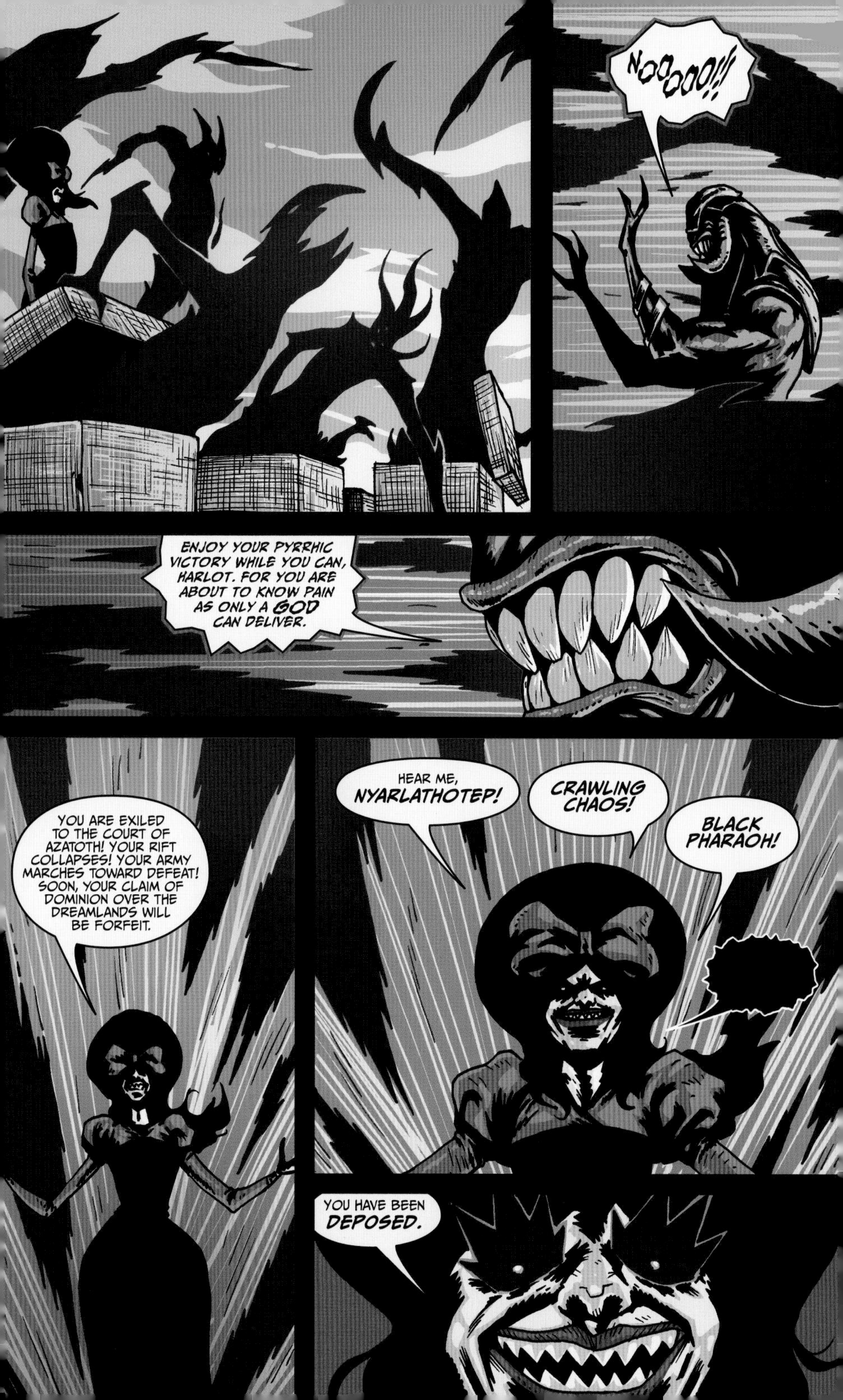
NOOOOO!!!
ENJOY YOUR PYRRHIC VICTORY WHILE YOU CAN, HARLOT. FOR YOU ARE ABOUT TO KNOW PAIN AS ONLY A GOD CAN DELIVER.
YOU ARE EXILED TO THE COURT OF AZATOTH! YOUR RIFT COLLAPSES! YOUR ARMY MARCHES TOWARD DEFEAT! SOON, YOUR CLAIM OF DOMINION OVER THE DREAMLANDS WILL BE FORFEIT.
HEAR ME, NYARLATHOTEP!
CRAWLING CHAOS!
BLACK PHARAOH!
YOU HAVE BEEN DEPOSED.

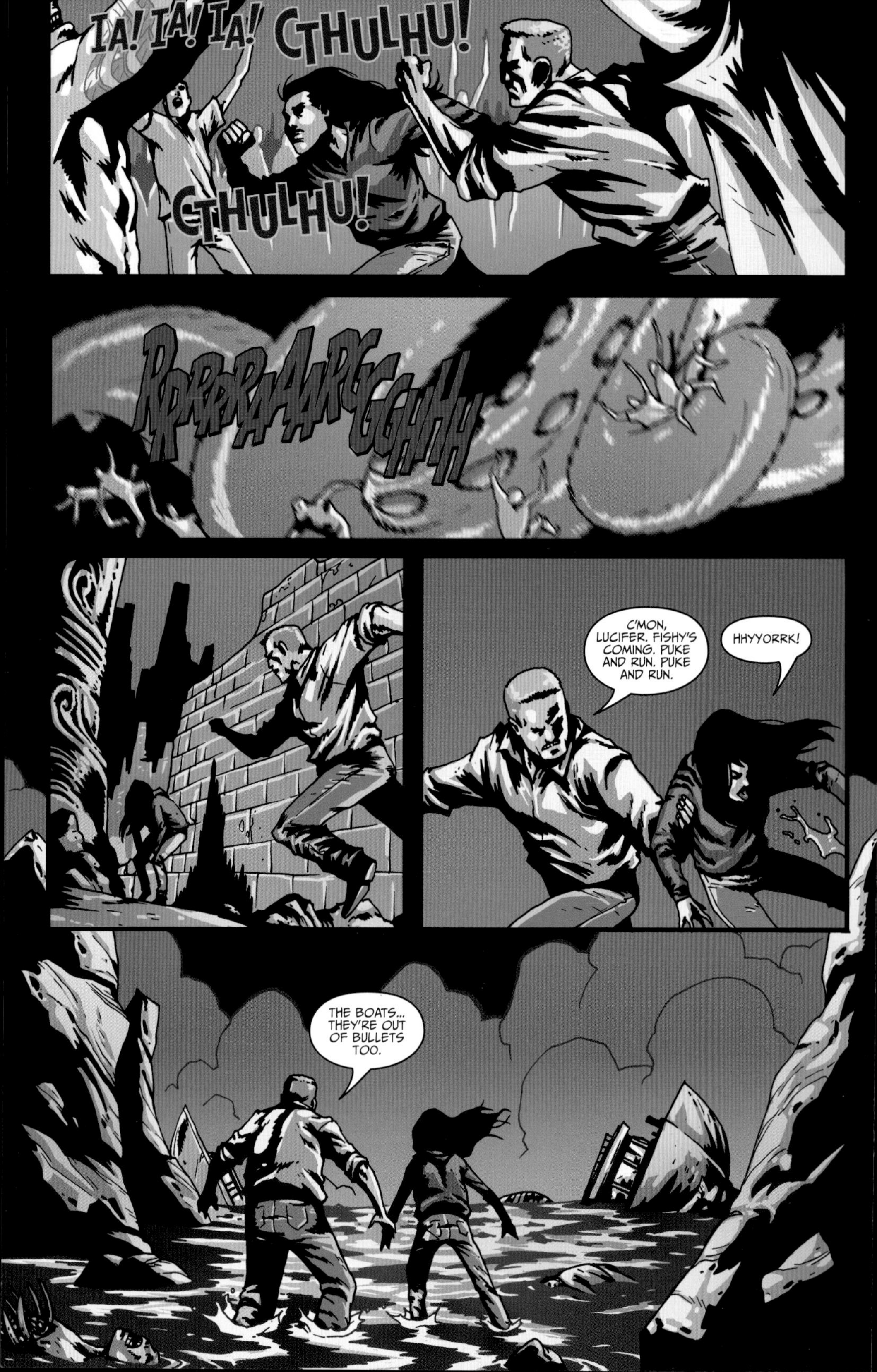
IA! IA! IA! CTHULHU!
CTHULHU!
RRRRRAAAARGGHHH
C'MON, LUCIFER. FISHY'S COMING. PUKE AND RUN. PUKE AND RUN.
HHYYORRK!
THE BOATS... THEY'RE OUT OF BULLETS TOO.

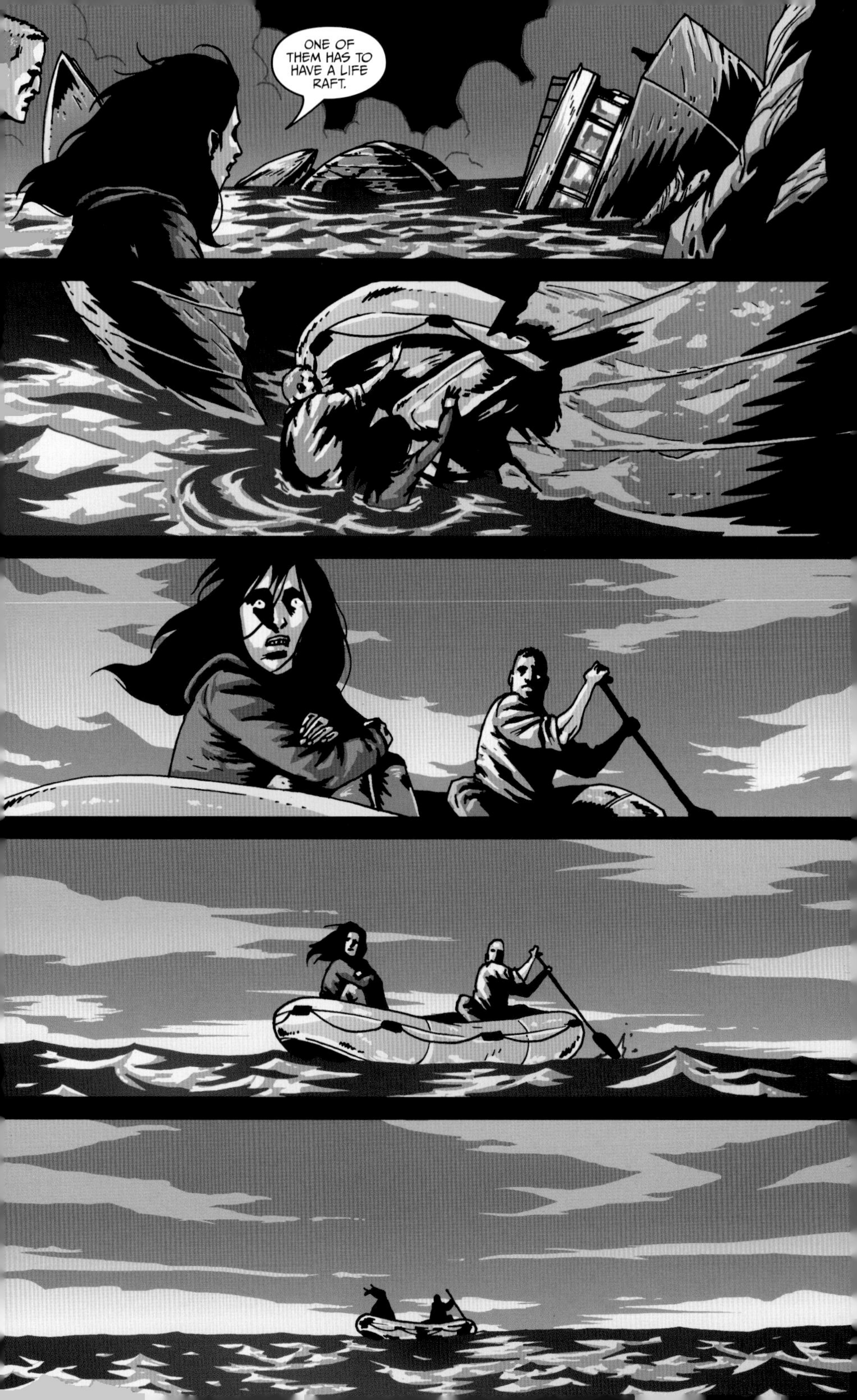
ONE OF THEM HAS TO HAVE A LIFE RAFT.

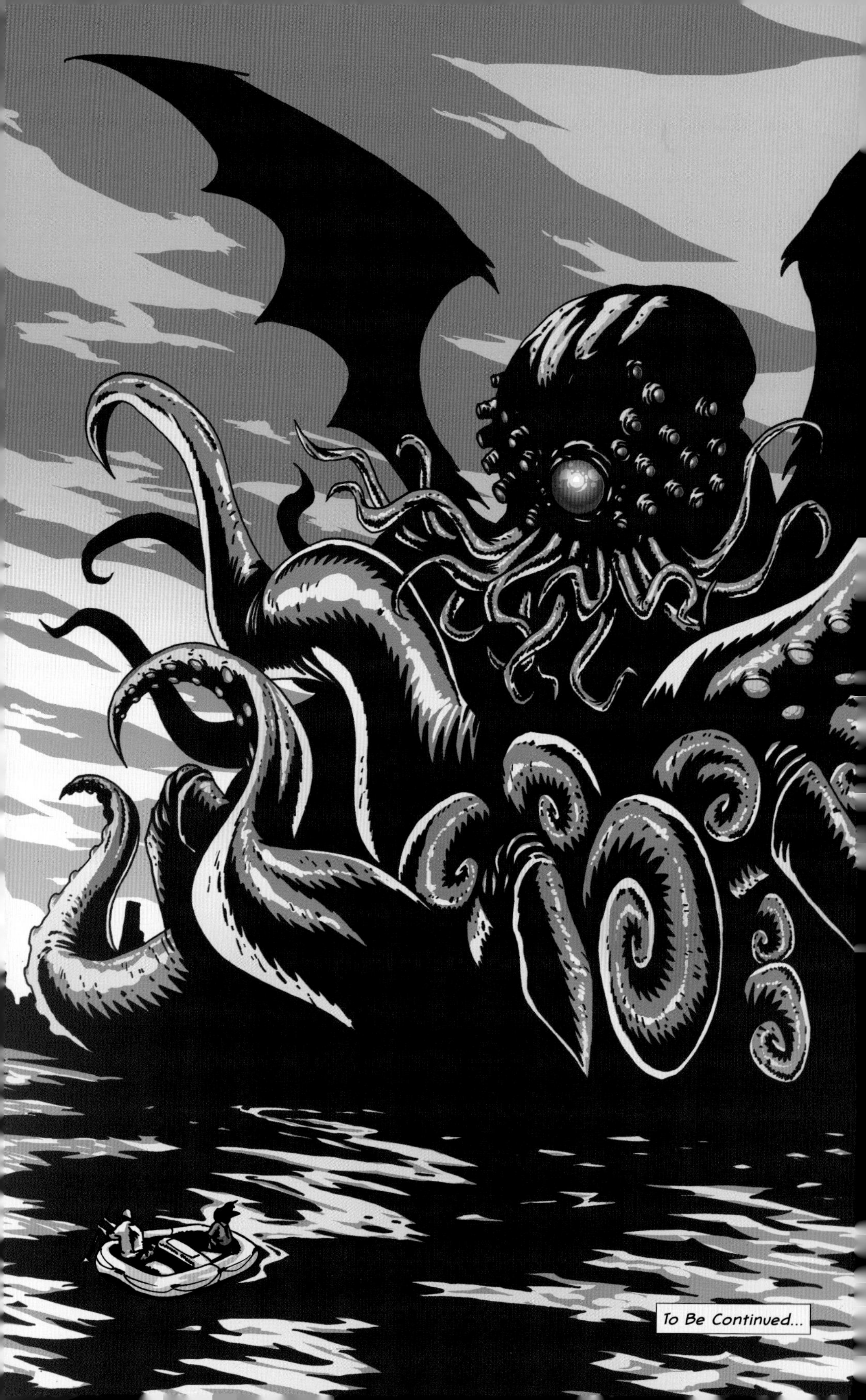
To Be Continued...

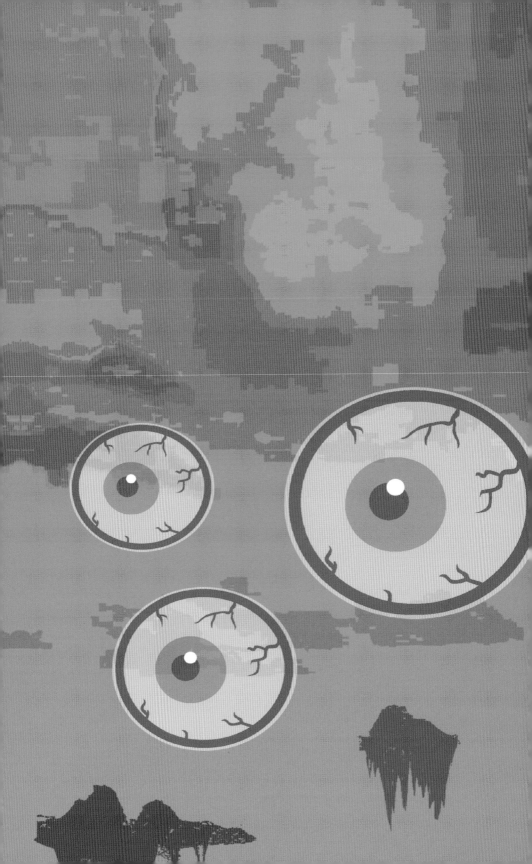

CHAPTER 4

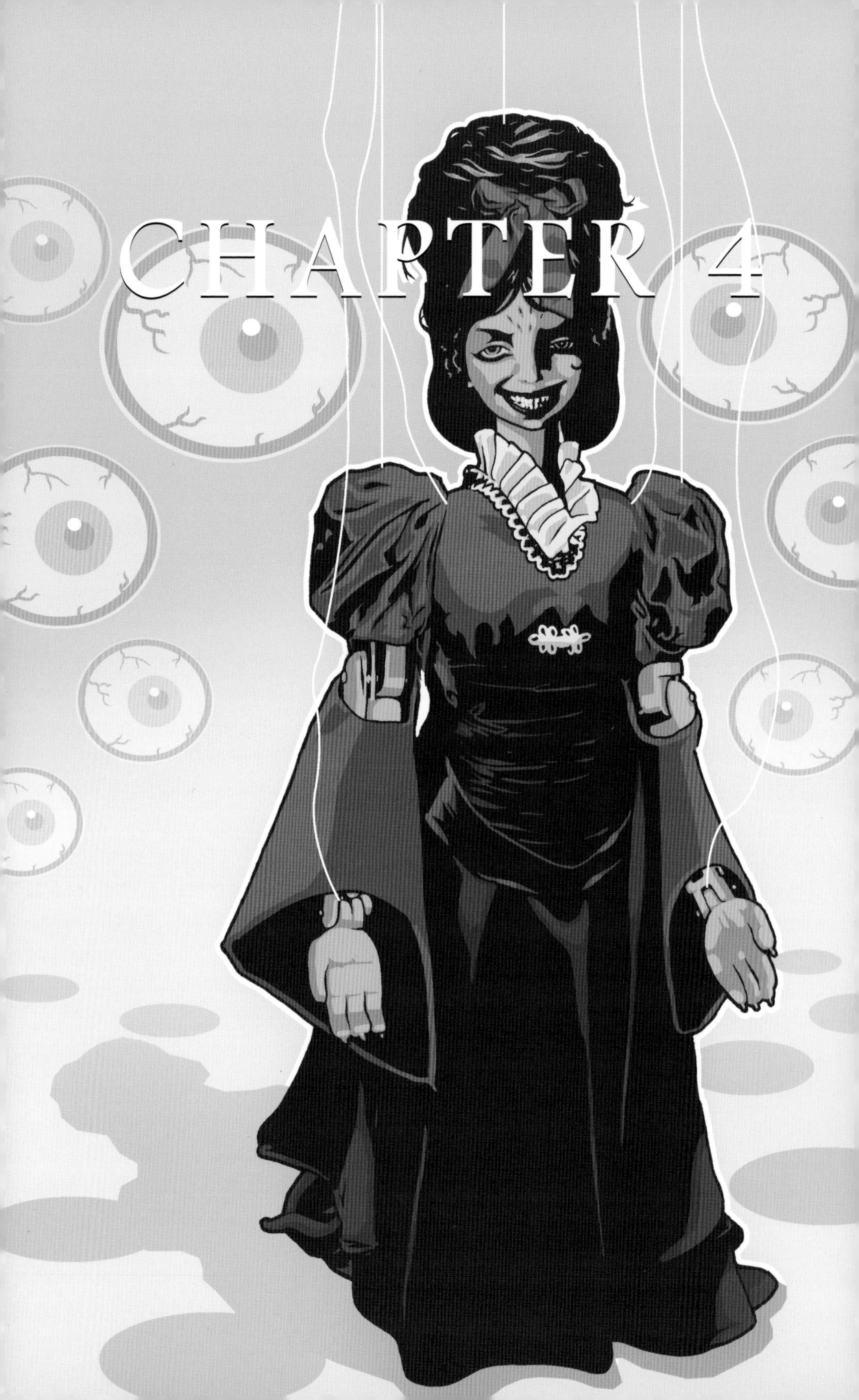

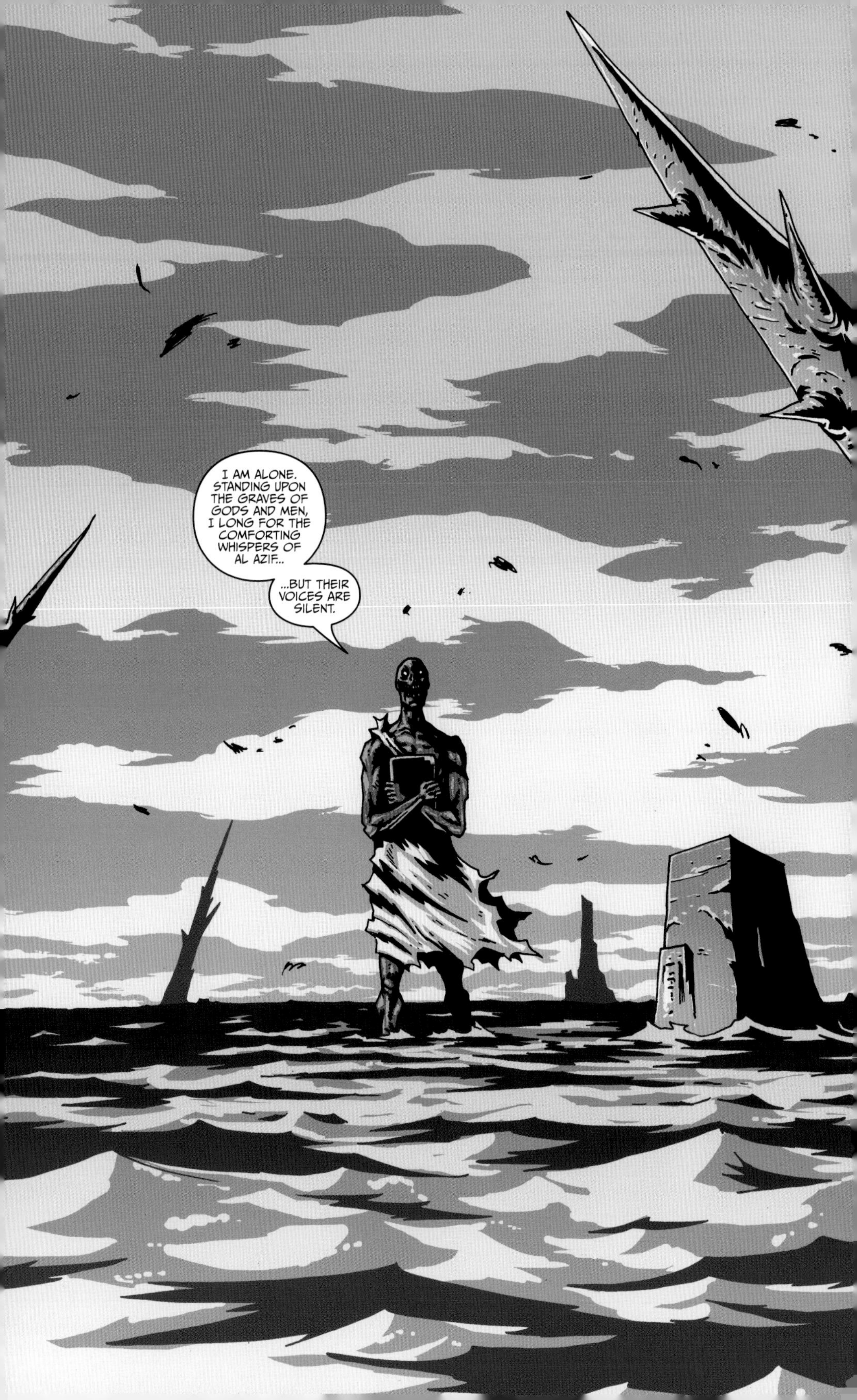
I AM ALONE. STANDING UPON THE GRAVES OF GODS AND MEN, I LONG FOR THE COMFORTING WHISPERS OF AL AZIF...
...BUT THEIR VOICES ARE SILENT.

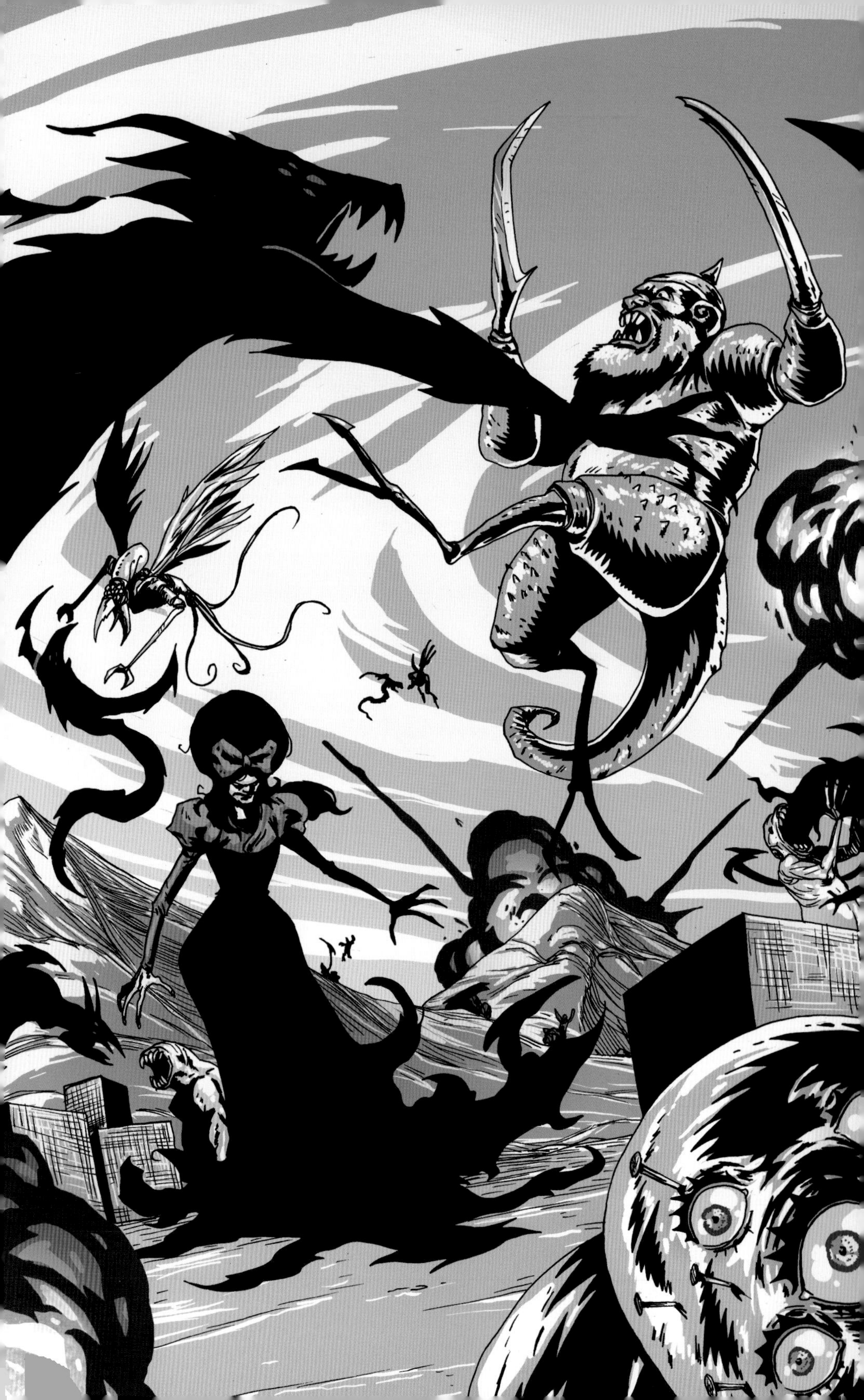

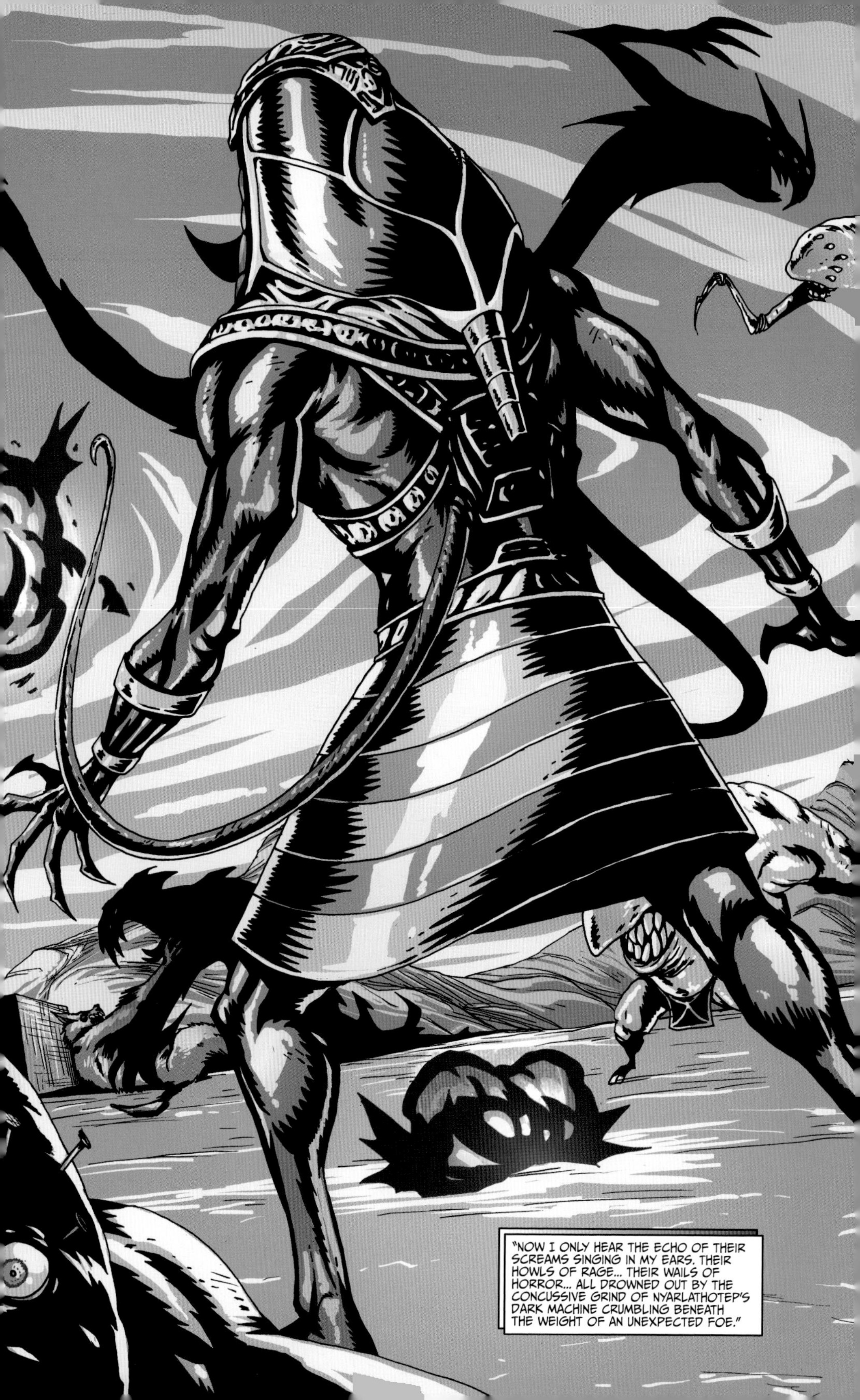
"NOW I ONLY HEAR THE ECHO OF THEIR SCREAMS SINGING IN MY EARS. THEIR HOWLS OF RAGE... THEIR WAILS OF HORROR... ALL DROWNED OUT BY THE CONCUSSIVE GRIND OF NYARLATHOTEP'S DARK MACHINE CRUMBLING BENEATH THE WEIGHT OF AN UNEXPECTED FOE."

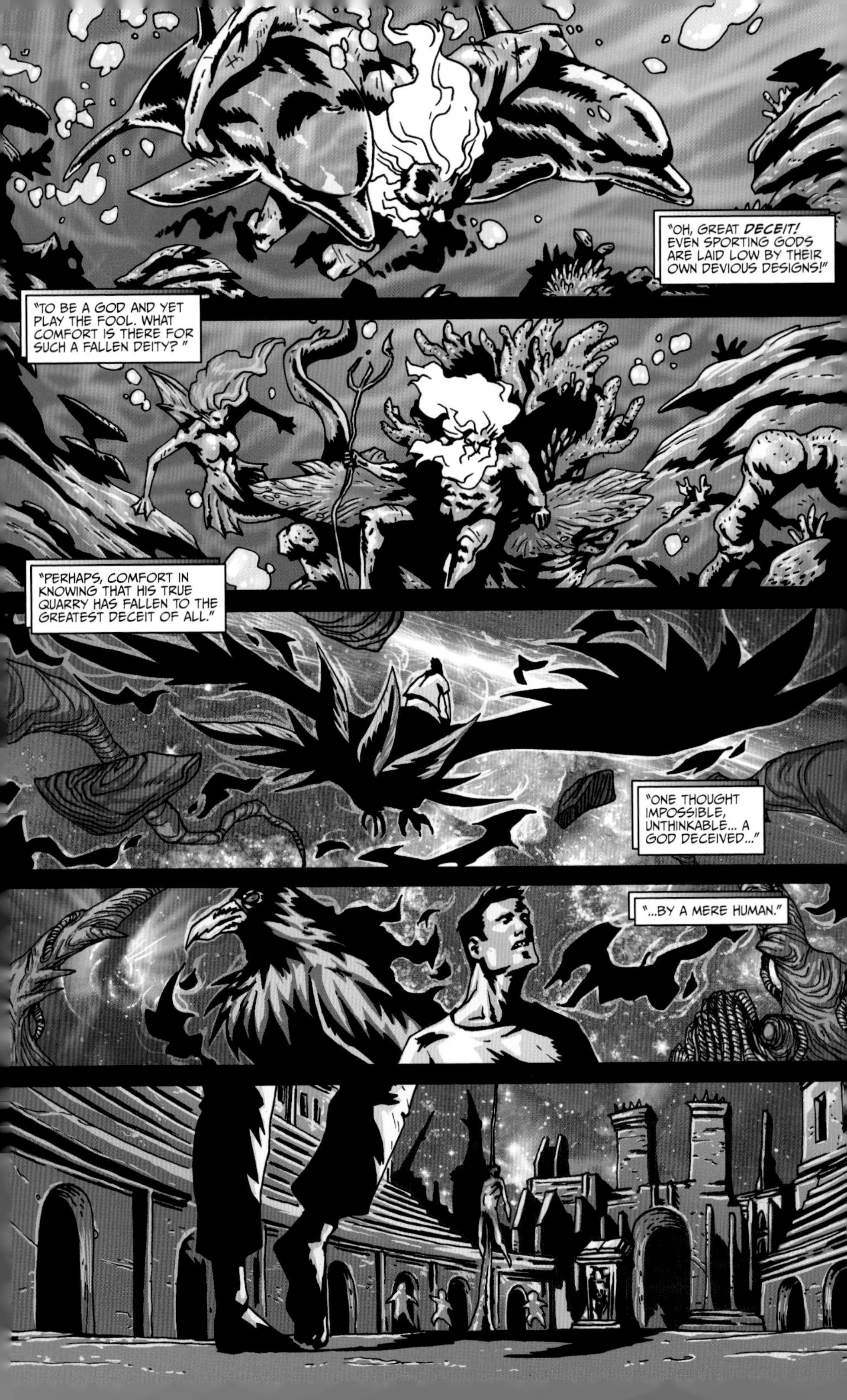
"OH, GREAT DECEIT! EVEN SPORTING GODS ARE LAID LOW BY THEIR OWN DEVIOUS DESIGNS!"
"TO BE A GOD AND YET PLAY THE FOOL. WHAT COMFORT IS THERE FOR SUCH A FALLEN DEITY?"
"PERHAPS, COMFORT IN KNOWING THAT HIS TRUE QUARRY HAS FALLEN TO THE GREATEST DECEIT OF ALL."
"ONE THOUGHT IMPOSSIBLE, UNTHINKABLE... A GOD DECEIVED..."
"...BY A MERE HUMAN."

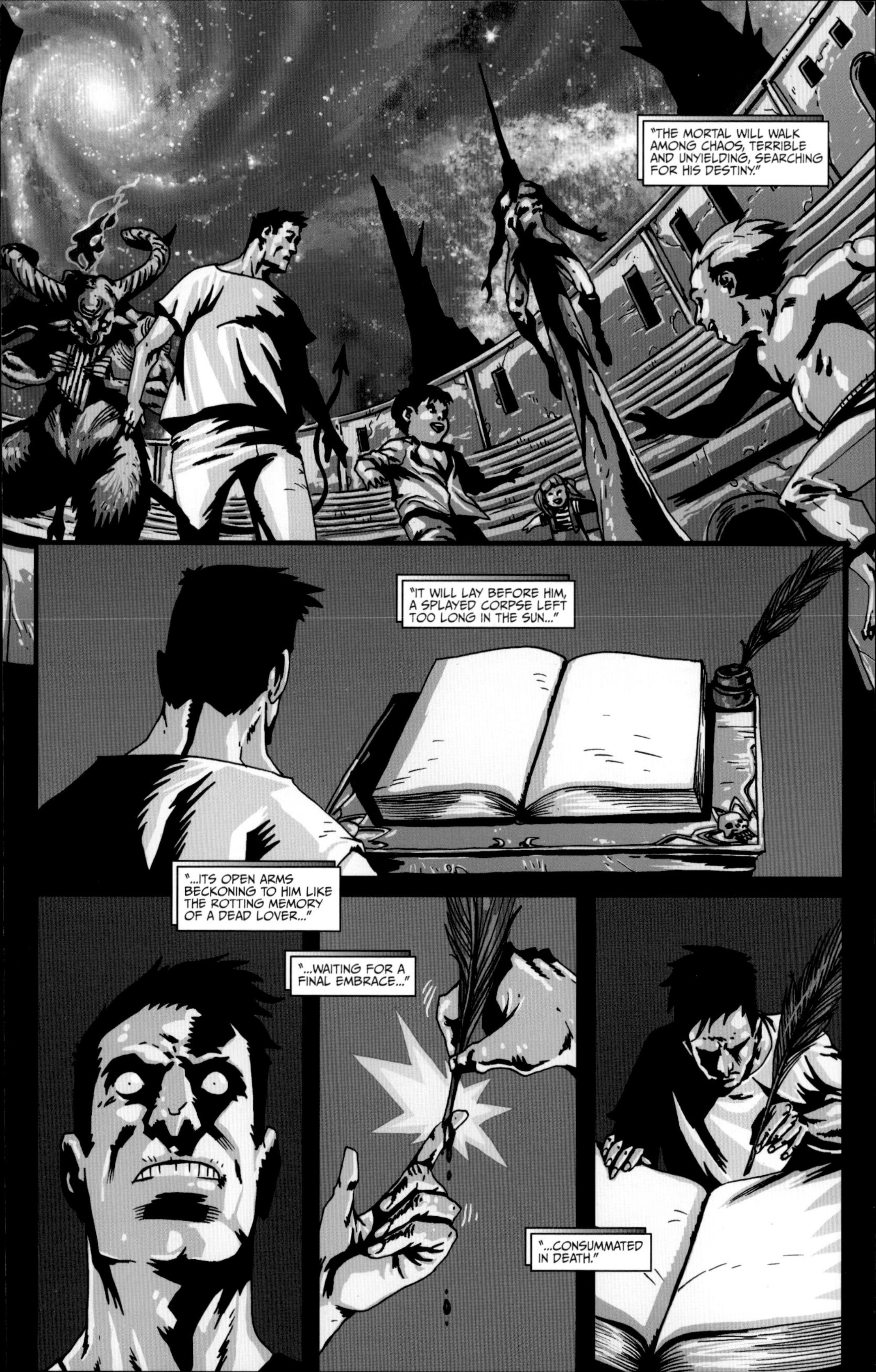
"THE MORTAL WILL WALK AMONG CHAOS, TERRIBLE AND UNYIELDING, SEARCHING FOR HIS DESTINY."
"IT WILL LAY BEFORE HIM, A SPLAYED CORPSE LEFT TOO LONG IN THE SUN..."
"...ITS OPEN ARMS BECKONING TO HIM LIKE THE ROTTING MEMORY OF A DEAD LOVER..."
"...WAITING FOR A FINAL EMBRACE..."
"...CONSUMMATED IN DEATH."

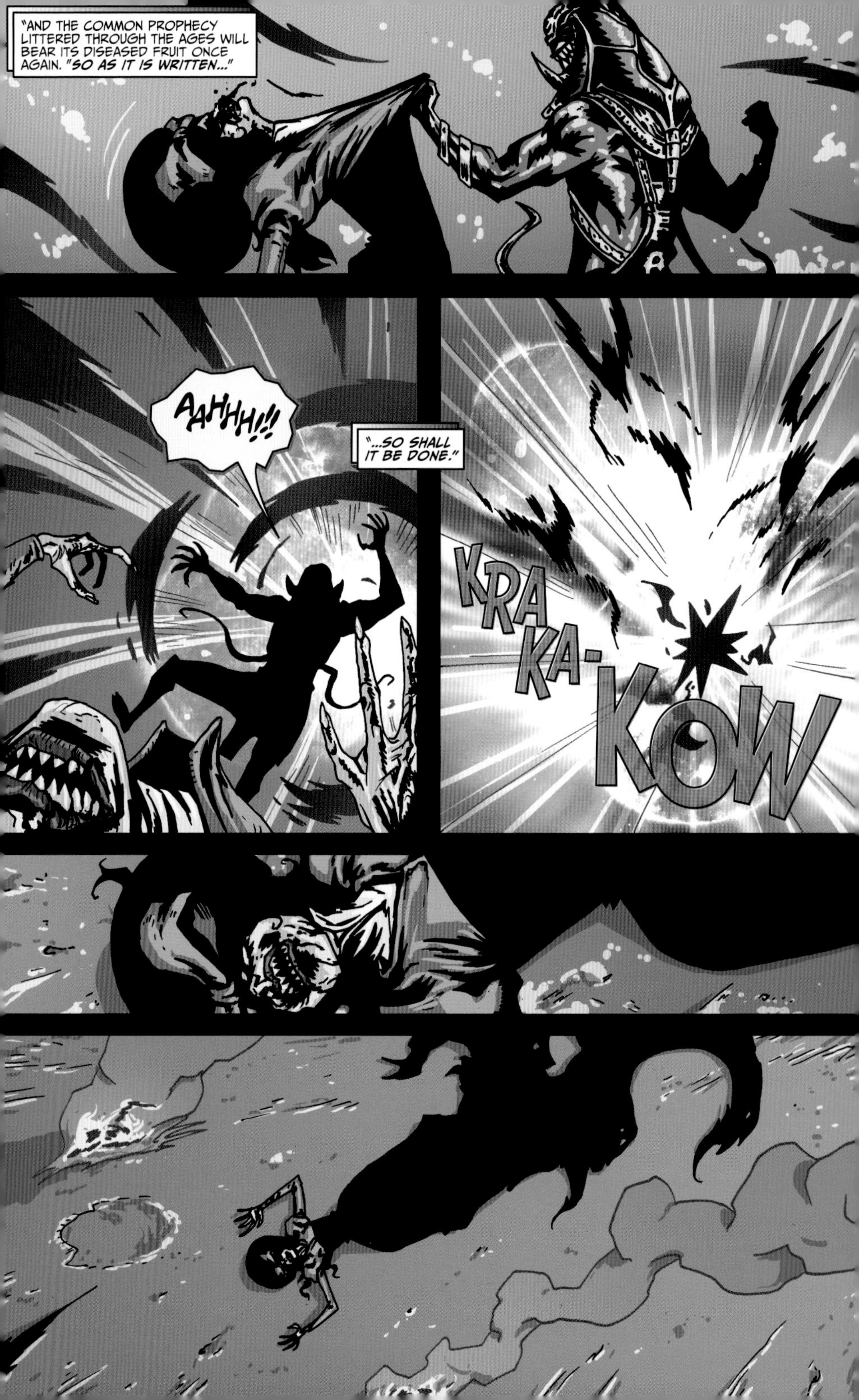
"AND THE COMMON PROPHECY LITTERED THROUGH THE AGES WILL BEAR ITS DISEASED FRUIT ONCE AGAIN. "SO AS IT IS WRITTEN..."
AAHHH!!!
"...SO SHALL IT BE DONE."
KRA KA-KOW

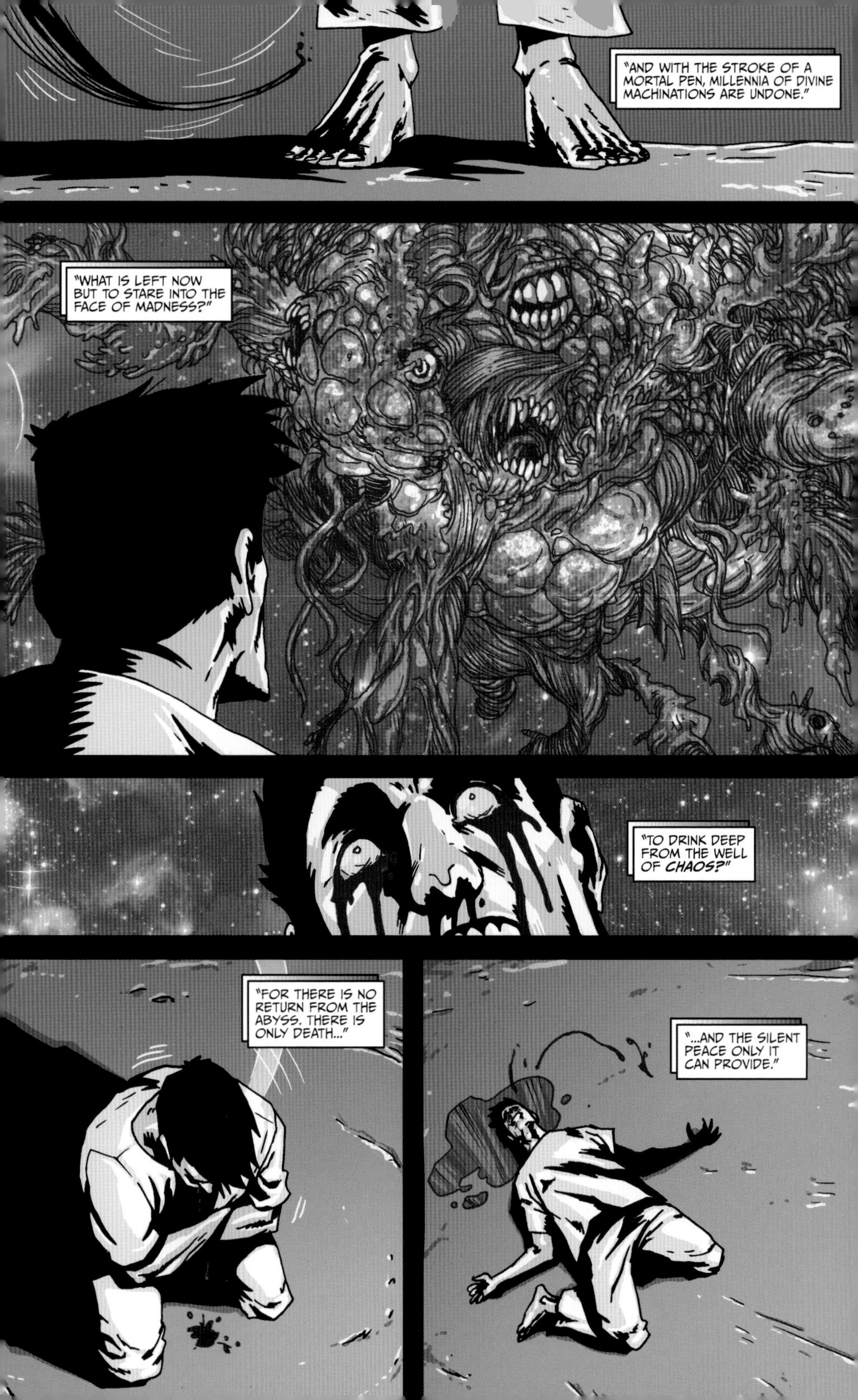
"AND WITH THE STROKE OF A MORTAL PEN, MILLENNIA OF DIVINE MACHINATIONS ARE UNDONE."
"WHAT IS LEFT NOW BUT TO STARE INTO THE FACE OF MADNESS?"
"TO DRINK DEEP FROM THE WELL OF *CHAOS?*"
"FOR THERE IS NO RETURN FROM THE ABYSS. THERE IS ONLY DEATH..."
"...AND THE SILENT PEACE ONLY IT CAN PROVIDE."

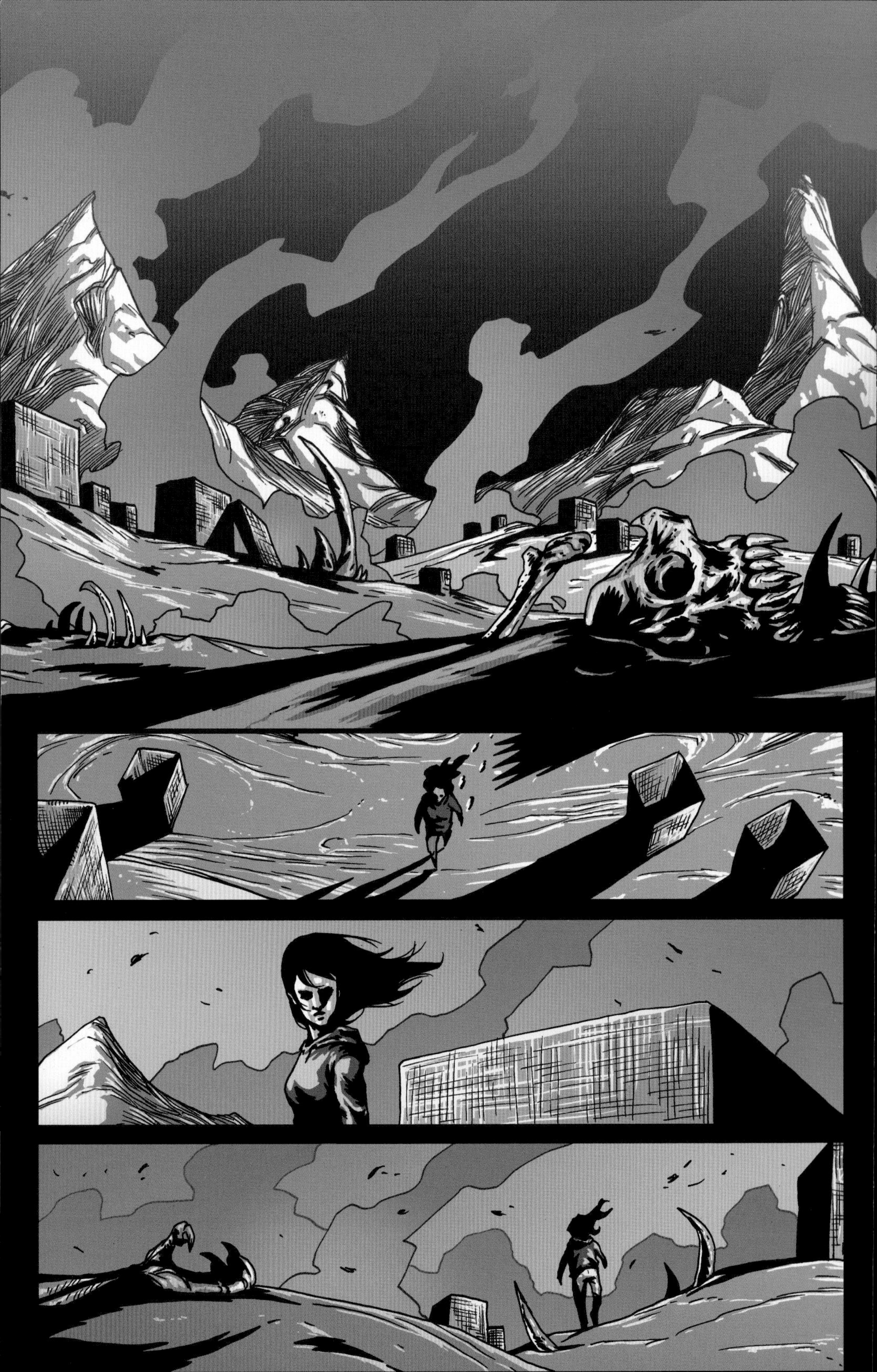

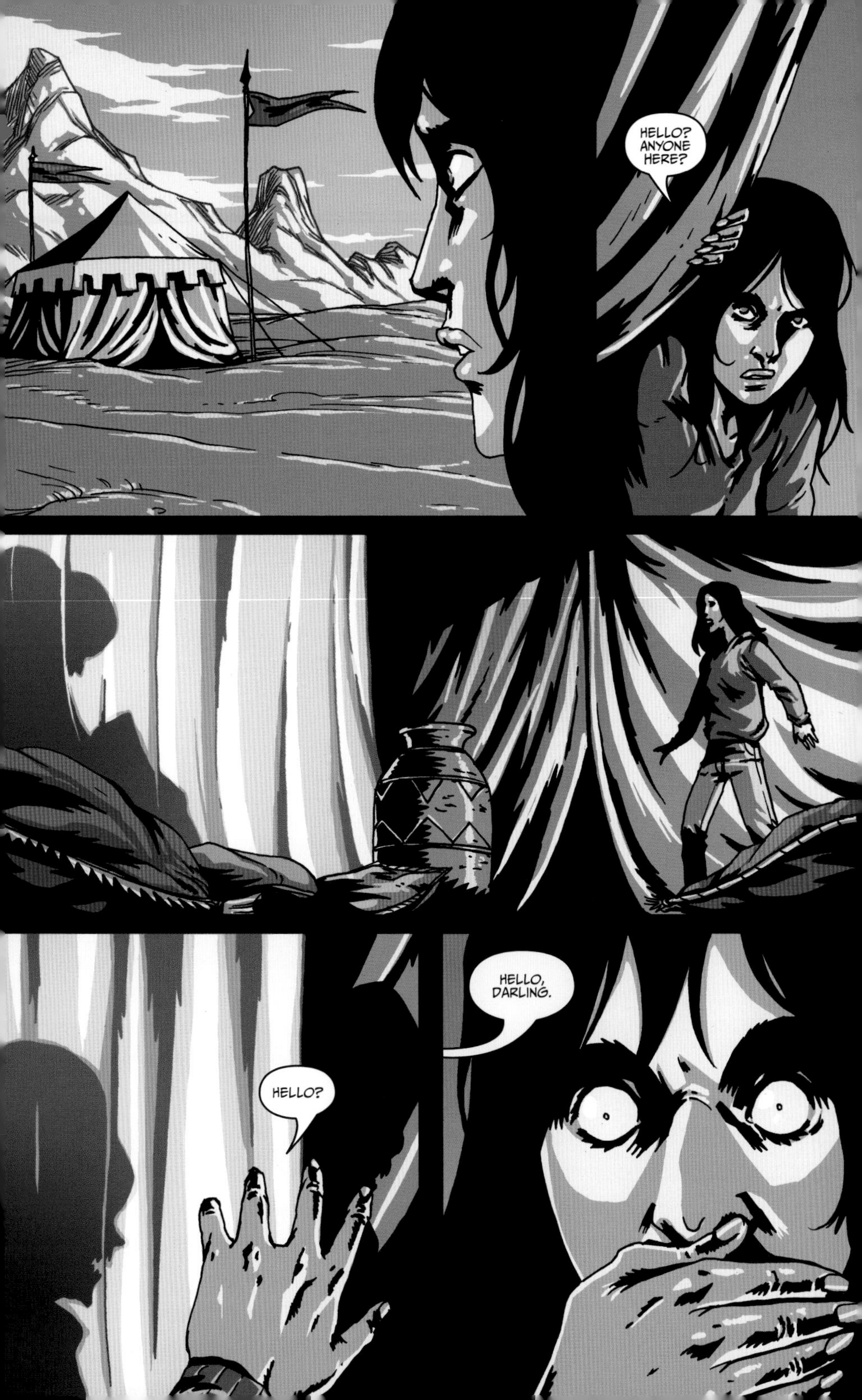
HELLO? ANYONE HERE?
HELLO?
HELLO, DARLING.

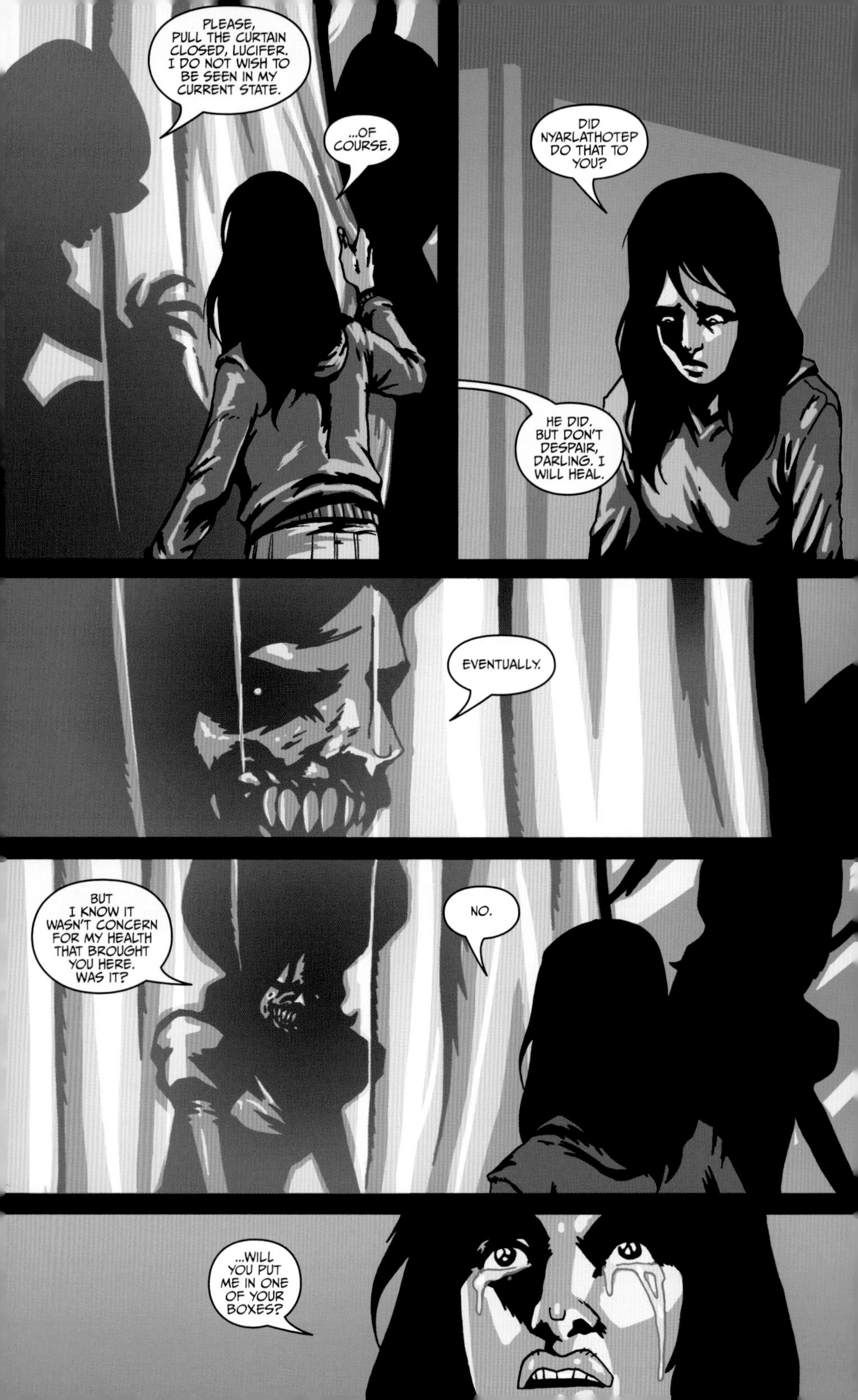
PLEASE, PULL THE CURTAIN CLOSED, LUCIFER. I DO NOT WISH TO BE SEEN IN MY CURRENT STATE.
...OF COURSE.
DID NYARLATHOTEP DO THAT TO YOU?
HE DID. BUT DON'T DESPAIR, DARLING. I WILL HEAL.
EVENTUALLY.
BUT I KNOW IT WASN'T CONCERN FOR MY HEALTH THAT BROUGHT YOU HERE. WAS IT?
NO.
...WILL YOU PUT ME IN ONE OF YOUR BOXES?

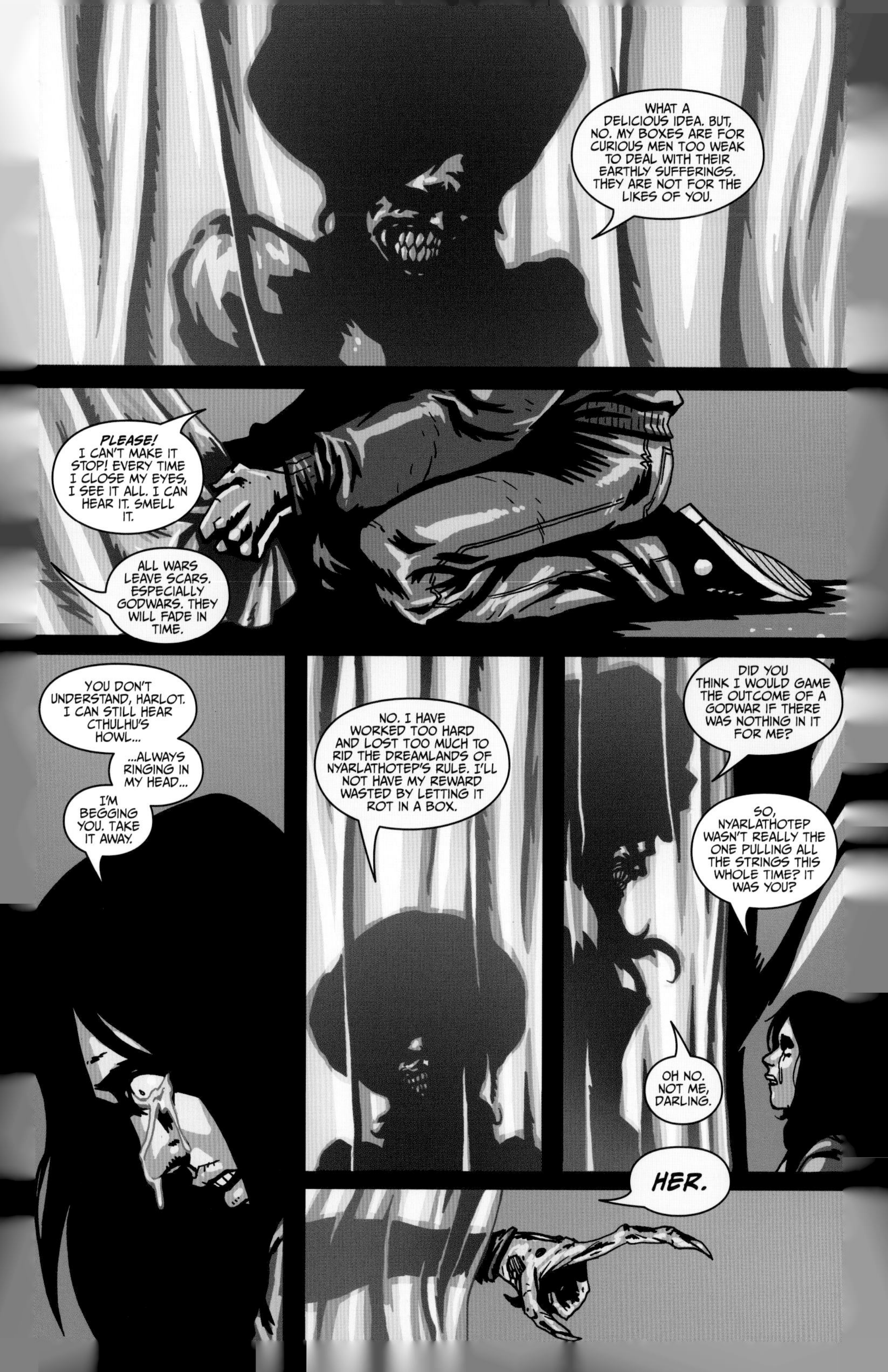
WHAT A DELICIOUS IDEA. BUT, NO. MY BOXES ARE FOR CURIOUS MEN TOO WEAK TO DEAL WITH THEIR EARTHLY SUFFERINGS. THEY ARE NOT FOR THE LIKES OF YOU.
PLEASE! I CAN'T MAKE IT STOP! EVERY TIME I CLOSE MY EYES, I SEE IT ALL. I CAN HEAR IT. SMELL IT.
ALL WARS LEAVE SCARS. ESPECIALLY GODWARS. THEY WILL FADE IN TIME.
YOU DON'T UNDERSTAND, HARLOT. I CAN STILL HEAR CTHULHU'S HOWL...
...ALWAYS RINGING IN MY HEAD...
I'M BEGGING YOU. TAKE IT AWAY.
NO. I HAVE WORKED TOO HARD AND LOST TOO MUCH TO RID THE DREAMLANDS OF NYARLATHOTEP'S RULE. I'LL NOT HAVE MY REWARD WASTED BY LETTING IT ROT IN A BOX.
DID YOU THINK I WOULD GAME THE OUTCOME OF A GODWAR IF THERE WAS NOTHING IN IT FOR ME?
SO, NYARLATHOTEP WASN'T REALLY THE ONE PULLING ALL THE STRINGS THIS WHOLE TIME? IT WAS YOU?
OH NO. NOT ME, DARLING.
HER.

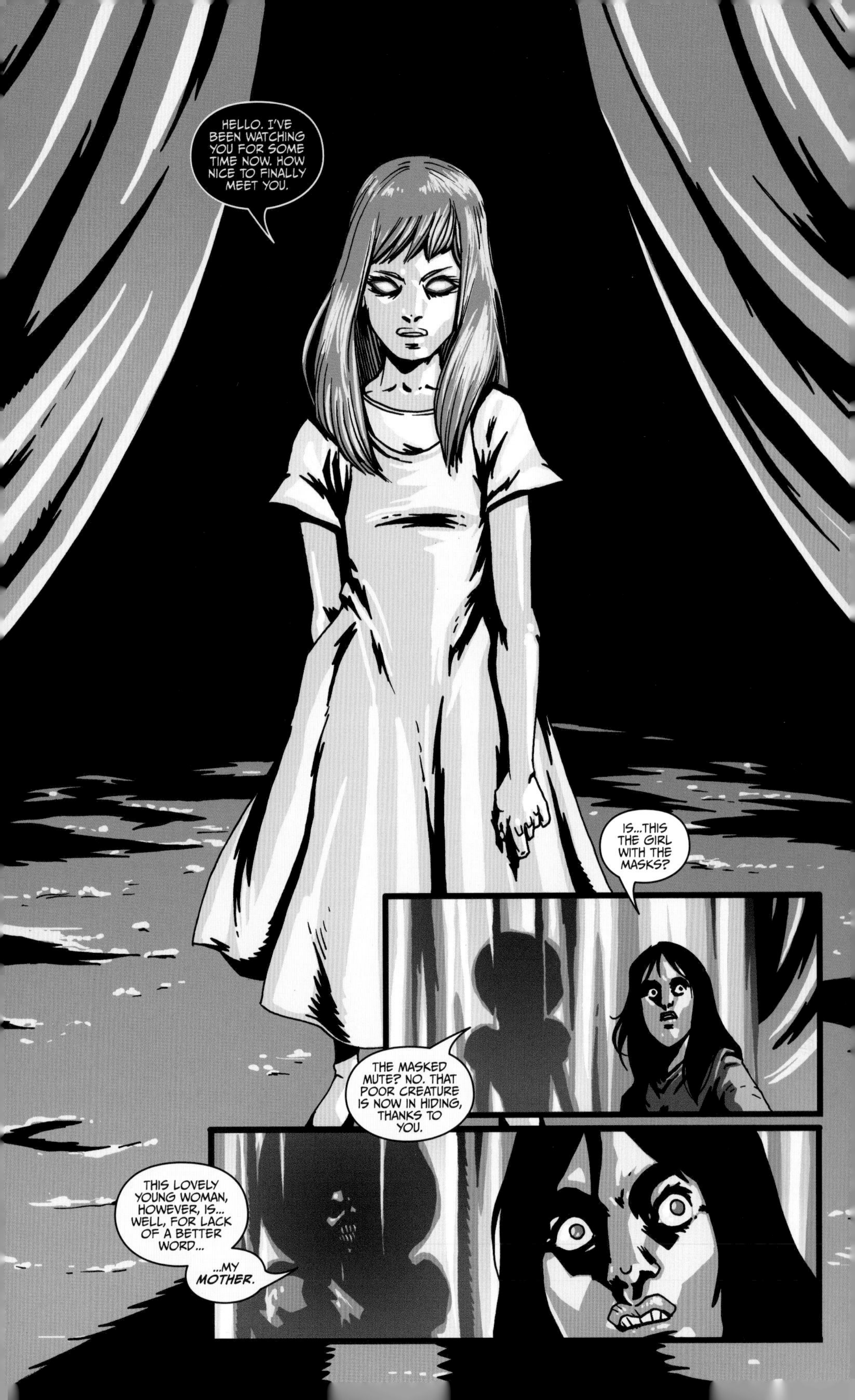
HELLO. I'VE BEEN WATCHING YOU FOR SOME TIME NOW. HOW NICE TO FINALLY MEET YOU.
IS...THIS THE GIRL WITH THE MASKS?
THE MASKED MUTE? NO. THAT POOR CREATURE IS NOW IN HIDING, THANKS TO YOU.
THIS LOVELY YOUNG WOMAN, HOWEVER, IS... WELL, FOR LACK OF A BETTER WORD...
...MY *MOTHER*.

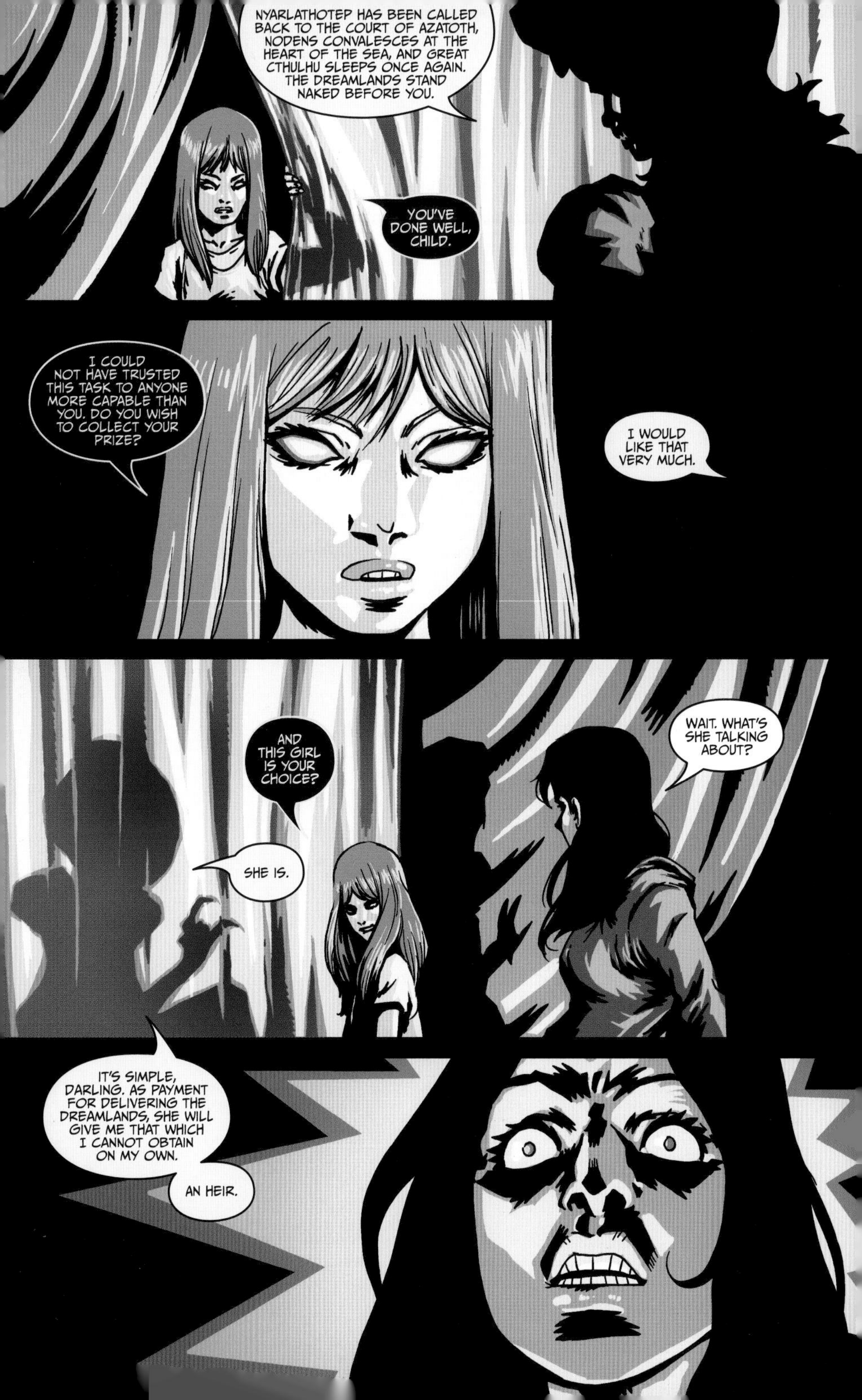
NYARLATHOTEP HAS BEEN CALLED BACK TO THE COURT OF AZATOTH, NODENS CONVALESCES AT THE HEART OF THE SEA, AND GREAT CTHULHU SLEEPS ONCE AGAIN. THE DREAMLANDS STAND NAKED BEFORE YOU.
YOU'VE DONE WELL, CHILD.
I COULD NOT HAVE TRUSTED THIS TASK TO ANYONE MORE CAPABLE THAN YOU. DO YOU WISH TO COLLECT YOUR PRIZE?
I WOULD LIKE THAT VERY MUCH.
AND THIS GIRL IS YOUR CHOICE?
SHE IS.
WAIT. WHAT'S SHE TALKING ABOUT?
IT'S SIMPLE, DARLING. AS PAYMENT FOR DELIVERING THE DREAMLANDS, SHE WILL GIVE ME THAT WHICH I CANNOT OBTAIN ON MY OWN.
AN HEIR.

STAY AWAY FROM--

AHHHH!!

SSKKK SSHHHH

...NNHHH...

THERE IS NO ESCAPING YOUR DESTINY, CHILD.

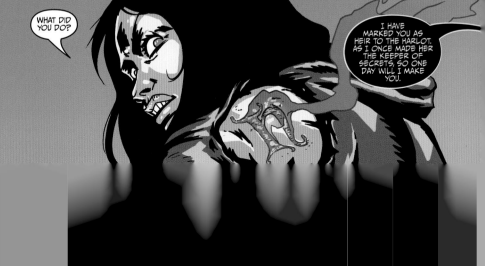

WHAT DID YOU DO?

I HAVE MARKED YOU AS HEIR TO THE HARLOT. AS I ONCE MADE HER THE KEEPER OF SECRETS, SO ONE DAY WILL I MAKE YOU.

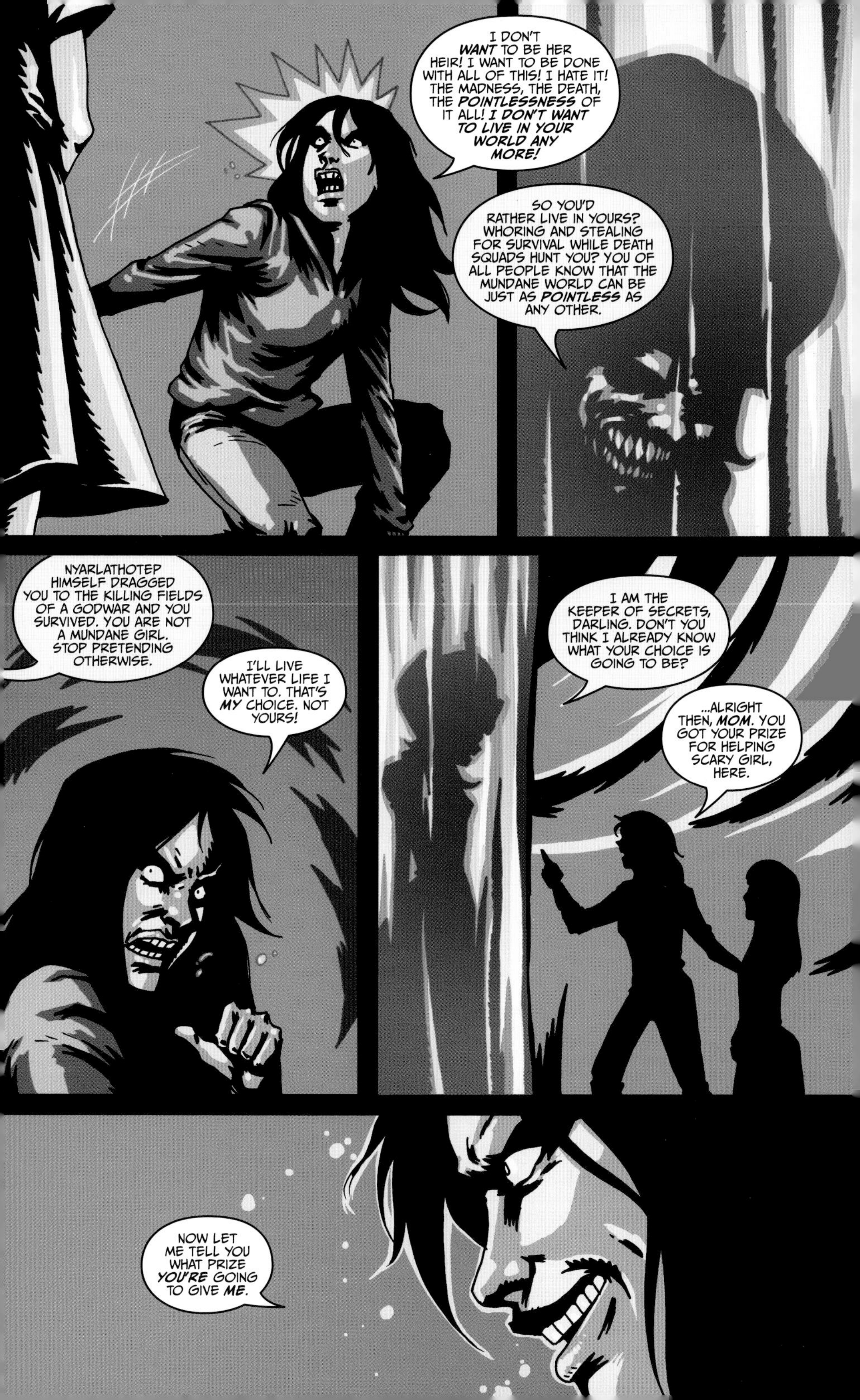
I DON'T *WANT* TO BE HER HEIR! I WANT TO BE DONE WITH ALL OF THIS! I HATE IT! THE MADNESS, THE DEATH, THE *POINTLESSNESS* OF IT ALL! *I DON'T WANT TO LIVE IN YOUR WORLD ANY MORE!*
SO YOU'D RATHER LIVE IN YOURS? WHORING AND STEALING FOR SURVIVAL WHILE DEATH SQUADS HUNT YOU? YOU OF ALL PEOPLE KNOW THAT THE MUNDANE WORLD CAN BE JUST AS *POINTLESS* AS ANY OTHER.
NYARLATHOTEP HIMSELF DRAGGED YOU TO THE KILLING FIELDS OF A GODWAR AND YOU SURVIVED. YOU ARE NOT A MUNDANE GIRL. STOP PRETENDING OTHERWISE.
I'LL LIVE WHATEVER LIFE I WANT TO. THAT'S *MY* CHOICE. NOT YOURS!
I AM THE KEEPER OF SECRETS, DARLING. DON'T YOU THINK I ALREADY KNOW WHAT YOUR CHOICE IS GOING TO BE?
...ALRIGHT THEN, *MOM*. YOU GOT YOUR PRIZE FOR HELPING SCARY GIRL, HERE.
NOW LET ME TELL YOU WHAT PRIZE *YOU'RE* GOING TO GIVE *ME*.

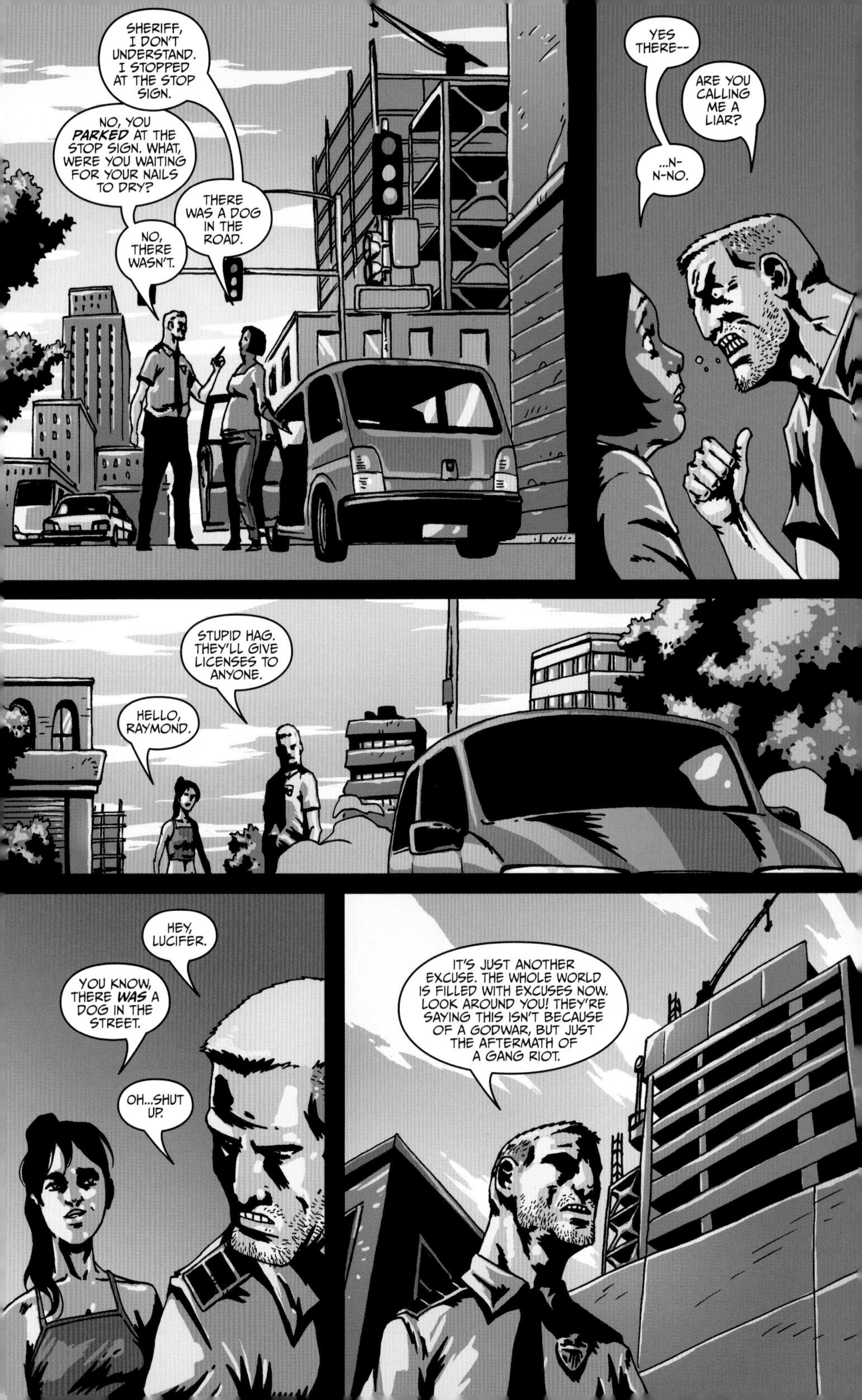

SHERIFF, I DON'T UNDERSTAND. I STOPPED AT THE STOP SIGN.
NO, YOU PARKED AT THE STOP SIGN. WHAT, WERE YOU WAITING FOR YOUR NAILS TO DRY?
THERE WAS A DOG IN THE ROAD.
NO, THERE WASN'T.
YES THERE--
ARE YOU CALLING ME A LIAR?
...N-N-NO.
STUPID HAG. THEY'LL GIVE LICENSES TO ANYONE.
HELLO, RAYMOND.
HEY, LUCIFER.
YOU KNOW, THERE WAS A DOG IN THE STREET.
OH...SHUT UP.
IT'S JUST ANOTHER EXCUSE. THE WHOLE WORLD IS FILLED WITH EXCUSES NOW. LOOK AROUND YOU! THEY'RE SAYING THIS ISN'T BECAUSE OF A GODWAR, BUT JUST THE AFTERMATH OF A GANG RIOT.

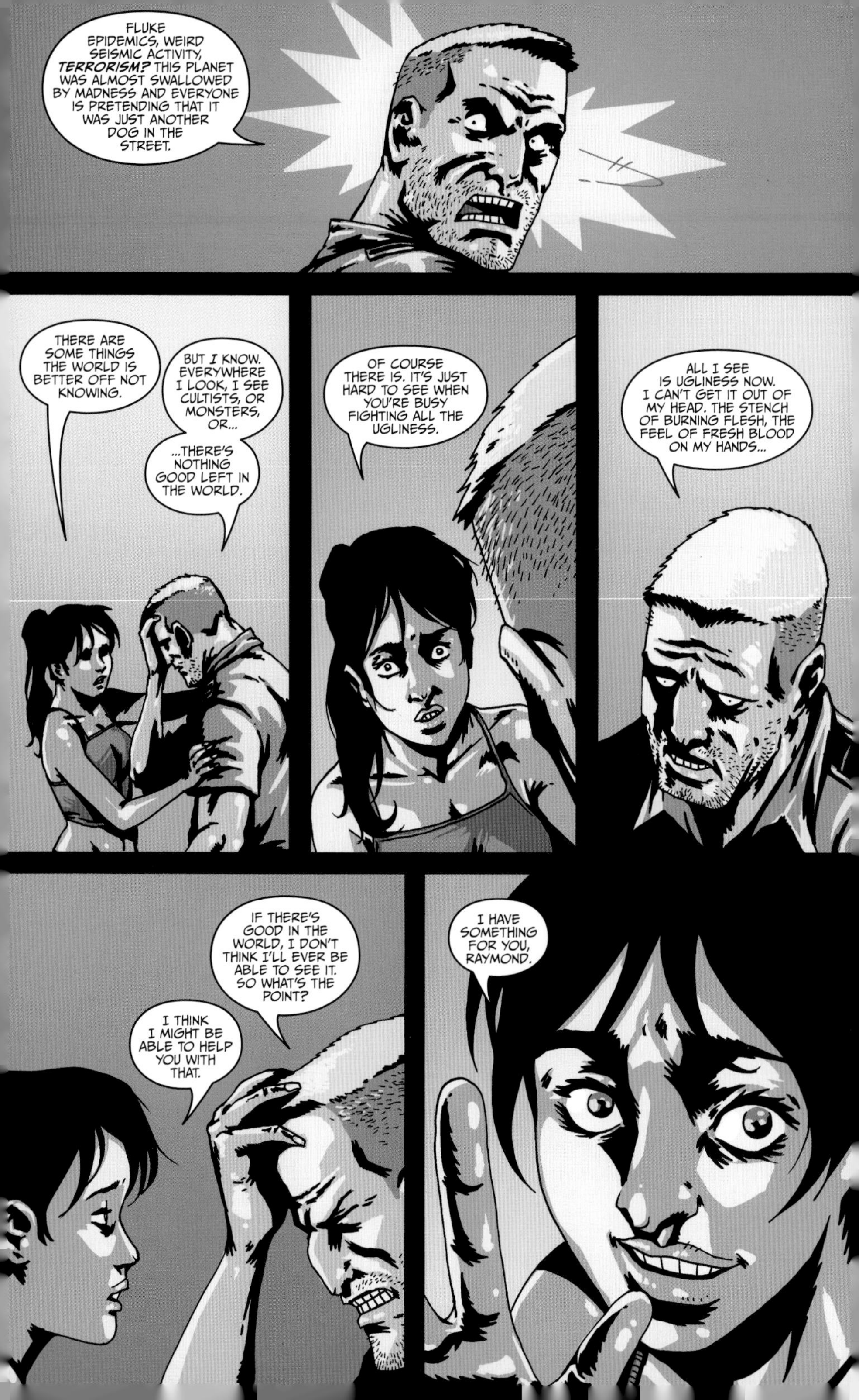
FLUKE EPIDEMICS, WEIRD SEISMIC ACTIVITY, TERRORISM? THIS PLANET WAS ALMOST SWALLOWED BY MADNESS AND EVERYONE IS PRETENDING THAT IT WAS JUST ANOTHER DOG IN THE STREET.
THERE ARE SOME THINGS THE WORLD IS BETTER OFF NOT KNOWING.
BUT I KNOW. EVERYWHERE I LOOK, I SEE CULTISTS, OR MONSTERS, OR...
...THERE'S NOTHING GOOD LEFT IN THE WORLD.
OF COURSE THERE IS. IT'S JUST HARD TO SEE WHEN YOU'RE BUSY FIGHTING ALL THE UGLINESS.
ALL I SEE IS UGLINESS NOW. I CAN'T GET IT OUT OF MY HEAD. THE STENCH OF BURNING FLESH, THE FEEL OF FRESH BLOOD ON MY HANDS...
IF THERE'S GOOD IN THE WORLD, I DON'T THINK I'LL EVER BE ABLE TO SEE IT. SO WHAT'S THE POINT?
I THINK I MIGHT BE ABLE TO HELP YOU WITH THAT.
I HAVE SOMETHING FOR YOU, RAYMOND.

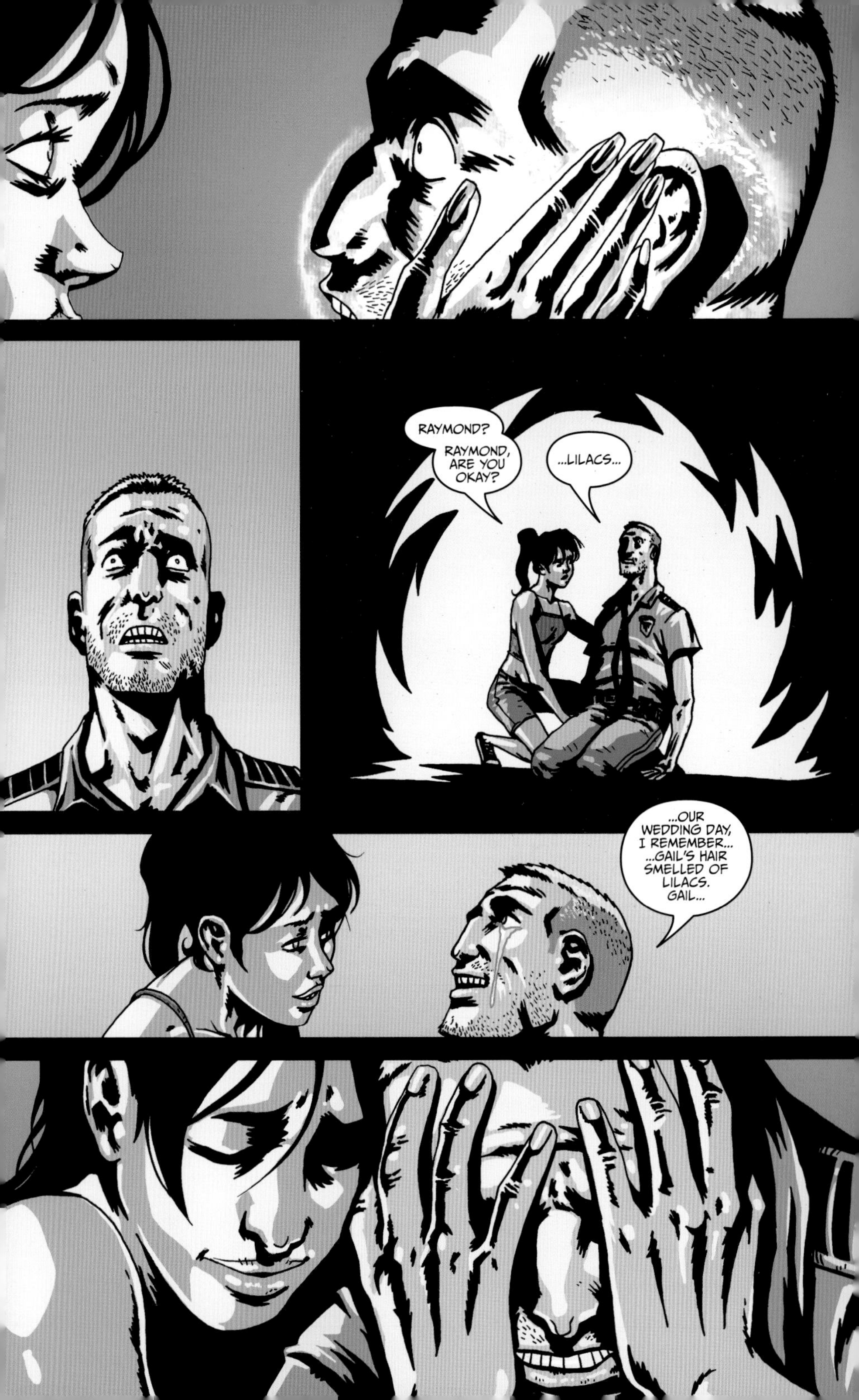
RAYMOND?
RAYMOND, ARE YOU OKAY?
...LILACS...
...OUR WEDDING DAY, I REMEMBER... ...GAIL'S HAIR SMELLED OF LILACS. GAIL...

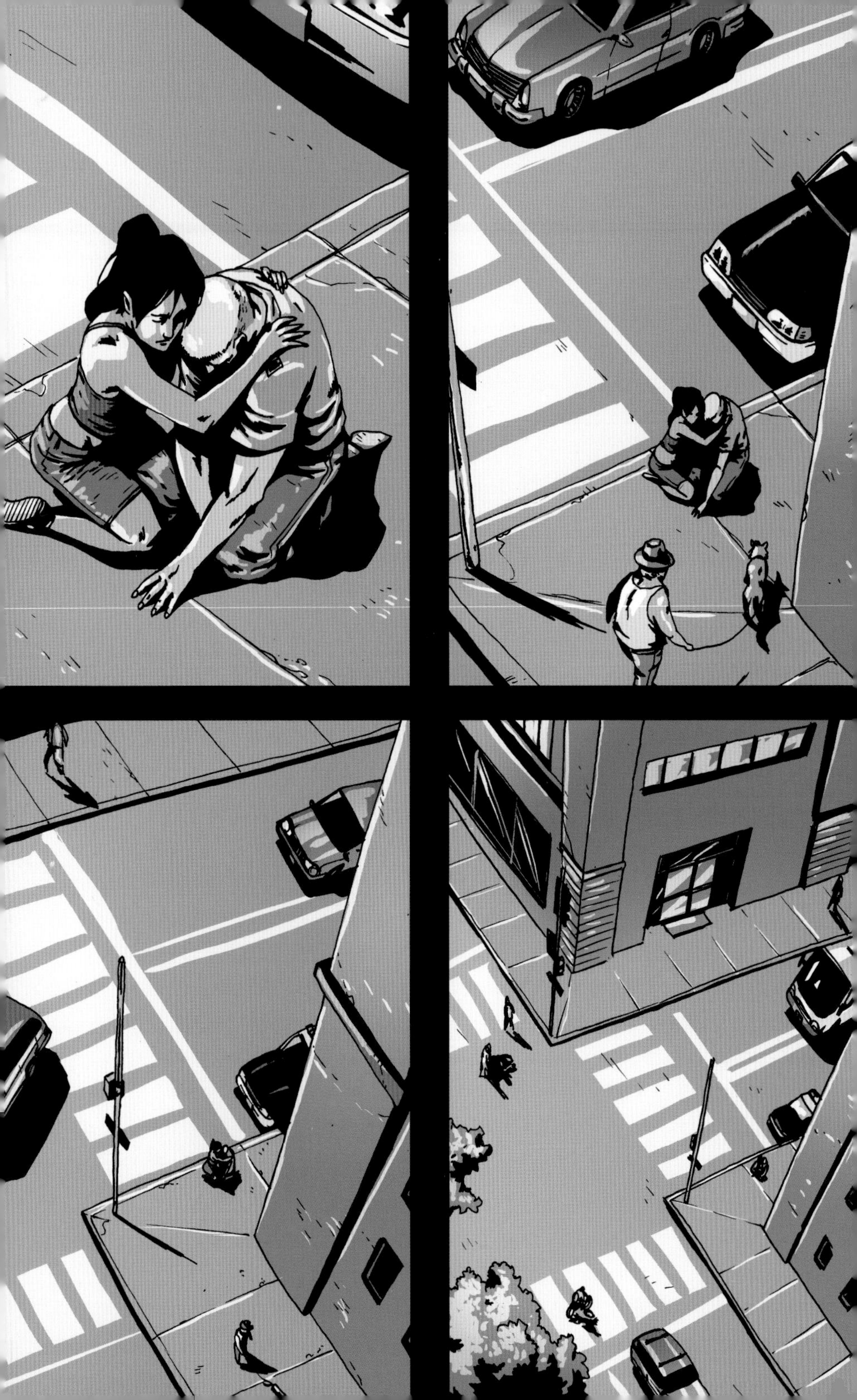

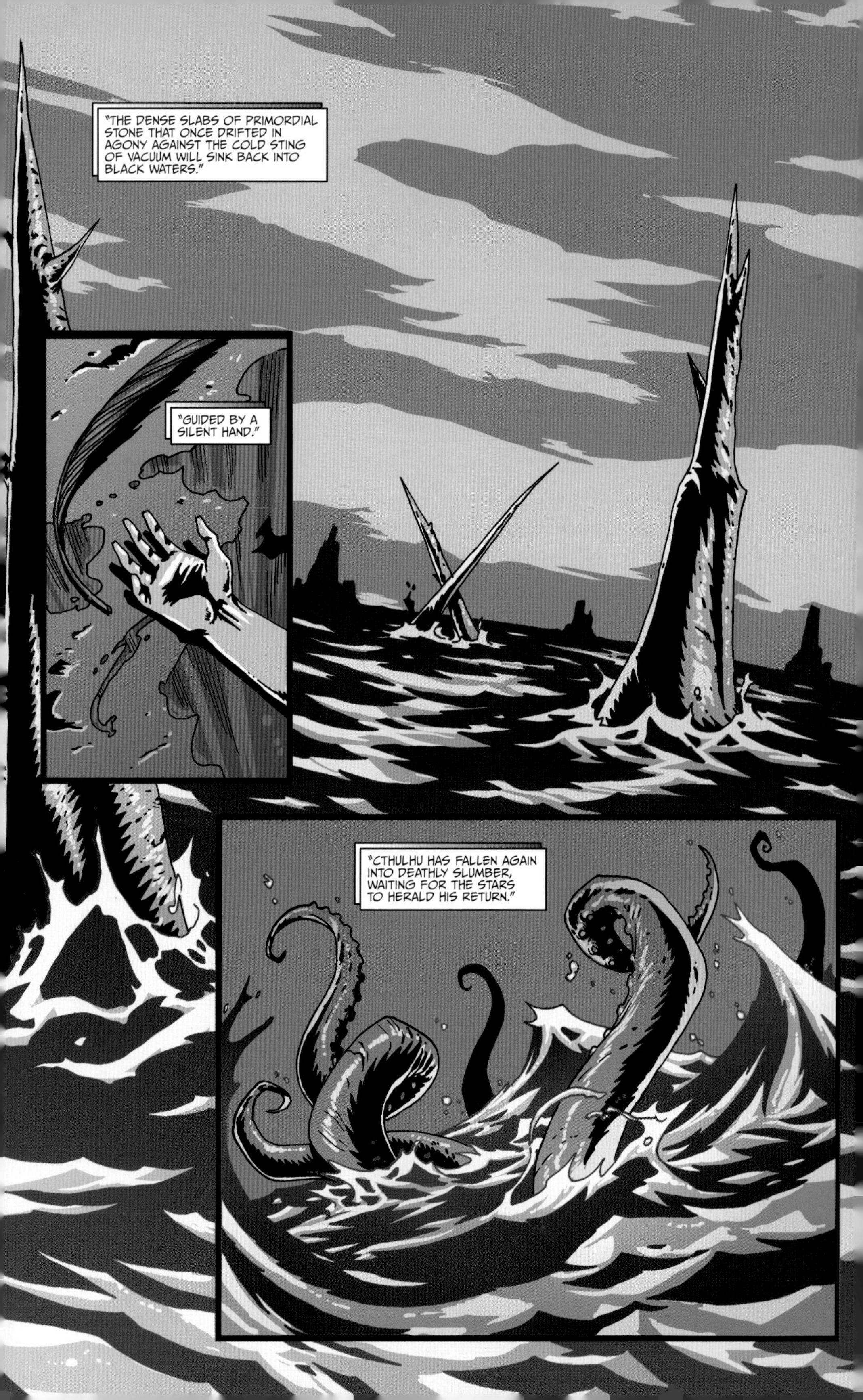
"THE DENSE SLABS OF PRIMORDIAL STONE THAT ONCE DRIFTED IN AGONY AGAINST THE COLD STING OF VACUUM WILL SINK BACK INTO BLACK WATERS."
"GUIDED BY A SILENT HAND."
"CTHULHU HAS FALLEN AGAIN INTO DEATHLY SLUMBER, WAITING FOR THE STARS TO HERALD HIS RETURN."

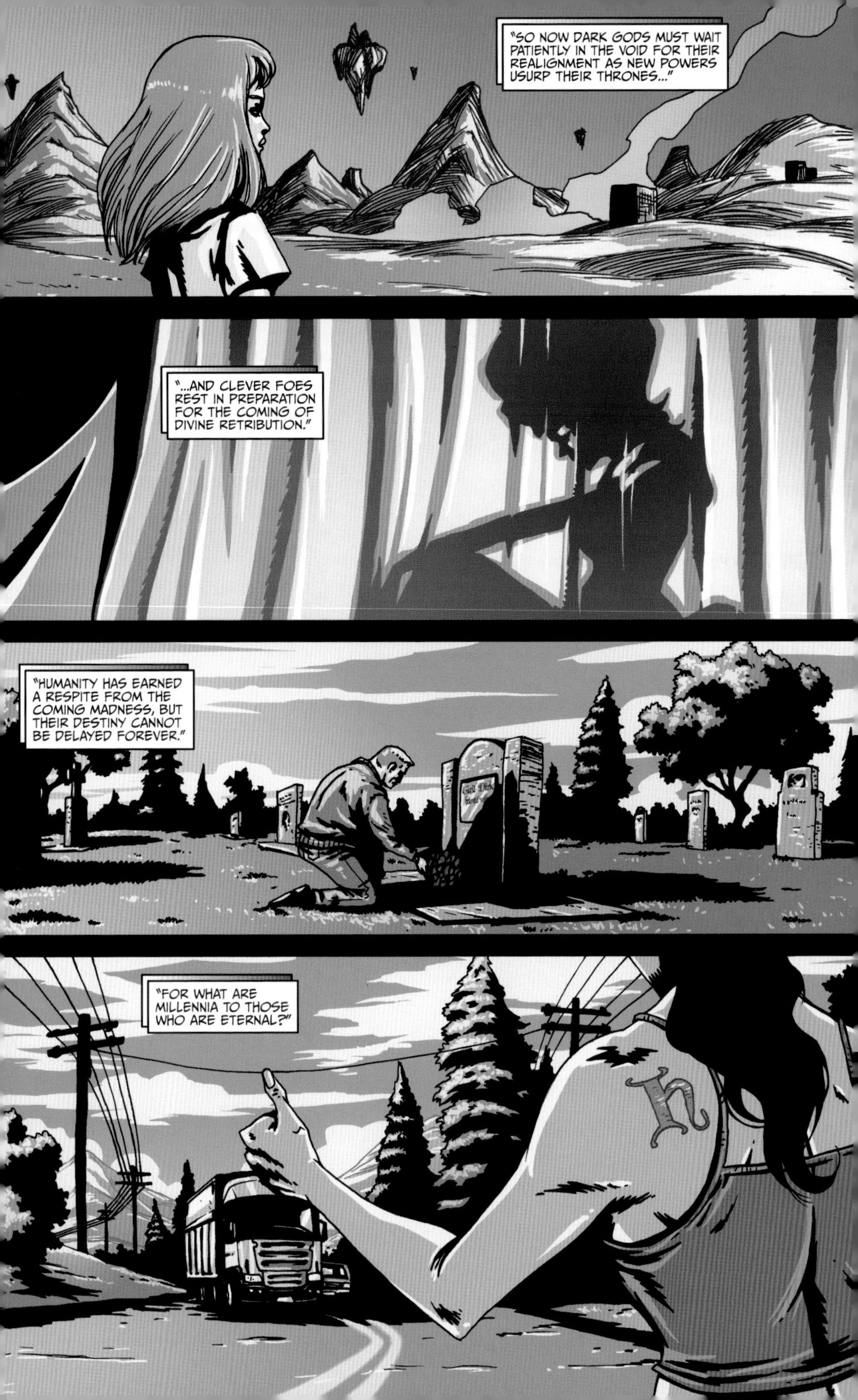
"SO NOW DARK GODS MUST WAIT PATIENTLY IN THE VOID FOR THEIR REALIGNMENT AS NEW POWERS USURP THEIR THRONES..."
"...AND CLEVER FOES REST IN PREPARATION FOR THE COMING OF DIVINE RETRIBUTION."
"HUMANITY HAS EARNED A RESPITE FROM THE COMING MADNESS, BUT THEIR DESTINY CANNOT BE DELAYED FOREVER."
"FOR WHAT ARE MILLENNIA TO THOSE WHO ARE ETERNAL?"

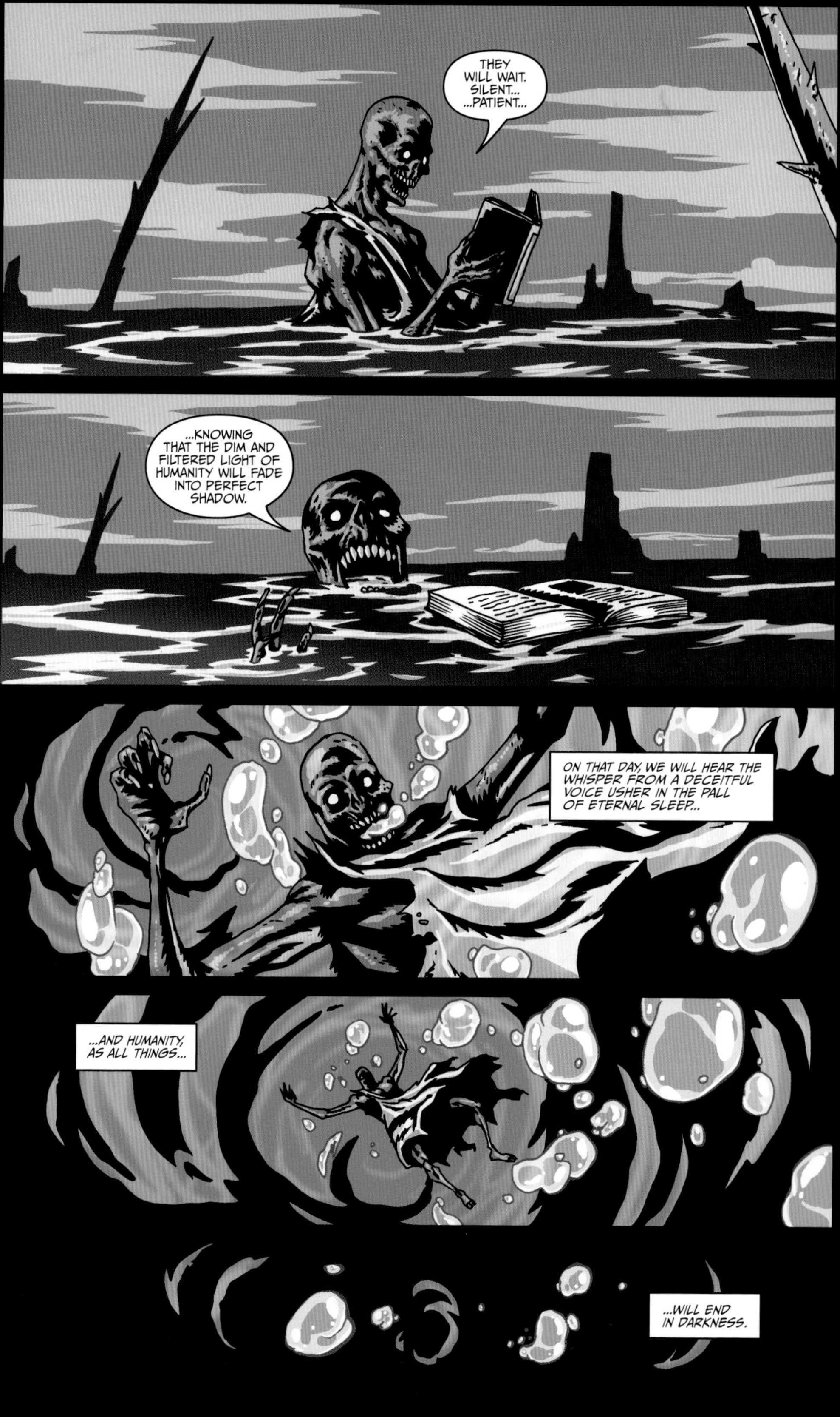
THEY WILL WAIT. SILENT... ...PATIENT...
...KNOWING THAT THE DIM AND FILTERED LIGHT OF HUMANITY WILL FADE INTO PERFECT SHADOW.
ON THAT DAY, WE WILL HEAR THE WHISPER FROM A DECEITFUL VOICE USHER IN THE PALL OF ETERNAL SLEEP...
...AND HUMANITY, AS ALL THINGS...
...WILL END IN DARKNESS.

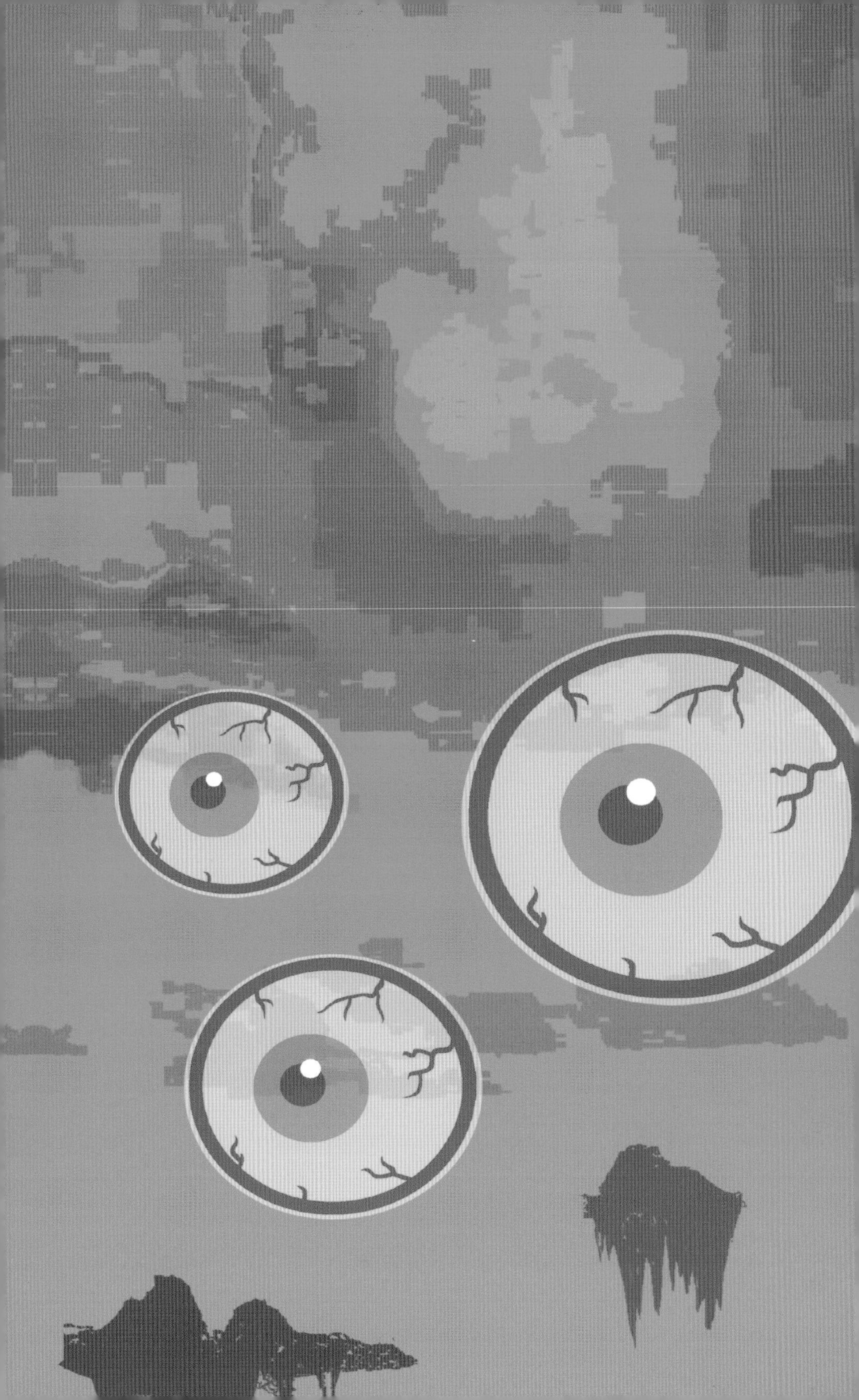

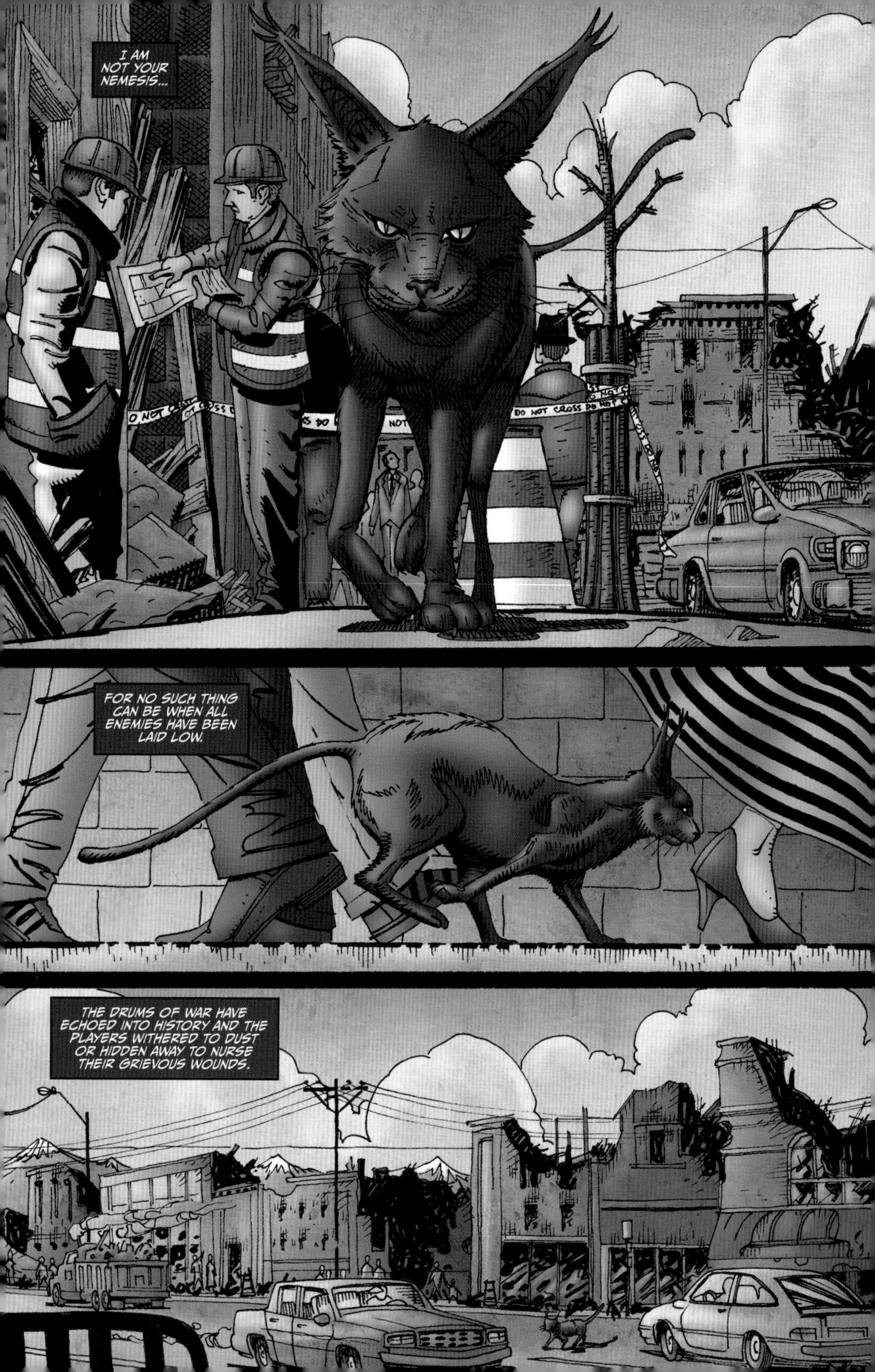
I AM NOT YOUR NEMESIS...
DO NOT CROSS
FOR NO SUCH THING CAN BE WHEN ALL ENEMIES HAVE BEEN LAID LOW.
THE DRUMS OF WAR HAVE ECHOED INTO HISTORY AND THE PLAYERS WITHERED TO DUST OR HIDDEN AWAY TO NURSE THEIR GRIEVOUS WOUNDS.

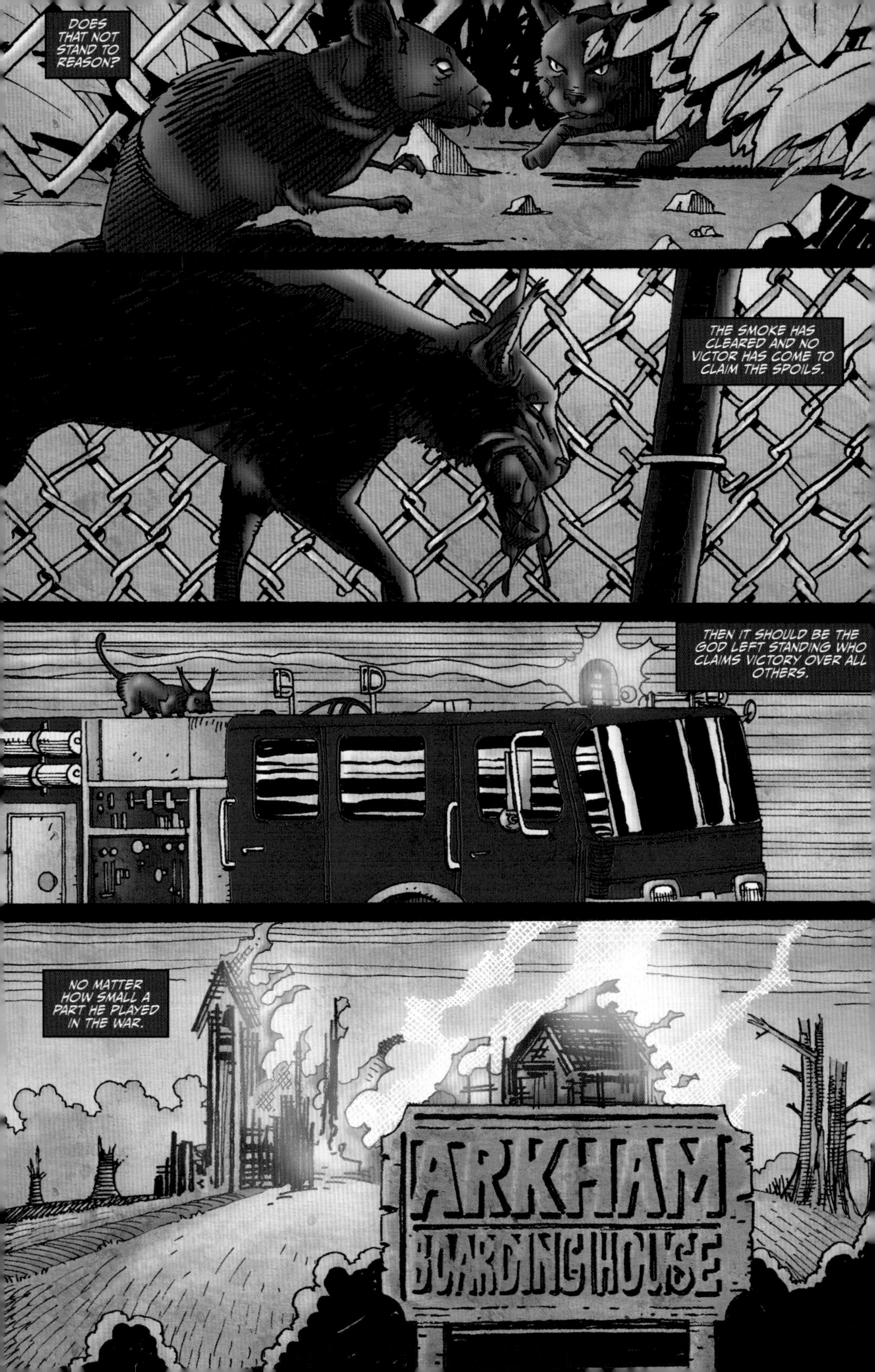
DOES THAT NOT STAND TO REASON?
THE SMOKE HAS CLEARED AND NO VICTOR HAS COME TO CLAIM THE SPOILS.
THEN IT SHOULD BE THE GOD LEFT STANDING WHO CLAIMS VICTORY OVER ALL OTHERS.
NO MATTER HOW SMALL A PART HE PLAYED IN THE WAR.
ARKHAM
BOARDING HOUSE

SO I WILL CLAIM VICTORY. THROUGH CHANCE, SUBTERFUGE, LUCK...IT DOES NOT MATTER.

I HAVE BUT TO SPEAK THE REASON AND IT WILL BE SO. WHO IS LEFT TO CHALLENGE MY ASSERTION?

THE STING OF OFFENSE HAS FESTERED WITHIN MY SOUL. BUT FATE HAS GRANTED ME THIS POTENT GIFT.

FINALLY, I MAY SPEAK THE VENGEFUL WORDS THAT HAVE LONGED TO SLIP FROM MY TONGUE AFTER MILLENNIA OF HUMILIATION. I AM NOT YOUR NEMESIS...

ARKHAM BOARDINGHOUSE!

ARKHAM BOARDINGHOUSE!

...I AM YOUR CONQUEROR.

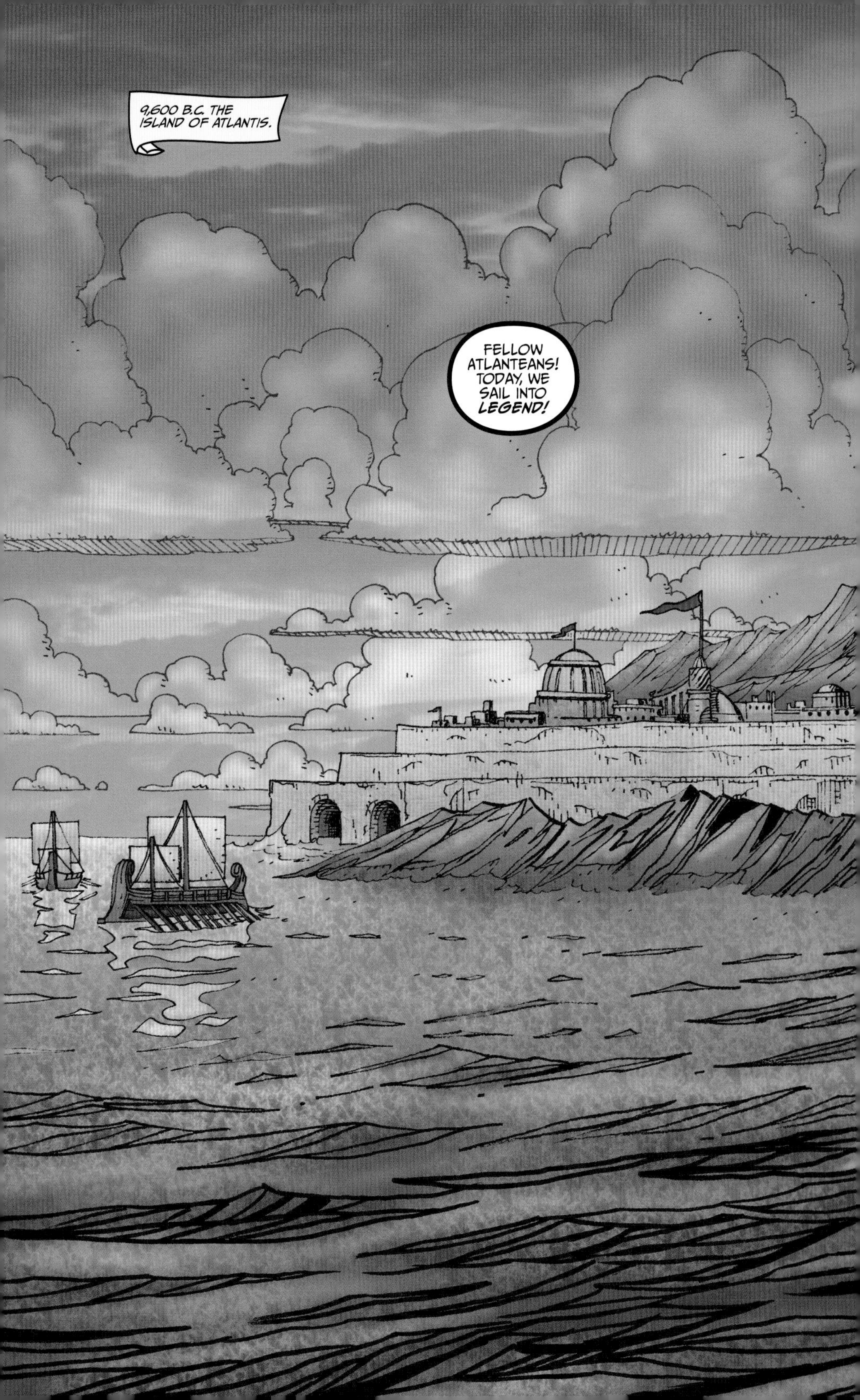
9,600 B.C. THE ISLAND OF ATLANTIS.
FELLOW ATLANTEANS! TODAY, WE SAIL INTO LEGEND!

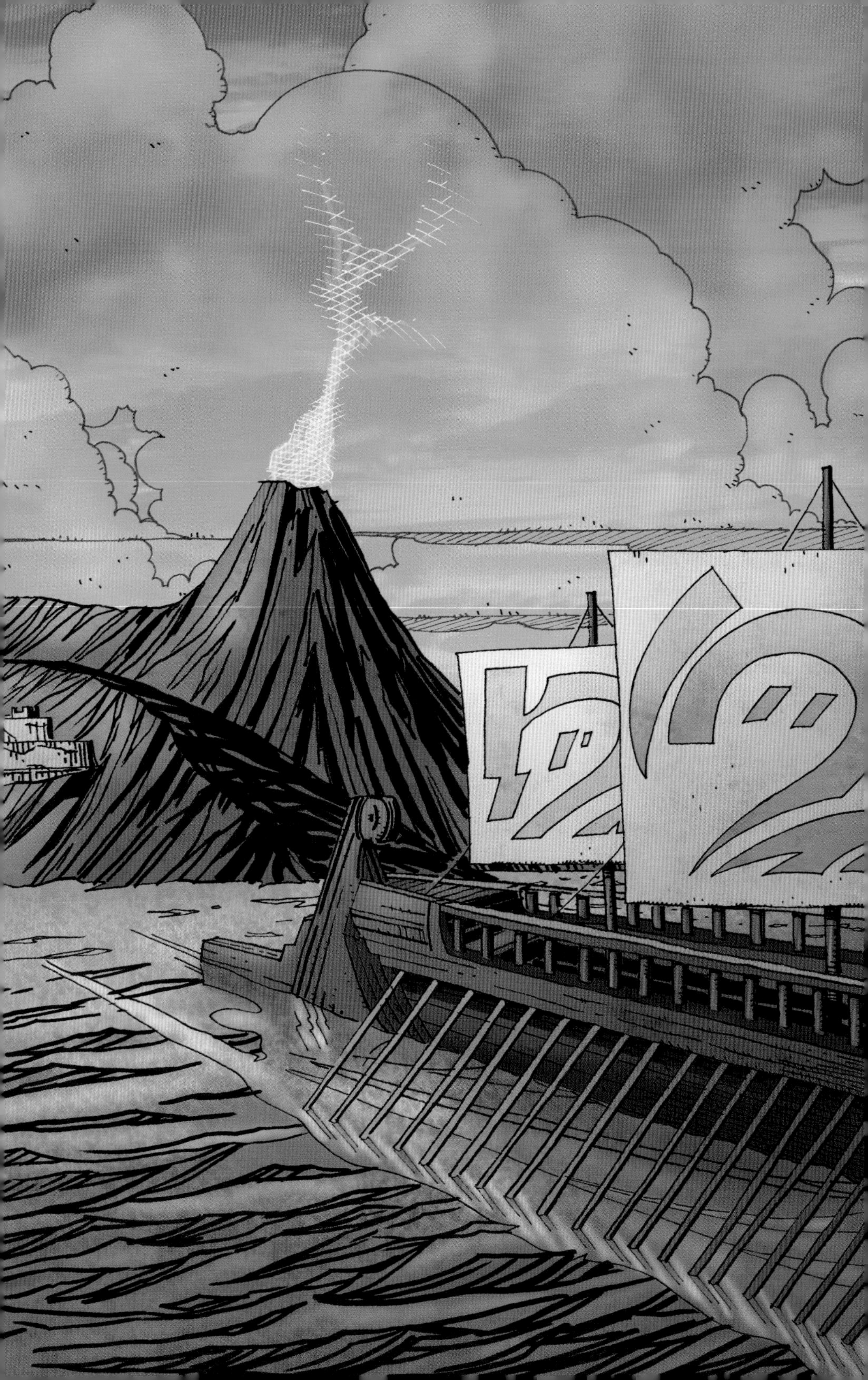

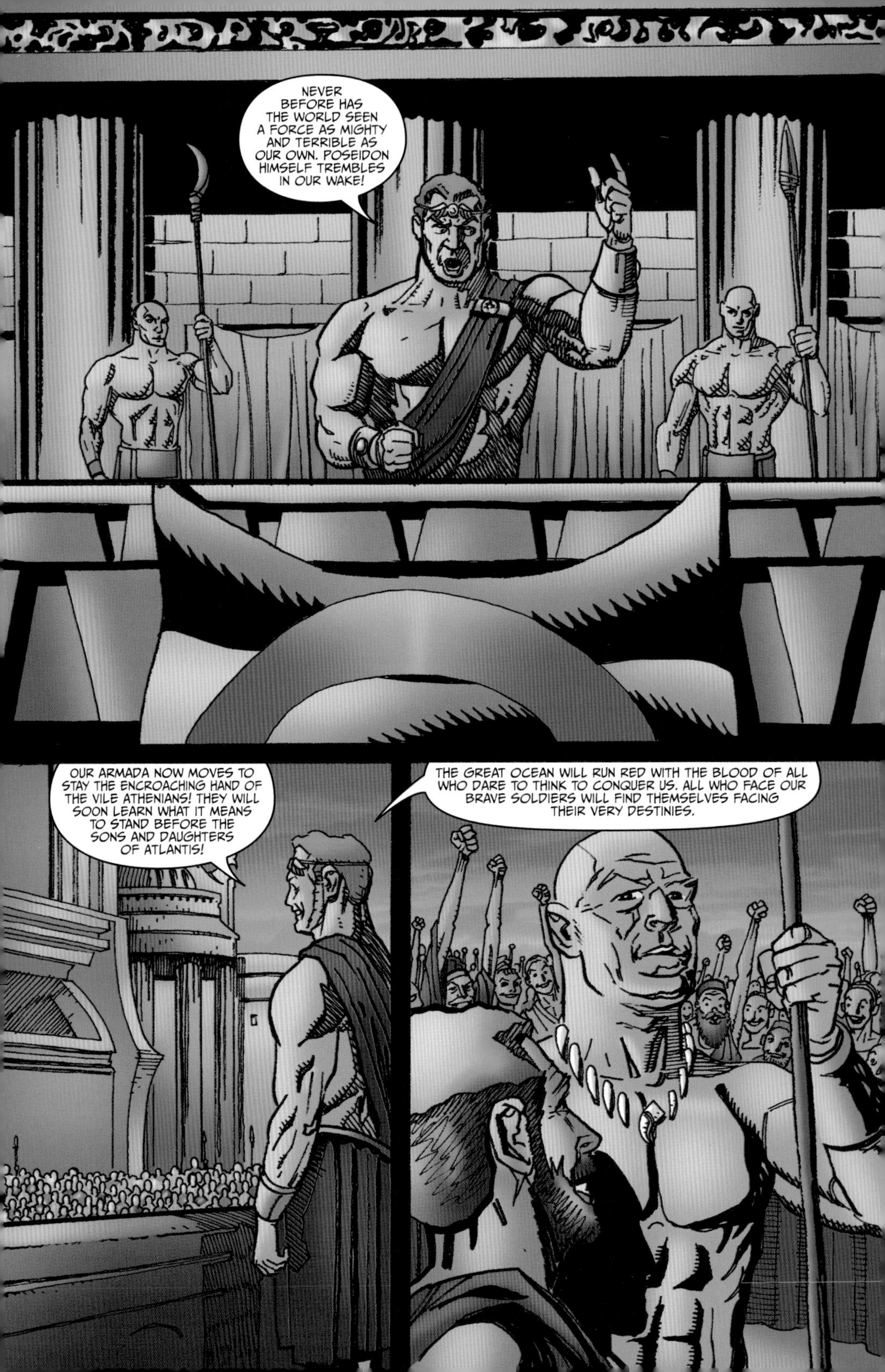
NEVER BEFORE HAS THE WORLD SEEN A FORCE AS MIGHTY AND TERRIBLE AS OUR OWN. POSEIDON HIMSELF TREMBLES IN OUR WAKE!
OUR ARMADA NOW MOVES TO STAY THE ENCROACHING HAND OF THE VILE ATHENIANS! THEY WILL SOON LEARN WHAT IT MEANS TO STAND BEFORE THE SONS AND DAUGHTERS OF ATLANTIS!
THE GREAT OCEAN WILL RUN RED WITH THE BLOOD OF ALL WHO DARE TO THINK TO CONQUER US. ALL WHO FACE OUR BRAVE SOLDIERS WILL FIND THEMSELVES FACING THEIR VERY DESTINIES.

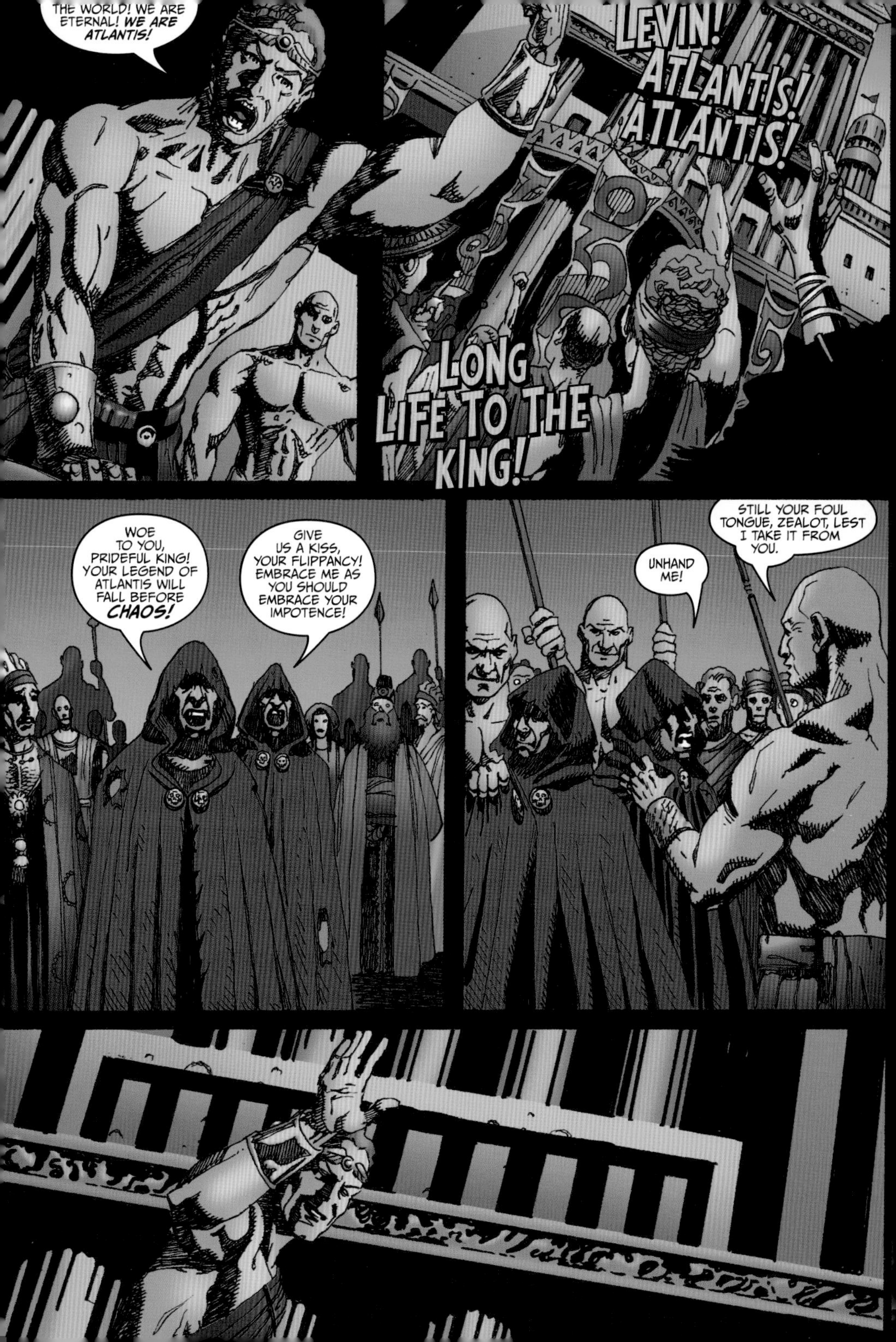
THE WORLD! WE ARE ETERNAL! WE ARE ATLANTIS!
LEVIN! ATLANTIS! ATLANTIS!
LONG LIFE TO THE KING!
WOE TO YOU, PRIDEFUL KING! YOUR LEGEND OF ATLANTIS WILL FALL BEFORE CHAOS!
GIVE US A KISS, YOUR FLIPPANCY! EMBRACE ME AS YOU SHOULD EMBRACE YOUR IMPOTENCE!
UNHAND ME!
STILL YOUR FOUL TONGUE, ZEALOT, LEST I TAKE IT FROM YOU.

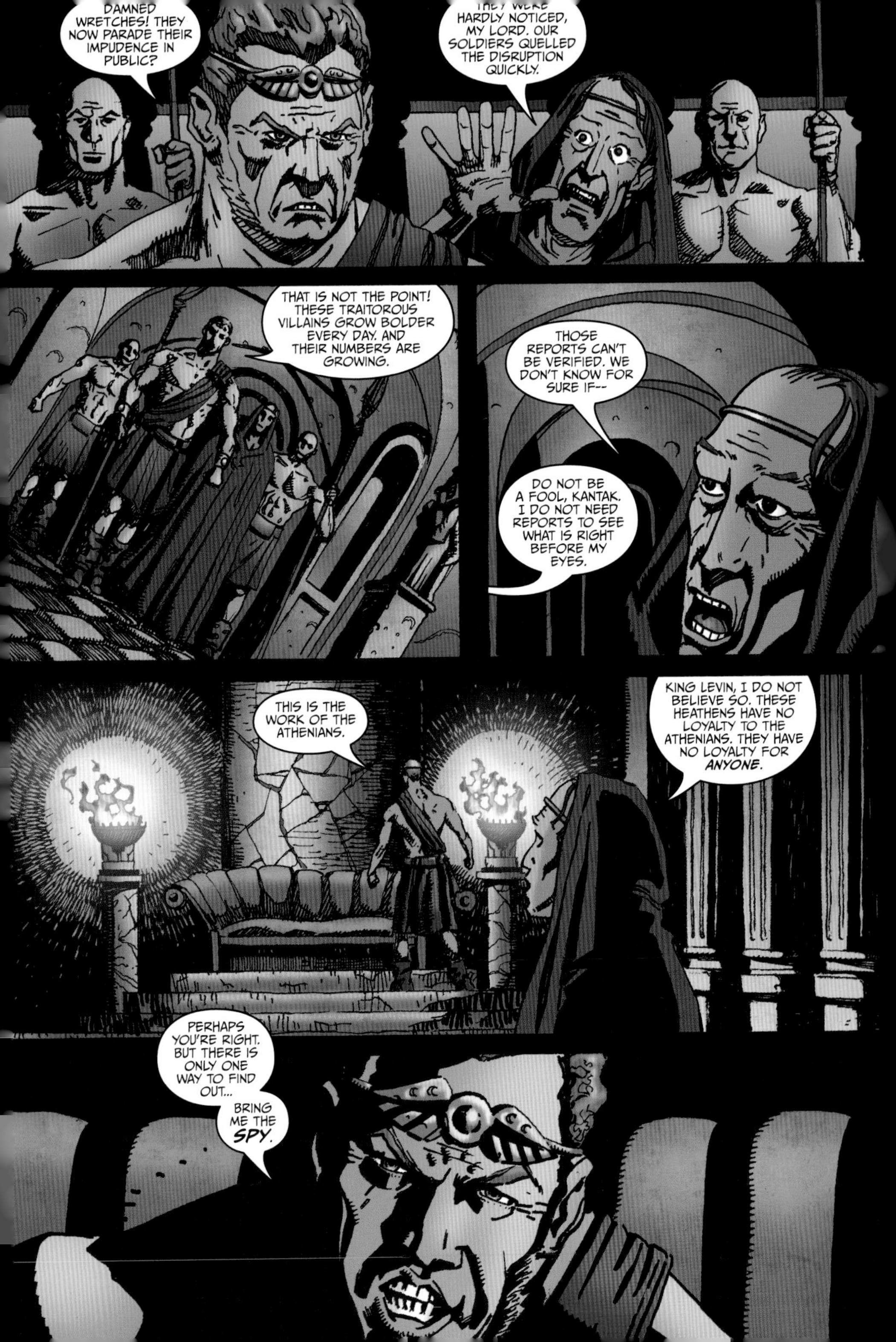
DAMNED WRETCHES! THEY NOW PARADE THEIR IMPUDENCE IN PUBLIC?
THEY WERE HARDLY NOTICED, MY LORD. OUR SOLDIERS QUELLED THE DISRUPTION QUICKLY.
THAT IS NOT THE POINT! THESE TRAITOROUS VILLAINS GROW BOLDER EVERY DAY. AND THEIR NUMBERS ARE GROWING.
THOSE REPORTS CAN'T BE VERIFIED. WE DON'T KNOW FOR SURE IF--
DO NOT BE A FOOL, KANTAK. I DO NOT NEED REPORTS TO SEE WHAT IS RIGHT BEFORE MY EYES.
THIS IS THE WORK OF THE ATHENIANS.
KING LEVIN, I DO NOT BELIEVE SO. THESE HEATHENS HAVE NO LOYALTY TO THE ATHENIANS. THEY HAVE NO LOYALTY FOR ANYONE.
PERHAPS YOU'RE RIGHT. BUT THERE IS ONLY ONE WAY TO FIND OUT...
BRING ME THE SPY.

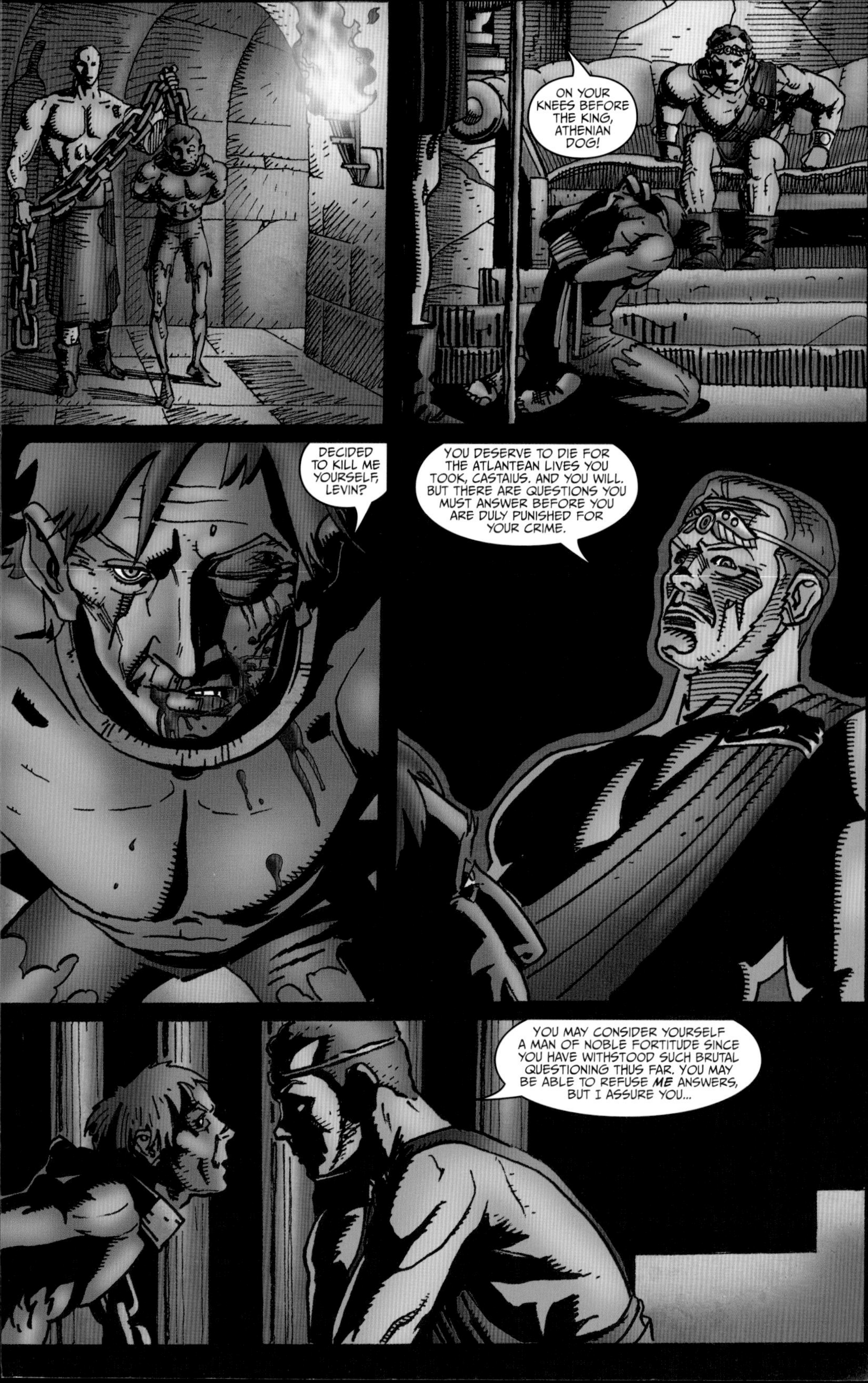
ON YOUR KNEES BEFORE THE KING, ATHENIAN DOG!
DECIDED TO KILL ME YOURSELF, LEVIN?
YOU DESERVE TO DIE FOR THE ATLANTEAN LIVES YOU TOOK, CASTAIUS. AND YOU WILL. BUT THERE ARE QUESTIONS YOU MUST ANSWER BEFORE YOU ARE DULY PUNISHED FOR YOUR CRIME.
YOU MAY CONSIDER YOURSELF A MAN OF NOBLE FORTITUDE SINCE YOU HAVE WITHSTOOD SUCH BRUTAL QUESTIONING THUS FAR. YOU MAY BE ABLE TO REFUSE ME ANSWERS, BUT I ASSURE YOU...

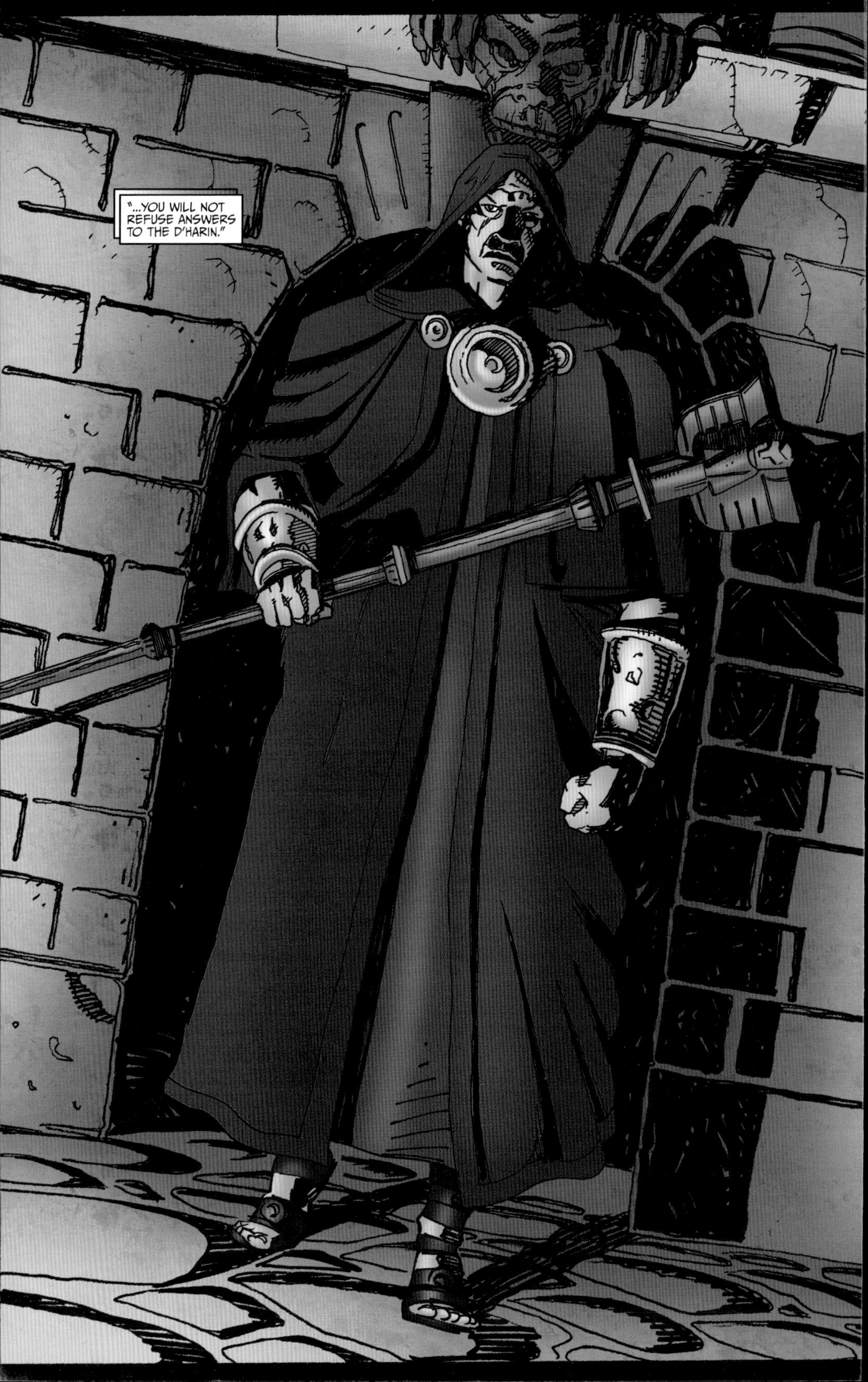
"...YOU WILL NOT REFUSE ANSWERS TO THE D'HARIN."

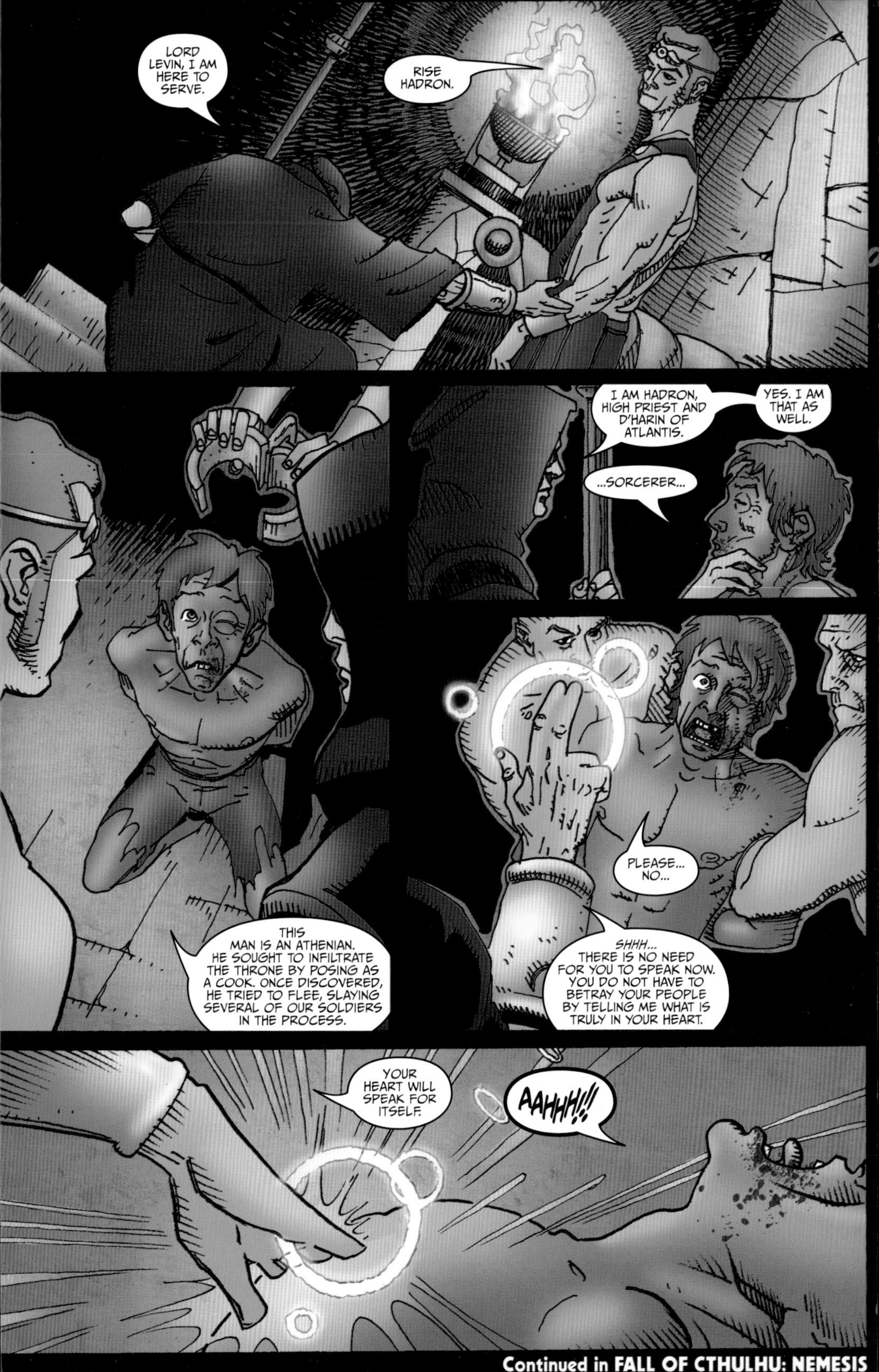
LORD LEVIN, I AM HERE TO SERVE.
RISE HADRON.
I AM HADRON, HIGH PRIEST AND D'HARIN OF ATLANTIS.
YES. I AM THAT AS WELL.
...SORCERER...
THIS MAN IS AN ATHENIAN. HE SOUGHT TO INFILTRATE THE THRONE BY POSING AS A COOK. ONCE DISCOVERED, HE TRIED TO FLEE, SLAYING SEVERAL OF OUR SOLDIERS IN THE PROCESS.
PLEASE... NO...
SHHH... THERE IS NO NEED FOR YOU TO SPEAK NOW. YOU DO NOT HAVE TO BETRAY YOUR PEOPLE BY TELLING ME WHAT IS TRULY IN YOUR HEART.
YOUR HEART WILL SPEAK FOR ITSELF.
AAHHH!!!

Continued in FALL OF CTHULHU: NEMESIS

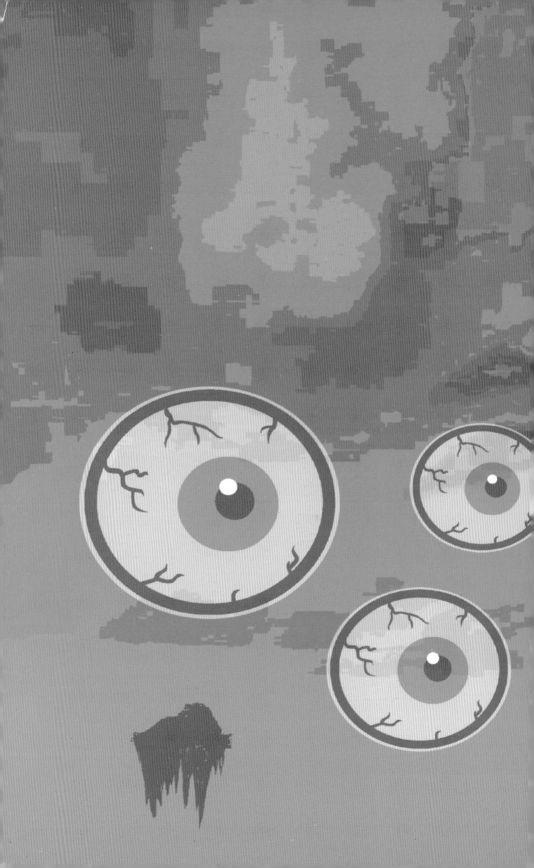